VESSELS OF EXCELLENCE

Ushering you into an experience of life in the presence of Almighty God.

Apostle Dr Max Matonhodze

Foreword by Apostle Dr Cephas Nyemba- Bishop (DTH)

Published by Max Matonhodze
Publishing partner: Paragon Publishing, Rothersthorpe
First published 2022

ISBN 978-1-78222-952-0

Book design, layout and production management by Into Print
www.intoprint.net
+44 (0)1604 832149

ACKNOWLEDGEMENTS

I would like to acknowledge the dedication and support from my wife Joyce and our children Tanashe Zoe, Tamiranashe Deborah and Maximilian Junior Taonashe during the writing of this book.

May the Lord God Almighty remember and reward you for the all the sacrifices you had to make.

I also would like to acknowledge the brethren who previewed the manuscript and made constructive suggestions and comments some of which are listed under "What others have said".

May the Lord God Almighty remember and reward you for the all the sacrifices you had to make.

To my father

What people are saying about *Vessels of Excellence*

"This book is designed to help anyone, irrespective of religion, denomination, nationality, or orientation who genuinely wants to know God. It is written by a colleague who had initially asked the question: *'Is there God?'*

He got his answer, and he has subsequently experienced Jesus's presence over four decades and has proven that God does exist, and that God wants humanity to seek Him.

There is manifest evidence of the Spirit of God at work through the author's Planet Ministries.

The book is designed to help anyone who really wants to know if God does exist and if it is possible to know Him personally. I hope whoever reads this book, it will make them a better person and that they will be able to overcome any problems/weaknesses that they may have. I believe that the book does what it says- lead you to know God intimately. God bless you."

Opeyemi Babatola
Birmingham, United Kingdom

"The Vessels of Excellence Book, written by Apostle Dr Max Matonhodze is the ultimate Christian Manual. Apostle Matonhodze is a humble servant of Our Lord Jesus Christ, who founded the Planet Ministries fellowship. A committed, diligent, and anointed servant of God, his Ministry has spread internationally, with a strong presence in the UK, Kenya, and Zimbabwe.

The author uses his personal life journey and how God called him into ministry to explore issues of religion that we can all relate to. Anyone with questions or doubts about religion or their purpose in life will benefit from reading this book. Likewise, practising Christians are also strongly recommended to read the book. It is the most comprehensive manual of the Gospel of Jesus Christ that I have come across, with detailed exposition of bible truths. It is packed with the revelation of God's word, and it certainly improves one's understanding of scriptures.

I highly recommend everyone to read this book. It is a powerful book indeed."

Blessing Magara
Birmingham, United Kingdom

"Once I started to read Vessels of Excellence, I couldn't put it down!!
Very good read.

Found the reading inspiring and enlightening.

It identifies the purpose of the teaching which is directed to the individual.

Personally I've found that it provided me with answers to questions I've been asking.

I also found it giving me knowledge and understanding in the meaning behind the scriptures. I have gained much knowledge and understanding.

I feel the author is right in saying that one needs to be under the guidance of a teacher.

I like the way the author addressed the individual on a personal level as this makes the teaching personal to the reader.

I would recommend this book to anybody seeking to have a personal experience with Jesus Christ, a deeper understanding of the word of God and as a resource tool for teachers and instructors of the word of God"

Jayne Powell
Walsall, United Kingdom

"If you're inquisitive about God, wanting a life transforming experience for yourself, or looking to learn about the word of God and become a vessel to teach others the Bible, this book compiles lessons in a manual/ textbook style into one place.

I would recommend this book for any teacher of the gospel of Jesus Christ, any Christian teacher needs to have this book it is an absolute classic in Christian literature, a sweeping multi-generational manual about the gospel of Jesus Christ and how to teach it. It's complex, nuanced, and simply put, a casual work of genius."

Brill Pongo
Telford, UK

"Apostle Dr Max Matonhodze is a trained medical doctor whom God called as a young man in medical training in Zimbabwe. He is one person who is so passionate about soul winning which is a mandate for every born again Christian and in seeing the Kingdom of God established here on earth. This is shown in his book "Vessels of Excellence". He operates in the Apostolic and Prophetic gifts. He is the founder of Planet Ministries with headquarters in the United Kingdom.

This book is a must read for both Christians and Non-Christians of all ages. For Non-Christians who want to know about the Almighty God and serious Christians who want to grow spiritually to sonship and maturity. Christians who want to experience God's manifestations in their walk with Him. It is an excellent book as a handbook for all Christians including those in leadership positions.

I strongly recommend that all Christians read this book".

Maria Sibanda
Harare, Zimbabwe

"Vessels of Excellence is an in-depth exploration of what it means to be a Christian.

The text is both passionate and rousing in its delivery and will help the reader build on their faith and spiritual maturity.

It is both instructional and insightful and I would recommend it for anyone who wishes to explore more about their own Christianity and faith."

Nicola Walker
Staffordshire, United Kingdom

"I felt so encouraged and uplifted in my spirit when I was reading Vessels of Excellence. It helped me and can also equips everyone who wants to grow in their Christian faith. The book contains basic truth which comes from the word of God.

The book explained in detail that reading the bible, praying and fellowship with one another as the foundation of our Christian walk. Again, the writer explained in a step-by-step manner how you can be born again through receiving Jesus Christ as our Lord and Saviour.

The writer clearly explained the idea that God doesn't want us to deal with the affairs of this life as though we don't have a Father.

We have a heavenly Father who wants to fellowship with us every day. I would encourage both young and old who are looking for the true meaning of life to read this book as it is life transforming."

Winston Matanda
Melbourne, Australia

"I have interacted with Apostle Dr Max through his devotionals, Planet Daily. He has demonstrated a high degree of consistency and commitment and I have found his teachings life transforming.

I have found the book *Vessels of Excellence* a stimulating read with scripture insights that will invigorate and strengthen the spiritual journey of any child of God.

It is a powerful tool to guide and equip teachers and trainers of the gospel while giving those searching for the truth and an experience of God.

It is a powerful tool and guide for discipleship that will transform Planet Earth. I would recommend this book to anyone genuinely asking the question: Is there God?

I would also recommend 'Vessels of Excellence' as a critical resource tool to those who teach and train church leaders at every level."

Gladys
Harare Zimbabwe

"Have you ever 'discovered' something new, then wonder how you ever lived without it? That's exactly what has happened since I read the manuscript of Apostle Dr Max's Vessels of Excellence. My first thought was... 'I now have everything I need in ONE place!'

I recommend this book to anyone wanting to discover and experience a personal God and for those church leaders seeking a comprehensive resource tool for teaching and equipping the saints for the work of the ministry. It is comprehensive and has instructions that are suitable for enabling one to understand not only the Bible but increase your knowledge of the gospel and love of Jesus Christ every single day."

Smollet Kalua
Birmingham, United Kingdom.

Foreword

Apostle Dr Cephas Nyemba- Bishop (DTH)

Former Vice President and Member of the Apostolic Cabinet at Grace Ministries
International Fellowship

It was an honour to be asked to write the foreword to the book *Vessels of Excellence* by Apostle and Dr Max Matonhodze. It is a blessing to me because I know that Apostle Matonhodze's ministry is impacting many people around the world, and it is great for me to be part of it even in a little way. I am happy to attest to the apostleship of Apostle Matonhodze, and to the value or worthiness of this book because I have grown to know him and what he has as part of his ministry. Please read this book and it will transform your life.

Let me reflect a little on myself although I am not the highlight. My reflection may, however, have a bearing on my testimony about Apostle Max Matonhodze and his ministry.

My ministry and apostleship is by the grace of God and has been etched in me by the personal and occasional voice of God to me, by the numerous engagements and by life experiences with God. My ministry activities often involve preaching the truth that brings people to salvation. By the working power of the Holy Spirit, my ministry identifies, affirms, and commissions modern day forerunners of the second coming of our Lord Jesus, and prepares people of God to be overcomers in the progressive trials and tribulations of our times.

I have known the apostle for the past 30 years and had fellowship with him being in the same church for about ten years. Apostle Matonhodze ministered to me in my own family life crisis. He was sent by God, to address my issue with the Word of knowledge and provided a resolution in my life.

I have, on occasions, been invited by Apostle Matonhodze to minister at his ministry's annual conferences where I shared the pulpit with him. I was personally blessed by his ministry as I ministered with him in Birmingham, in the United Kingdom.

I sincerely believe that God prepared me to give witness to Apostle Matonhodze and his ministry. You will also notice that there are several other witnesses to the calling of Apostle Dr Max Matonhodze and the life changing impact of this book under "What other people are saying about *Vessels of Excellence*" at the beginning of this book.

A couple of years ago, one day as I was intensely engaged in some home activities, my cell phone began to play a wonderful story. A narrator stated that he saw in a dream a man that was on a dazzling white cloud and was elevated high up above the clouds. This man was reported to have pulled out a trumpet as he stood there above the clouds and blew it to be heard by multitudes of people around the Planet Earth.

I must briefly state that (and I paraphrase), from the trumpet, the narrator heard the sound, a word, a message given to Planet Earth. The message carried in it a charge to those that heard it, to pass it on to the rest of the world. That means that the message had a multiplier effect. It carried in it the power to spread. This means that you the reader of this book will be used by God to carry the message and impact many lives.

As the story was being narrated, there was something ignited in my spirit, and there was a burning in me, and I was totally captivated with the narration. The reporter whom I later learnt to be Dr Brilliant Pongo, pronounced that he had the same dream on three consecutive nights, and that this man that was raised on a dazzling cloud was Dr, and Apostle Max Matonhodze. The mention of his name was stunning because it was a name that I knew.

When I pulled out my cell phone, I searched the phone to see where the message was being played, but I failed to identify the source. The message continued to play starting again several times, at intervals, through the day, and I had no control of it. Every time he retold the story, I was captivated, and I continued to marvel at what a wonderful story that was. Surprisingly, I still could not identify the source of the message on my cellphone. I, therefore, concluded that God was sending a message to me, and to the world. This was not a systematic accident because there is no such a thing. It was God. I later realised that this testimony is recorded in a documentary by Planet Ministries available on YouTube entitled "Who is Max Matonhodze".

I therefore conclude that I am more than qualified to boldly affirm of Apostle Matonhodze's mantle because I believe that God has prepared me to be such a witness. I urge readers to open their lives and receive his ministry and the impartation of power and transformation through the Word that he shares in this book.

Based on how God has manifested Himself in Apostle Matonhodze's life, and the mantle that He has put upon him, I assert that his ministry is both prophetic and apostolic. That means that God has spoken to him directly and he has been sent into the world with a life changing Word that transforms lives. That is what you get in the book *Vessels of Excellence*. The message of this book is a Word that is active, life giving, and life changing.

If you want to draw meaning from my cellphone experience, and from Dr. Pongo's testimony and his quest to discover the Apostle, you will project that the message of this book will have a life of its own. It means that as this book is released in its written form, it will make things happen far and wide and specifically in your life. Your life and the lives of many will change for the better and they will mature in Christ. Miraculous things will happen in accordance with the scope of God's mind who conceived the vision that He has given the Apostle.

The charge was given by God and the message will cover the Planet. Multitudes will be ignited with the fire of God as Jesus said in Luke 12:49 (NKJV): "I have come to set fire on earth, and how I wish it were already kindled! ...". That fire is the conviction of the word in this book, that generates results in your life and the lives of others impacted by the same word.

That is what I discern from a comprehensive perspective of understanding the inspiration that produced this book and the detailed Word rich content of this book.

Having gone through the outline and content of this book chapter by chapter to get a good understanding of the *Vessels of Excellence*, this is my conclusion. This book is rich with empowering and life changing Word.

Chapter 9 on "Holiness" caught my immediate attention, and I retrieved it for my own reading and benefit. It was so because I value and prioritize holiness because it is, as Apostle Matonhodze says, "a central attribute of God" without which no man can see Him. I read this chapter in its entirety first, and I was blessed. The chapter gives a comprehensive teaching on the subject and equips the believer to become holy by the working of the Holy Spirit in one's life.

The *Vessels of Excellence* is a manual for life. Every chapter of the 34 chapters is equipped to give practical guidelines to live a successful life in God. You will receive an impartation of the power of God upon your life. You will receive wisdom, knowledge, understanding, counsel, might/power, and the understanding of the "Fear of God".

This book is complete in its potential and capability to equip you, the reader, to live your life in a wholesome way in the fullness of God's presence.

This is my conclusion. There is no doubt that Apostle Matonhodze effectively narrates his testimonies about what God has done in his life. It is, however, necessary that the Apostle hears the witness of those who have been impacted by his ministry, and that the multitudes hear the confirmation of other witnesses other than himself. This is where my contribution comes in.

I, therefore, conclude that it is evident that Apostle Matonhodze and all that he represents, his ministry, his publications, his music, and everything that he will do, will carry unlimited possibilities. Bear this in mind as you read this book and open your life to the limitless potential. Allow God to transform you, equip you, bless you, and make you a great asset in His kingdom.

Cephas Nyemba

Contents

Foreword: xi

Preface: How this book came about xxv

How to use this book and who it is for xxix

Introduction..xxxi

Section 1: Turning Your Situation Around; Experiencing The God Of Jesus Christ

Chapter 1: Turning To God; Calling Upon His Name 3
Chapter 2: Be Under A Servant Of God.....................................11
Chapter 3: You Need To Learn To Pray.....................................14
Chapter 4: Reading And Meditating On The Word.....................19
Chapter 5: You Need To Be Baptised Under Water.....................23
Chapter 6: Grow Into Christ And Put Off The Old Man 26
Chapter 7: You Need To Be Filled With The Holy Spirit.............29

Section 2: What You Need To Know And Understand; Critical Areas Of Knowledge For The Child Of God.

Summary of Section 2 37

Chapter 8: Understanding Righteousness.....................................39

Summary Of Chapter.. 39

Covered In This Chapter:

8.1. Understanding righteousness...40
8.2. The prayer for righteousness and salvation.......................41
8.3. How do I know I have received salvation 42
8.4. With salvation comes eternal life 42
8.5. With salvation comes forgiveness of sin 44
8.6. Salvation is a gift from God to you- it is for free-
receive it 45
8.7. The package of salvation..45

Chapter 9: Understanding Holiness...47

Summary Of Chapter 47

Covered in this Chapter:

9.1 Definition of holiness 47

9.2 Understanding the necessity for holiness. 48

9.3 Holiness is a central attribute of Almighty God.....................49

9.4 The Holy Spirit is the standard for holiness.........................50

9.5 Knowledge of the word of God is critical for holiness 51

9.6 He wants to write His laws in your heart..............................51

Chapter 10: Understanding Sonship..53

Summary of Chapter...53

Covered in this Chapter:

10.1 You received the right, power and privilege to be a child of God54

10.2 You were adopted to be a child of God...............................54

10.3 You are heir of God and joint heir with the Lord Jesus Christ...54

10.4 You are God's own special person, a chosen generation and
belong to the royalty of Heaven......................................55

10.5 When you pray address God as Father 55

Chapter 11: Understanding Redemption...56

Summary Of Chapter...56

Covered In This Chapter:

11.1 Understanding the origins of sin and the redemption from sin. 57

11.2 Understanding the consequences of judgement and our
redemption from the consequences of judgement.......................59

11.2.1 Understanding redemption from mental oppression. ...60

11.2.2 Understanding redemption from disease and sickness..61

11.2.3 Understanding redemption from poverty, lack, toil and
barrenness...63

11.2.4 Redemption means Jesus Christ opened the door for
receiving the holy spirit and through him the blessing of
Abraham...63

Chapter 12: Understanding The Power Of A Continuous Positive
Attitude 66

Summary Of Chapter...66

Covered In This Chapter:

12.1 Understanding a positive attitude..67

12.2 Celebrating life in a positive attitude 68

12.3 A positive attitude is not easily offended and brings down
barriers...69

12.4 A positive attitude overcomes adversity 70

12.5 A positive attitude releases the delivering power of God.............73

Section 3: Almighty God's Promises To You

Summary of Section 3 79

Chapter 13: The Promised Land 81

When you live and walk in my presence - God says I will give to you the Promised Land, an experience of God's love and kindness.

Summary Of Chapter..81

Covered In This Chapter:

13.1 He wants us to experience His goodness...82

13.2 The Lord God wants us to experience His compassion, mercy
and loving kindness every day of our lives 82

13.3 God wants you to experience His peace 83

13.4 He wants you to experience His joy 84

13.5 As we trust in the Lord He gives us hope with which we can face
every situation..85

13.6 The Lord God wants to give us capacity to love and care for
others **unconditionally.**...85

Chapter 14: Character, Stature And Achievement 87

God said if you walk and live in my presence I will make you a person of character, stature and achievements.

Summary Of Chapter..87

Covered In This Chapter:

14.1 Learning from Abraham the father of those who believe-the
qualities he possessed. 88

14.2 To receive His promises you need to understand the need to
know God and His essential attributes. 90

14.3 To receive His promises you need to understand the need to
have the knowledge of the word of God. 91

14.4 To receive His promise you need to understand the need to have a strong conviction, a high degree of being persuaded concerning His promises..92

14.5 To receive His promises you need to understand how to overcome the wicked one. 93

    14.5.1 To overcome the wicked one you need to understand the nature of satan. 94

    14.5.2 To overcome the wicked one you need to understand the origins of satan. 94

14.6 Understanding the believer's victory over satan............................96

    14.6.1 Understanding the authority of the believer to bind and rebuke satan in the name of The Lord Jesus Christ.........97

    14.6.2 Understanding the victory over satan through the confession of the blood of the Lord Jesus Christ.............98

Chapter 15: I Will Be God To You... 100

Almighty God promises: When you live and walk in My presence, I will be God to you.

Summary of Chapter... 100
Covered In This Chapter:

15:1 To be your everything - He says when I am in relationship with you, you have everything you need through Jesus Christ....... 101

15:2 To be your guide as you make important decision of your life, career and relationships including marriage through Jesus Christ 102

15.3 To be your healer and source of well-being, through Jesus Christ 103

15.4 To be your giver of righteousness through Jesus Christ. 103

15.5 To give you victory in every situation you face through Jesus Christ 104

15.6 To be present with you in every situation you face through Jesus Christ. 105

15.7 To give you His kingdom – His righteousness, peace and joy in your life through Jesus Christ. 106

15.8 To be your ultimate source and provider through Jesus Christ. 107

Chapter 16: I Will Multiply You Exceedingly.. 108

*Almighty God promises: As you live and walk in my presence, I will
multiply you exceedingly. He needs first of all to make you feel secure- to uplift
you and fortify you. Then He needs to make you a type or a kind called the
God-kind- He will then multiply the God kind in you after its kind.
These three steps often happen concurrently.*

Summary of Chapter.. 108
Covered In This Chapter:

16.1 As you walk in His presence God has promised to shield you,
    fortify you, lift you up, increase and multiply you exceedingly
    and in every area of your life... 109

16.2 As you walk in His presence God desires that you produce after
    your kind- the God kind. God has a principle that every living
    creature produces after its kind. 112

16.3 As you walk and live in His presence His word will prevail and
    grow as you share and speak that word to your family, friends,
    colleagues, and community. His word accomplishes the mission
    for which it is sent and does not return void............................. 117

16.4 As you walk and live in His presence, He declares that righteous-
    ness and praise shall spring forth before the nations until the
    earth is filled with the knowledge of the glory of God as the
    waters cover the sea... 118

16.5 Bear witness to what the Lord Jesus Christ has done in your life.
    A witness speaks what he/she has seen, heard, touched, and
    experienced.. 119

16.6 As you walk and live in His presence, He desires to multiply
    grace and peace upon your life. 121

Chapter 17: He Promises To Make You Exceedingly Fruitful 124

*He said when you live and walk in my presence I will make you exceedingly
fruitful.*

Summary of Chapter.. 124
Covered In This Chapter:

17.1 Understanding the context in which we become exceedingly
    fruitful.. 125

17.2 Understanding that the source of our fruitfulness is abiding in
    obedience to the Lord Jesus Christ.. 125

17.3 Understanding that we bear fruit for the Lord God as we give flavour to society in as much as salt and condiments flavour food. 126

17.4 Understanding that we bear fruit for the Lord God as we let the light of Christ shine through us to the world. 127

Section 4: Growing Into Maturity In The Service Of Almighty God.

Chapter 18: It Is By Grace - Understanding Dimensions Of Grace. 131

Chapter 19: Grace Makes You An Extension Of God On The Earth. 135

Chapter 20: When Almighty God Says You Are His Portion 138

Chapter 21: Becoming God's Own Special Person. 140

Chapter 22: God's Promise To The Set Apart Ones: No Weapon To Prevail Against You 142

Chapter 23: Vessels Of Excellency Receive The Help Of God - God Is Their Ally 145

Chapter 24: Vessels Of Excellence Commit Emotionally 147

Chapter 25: Vessels Of Excellency Are Committed To A Godly Vision .. 149

Chapter 26: Vessels Of Excellency Wholly Follow The Lord Their God. 151

Chapter: 27: Other Attributes Of Vessels Of Excellence 157

27.1 Vessels of excellence are builders of the house of God 157

27.2 Vessels of excellence are granted by Almighty God victory against skilled archers 158

27.3 Vessels of excellence are distinguished by God and receive blessing unlimited in scope and in time. 160

27.4 Vessels of excellence are honoured by Almighty God in this life. 161

27.5 Vessels of excellence enter maturity, behave with maturity, and show maturity. 162

Section 5: Activities Of Excellence

Chapter 28: Your Calling To Intercede 167

Summary Of Chapter 167

Covered In This Chapter:

28.1 At the centre of the will of Almighty God is salvation of souls 167

28.2 He desires that we pray for the opening of eyes. 168

28.3 Almighty God desires that we plead on behalf of people
who do not know Him. 168

28.4 You are qualified to plead on behalf of Planet Earth because
of Jesus Christ. 170

28.5 You are qualified to join brethren in corporate prayer for God
to spare His people and not give them to reproach................. 170

28.6 The power of prayer with fasting... 172

28.7 Learning from the Lord Jesus Christ. 174

Chapter 29: You Are Witnesses To These Things................................ 176

Summary Of Chapter.. 176

Covered In This Chapter:

29.1 We are sent and commissioned by Jesus Christ to be
witnesses.. 177

29.2 A witness speaks about what they have seen, heard,
and handled.. 179

29.3 As you witness the power of Jesus Christ, He turns up to
confirm His word with undeniable miracles............................ 179

29.4 We have been sent to set the captives free. 181

29.5 Sent to open eyes 183

29.6 When you live and speak His word it will go and accomplish
the purpose for which He sent it. 183

29.7 As you witness the power of Jesus Christ, you cause desolate
cities to be inhabited. 184

29.8 Sent to comfort those who mourn- healing to those who are
hurting.. 186

Chapter 30: Faithful Stewardship... 187

Part 1: *God wants you to prosper, understanding God's position.* 187

Summary Of Chapter 187

Covered In This Chapter:

30.1 He wishes above all things that you may prosper and be in
health as your souls prospers.. 188

30.2 Jesus Christ redeemed you from the curse of the law, so that
the blessing of Abraham may come to you. 189

30.3 God in Jesus Christ is bringing you into a good land in which
you shall eat bread without scarcity... 190

30.4 He wants to command His blessing in your storehouses.......... 192

30.5 Jabez asked God for a blessing indeed and God granted
      his request.. 193
30.6 Use Almighty God given potential and capabilities to make
      livelihood and wealth creation happen. 194

Chapter 31: Faithful Stewardship 196
   Part 2: *Understanding the spiritual basis of tithing.* 196
   Summary Of Chapter.. 196
   Covered In This Chapter:
   31.1 Tithing is honouring God with our substance............................ 197
   31.2 The purpose of tithes is to support the work of the ministry... 197
   31.3 The first tithe was given by our father of faith Abraham to
         Melchizedek- it was an act of faith, not under the law
         of Moses. 199
   31.4 Jacob the patriarch pledged tithes to God well before the
         Law of Moses was given- this was an act of faith...................... 202
   31.5 Jesus Christ commended tithing....................................... 203
   31.6 Tithe prayerfully, of the Spirit not of the letter because the
         letter kills but the Spirit gives life. 204
   31.7 Where to put the decimal point....................................... 205

Chapter 32: Faithful Stewardship 206
   **Part 3: *Understanding worshipping God with the offering of
         substance.* ***.. 206
   Summary Of Chapter.. 206
   Covered In This Chapter:
   32.1 Jesus Christ offered Himself as an offering for sin..................... 207
   32.2 When you give an offering of substance, you are giving of
         yourself, your worth and value to God. 208
   32.3 Your offering appears before God as a sweet-smelling aroma .. 208
   32.4: Always aim to give an excellent offering, from the heart, learn
         from Abel, King Solomon and Cornelius............................... 208
   32:5 Giving is sowing a seed and Almighty God has made a
         hudred-fold return promise to your giving to the gospel. 210
   32.6 As the earth remains, seed time and harvest time shall not
         cease 211
   32.7 Apply diligence to your giving... 212

32.8 Purpose and give prayerfully knowing that he who sows
    bountifully will reap bountifully, he who sows sparingly
    will reap sparingly.. 214

32.9 Your giving needs to be in proportion to what you have- the
    widow who gave two mites, gave more than all........................ 215

32.10 Give yourself first to God then to His servants 215

32.11 Lay your treasures in heaven, where your treasure is, that is
    where your heart will be also. 216

Chapter 33: Faithful Stewardship... 218

Part 4: *Making prosperity to happen*.................................. 218

Summary Of Chapter... 218

Covered In This Chapter:

33.1 Almighty God desires you to prosper and be in health as your
    soul prospers. 218

33.2 God can prosper you anywhere 219

33.3 Understanding the principle of seed time and harvest time..... 221

33.4 Use sound financial principles. 222

33.5 The wealth of the wicked shall be laid up for the just. 223

33.6 Give it a fight - You need a strong conviction about the
    following: 226

    33.6.1 God wants you to prosper, He desires you to prosper
        above everything else. 227

    33.6.2 He wants you to experience the promised land -
        both spiritually (His love, peace and joy) and physically
        (His provision, health and victory). 227

    33.6.3 Almighty God desires every positive outcome for you
        in Jesus Christ... 229

    33.6.4 Remember - Jesus Christ redeemed us from the curse of
        the law and opened access for us to receive the Holy Spirit
        through faith, the Holy Spirit in turn opens the way for
        gentiles to receive the blessing of Abraham. 270

    33.6.5 It was necessary for the Christ to suffer- so that you can
        have not only forgiveness of sin but also blessing. 231

References **233**

Chapter 34: Conclusion... 234

About the Author 237

Preface

How this book came about

This book is a product of a series of extra-ordinary experiences with Almighty God which I have had over the last 40 years. As an academically bright and gifted young undergraduate medical Student at the University of Zimbabwe, I did not know God and I was getting more and more disillusioned.

I had obtained a good scholarship as a Ministry of Health Cadet. This cadetship paid me a salary every month and paid my University Tuition fees. On average I was being paid twice what my other fellow students were being paid. I was comfortable financially and knew that if I continued to focus on my studies as I had done before, I would complete my medical degree without struggle.

Then what, I asked myself? A job, buy my dream house in a good sub-urban area in Harare, drive a good car- is that all to this life? Surely there must be more to this life I thought.

I had been brought up as a Catholic, been to a Catholic High School for six years, but did not know God. I had no personal experience of God at all. At that time, I started asking: God are You there? If you are there, would You reveal yourself to me?

As I asked these questions one Saturday morning in August 1980, I went to the University chapel and met a friend who was one year ahead of me at the same, High School and had spent a year at the University. Unknown to me, he had become a born-again Christian at University. He asked me a question: Max do you want to receive Jesus Christ as Lord of your life?

I pondered for a minute- what is receiving Jesus Christ? He explained to me briefly: "Max when I came to University, I received Jesus Christ as my Lord and Saviour, and my life is not the same anymore".

I remembered then that I had been asking earlier that morning- "God are you there, if you are there reveal yourself to me."

So, I agreed, my heart was ready and seeking, and Nicholas as his name is, led me into a simple prayer of receiving Jesus Christ as Lord and Saviour. As I left the university chapel- something very profound had happened to me and I did not really understand what it was.

In the months that followed, I understood that experience more and more- I had become a born-again child of God and my life was never the same.

The following year, I felt God was calling me to be a preacher. I was not quite certain what this meant then. I was not sure at that time whether I was meant to complete my medical degree or whether God wanted me to leave and start preaching. I was ready to do His will either way.

On the 26th of January of 1982, while praying for the Lord's direction, I had an experience with God in which I was shown three stations of my life, in the now. It was like being shown a video of my life and being fast forwarded to events to happen in the future, these events were shown to me as if they were happening now. It was vivid, extra-ordinary and breath-taking. I was shown my graduation ceremony which was to happen in three years from then, then I was fast for-warded to events which were to happen in ten years from then- 1992 when I was elected National President of the Hospital Doctors Association of Zimbabwe and then finally I was shown a station later on, the time was not defined but I was shown events that would trigger my retirement from practising medicine to become a preacher of the gospel full time.

I was shown in that vision what I estimated to be about 40 years of my life in three stations. This event clarified to me a lot of things and while the exact timing of the last station I was shown was not revealed, I had a very clear idea of what events would happen to lead to it.

On the 19th of April 1982 in another extra-ordinary occurrence, the Lord showed me that the calling He had put upon my life was in the capacity of an Apostle- I did not understand fully what this meant until later on, however it did put some fear and dread in me. The way however in which this was spoken to me was dramatic. The details of this event will be covered in the book "The Calling".

On the 16th of November 1984, I qualified as a medical doctor and had my graduation ceremony subsequently as I had been shown in the vision. I did my internship in the University Hospitals in Harare rotating through General Sur-gery, Internal Medicine, Neurosurgery, Accident and Emergency, Paediatrics, Obstetrics and Gynaecology and Anaesthetics on a two-year program, before being posted to a District Hospital in Mutare in Eastern Zimbabwe as a Govern-ment Medical Officer (GMO) on the 1st of February 1987.

On the 30th November 1987, while working as a Government Medical Of-ficer in Mutare District Hospital in eastern Zimbabwe, I had another unforget-table and defining experience of my life. The Lord Jesus Christ appeared to me visually, spoke to me and commissioned me to take the message of the gospel to Planet Earth. The name Planet Ministries came out of that experience.

He took a black board and wrote five scripture which He explained in some detail. When He finished explaining those scriptures, where he stood, He was replaced by a picture of the globe, Planet Earth as seen from outer space spinning on its axis. A voice then spoke to me: "Go to that Planet and tell them what I have told you."

It was clear to me that the person who had appeared to me was the Lord Jesus Christ as His appearance was like the one described Revelations 1:14 and the white incandescent light was like what happened when Jesus Christ was transfigured as described in Matthew 17:2 and Mark 9:2

I went to bed in awe. The next day I did not know who to tell- I only confided to one sister-in-Christ, in the church.

Over the coming months the Lord spoke to me in a very detailed way about not talking about this experience until the appointed time.

The following year on the 16th of August 1987, on a Sunday afternoon, God spoke to me that He wanted me to go to England. It was not revealed to me at that time how this was going to happen, for how long and to do what.

I returned to Harare in January 1989 to do a Master's Degree in Medicine (M Med) with the University of Zimbabwe as part of continuing medical education.

I completed a Master's Degree in Medicine in November 1993 with the University of Zimbabwe. On the Lord's instruction I left Zimbabwe for England in December 1993. I took Membership examinations in Dublin in 1995 becoming a Member of the Royal College of Physicians of Ireland (MRCPI) and subsequently joined the West Midlands Deanery Respiratory Training scheme to train as a Respiratory Physician. I qualified with dual accreditation for General Internal Medicine and Respiratory Medicine in April 2002 with a Certificate of Completion of Specialist Training (CCST-UK) from the Joint Royal Colleges of Physicians Training Board (JRCPTB).

I was appointed as Consultant Physician in Respiratory and General Medicine for Walsall Healthcare NHS Trust on the 10th of June 2002.

In July 2007 I was elected a Fellow of the Royal College of Physicians of London (FRCP).

In 2013 I completed a three-year part time Masters in Arts in Medical Education (M A Med Ed) degree with Keel University.

On the 18th April 2012, I had another major encounter with God. The Lord woke me up in the middle of the night and asked me to open my bible to Genesis 17:1-8.

The Lord God spoke to me that night that I was to start a Ministry, Planet Ministries and begin the work of sending the message of the gospel to the nations of Planet Earth. On that night, God spoke to me in detail about the key message of Planet Ministries- the invitation to live life in the presence of God. He spoke to me about the Apostolic capacity in which He was sending me, effective from that moment.

He spoke to me also about the ten foundational messages of Planet Ministries, the five needs (covered in Section 2 Chapters 8-12) and the five promises (covered in section 3 chapters 13-17). One of the most extra-ordinary features of this encounter was that God revealed the full message of the gospel starting from the first 8 verses of Genesis chapter 17!

The next morning, I woke up to a completely different reality and it was hard to explain to my wife this encounter and that we had started a ministry with Almighty God in the middle of the night. Extra-ordinary!

We started having Sunday services and conventions at Easter time, Summer-time (August) as well as Christmas time. We also put up a website https://planetministries.org.uk.

On the 11th of August 2015 while in Kilkeel in Northern Ireland, I had taken my family on holiday while also visiting my mother who lived with my sister in Kilkeel. The Lord spoke to me: "From today I will give you a message everyday which I want you to package and send out".

Since that day I have been sending out Planet Daily, a devotional message from our website as well as through social media, Facebook and WhatsApp as well as Twitter and Instagram.

The Lord Jesus Christ has done extra-ordinary things through Planet Daily, including the dramatic and extra-ordinary healing of a 69-year-old man on the 29th January 2016 in Walsall, West Midlands, United Kingdom.

A documentary on his story can be viewed on YouTube by searching "arrested for being healed" and also in my coming book- "Arrested for being Healed".

Section 4 "Growing into maturity in the service of Almighty God" and parts of section 5-"Activities for excellence" are taken from the Planet Daily.

This book is therefore written wholly from what God has inspired me over the last 40 years. As you read with an open and receptive heart, it is certain to impart to you, positive change and impower you for life's challenges and more.

I will welcome your feedback by emailing: apostle@planetministries.org.uk

How to use this book and who it is for

This book is written for anyone of any age who would like to know the God of Jesus Christ and experience forgiveness of sin and the gift of eternal life through Him irrespective of your nationality, language, or tribe. Also, irrespective of whether your parents raised you up as a Protestant, Catholic, Sikh, Muslim, Hindu, Buddhist, Communist or any other religion not mentioned. Irrespective also of whether you consider yourself Atheist or Agnostic. The focus of this book is on finding a God who enriches and equips you for this life as well as the life to come.

You may be asking questions:

Is there God?
Is it possible to know Him intimately?
How can I become a better person?
How can I overcome some of the human weaknesses I have?

If that's you and you are looking to produce the best you there can be- read on, this book will help you become a vessel of excellence.

This book is also written to be used by any Christian as a training manual or resource book for personal growth and also for teaching and training church leaders and pastors.

Almighty God said to me: "Go tell My people I am giving them an invitation to live their lives in My presence".

"As they live in My presence, I will make them to experience My loving kindness, My mercies which are new every morning, My peace and My joy.

I will make them a person of stature, character, achievement, and self-assurance. I will make them a fruitful person who exudes and imparts hope, life, and goodness.

I will be their God and will multiply them exceedingly." This is a summary of the promises which Almighty God gives to every person who lives their lives in His presence. They are covered in Section 3 chapters 13-17.

"To access My presence, they need to believe in the sacrifice made by My Son Jesus Christ who died for them and rose again. They will need to know and understand righteousness through Jesus Christ, understand the redemption they receive through Him, understand the need to live a holy life in my presence, they also need to understand Sonship and the need to have a continuous positive attitude in My presence." This summarises "The needs" or critical areas of know ledge which every person should have as they live in His presence. 'The needs' are covered in Section 2 chapters 8-12 of this book.

More details on accessing the presence of God are covered in Section 1 – Turning Your Situation Around Chapters 2-7.

Section 4 covers "Growing into maturity in the service of Almighty God"- chapters 18-27. This section explains critical areas of setting yourself apart for God also known as consecration and how this spurs you into maturity and over-coming of the wicked one satan.

Section 5 covers being a partner with Almighty God on the earth in activities of excellence which are being an intercessor- praying for people everywhere including leaders and interceding for salvation of souls (chapter 28).

It also covers being a witness for Jesus Christ (chapter 29) and being a faithful steward of substance (chapters 30-33).

Throughout this book quotations from the Holy Scriptures are mostly from the New Kings James Version (NKJV). Others are from the Amplified Bible (AMP), King James Version (KJV) and New Living Translation (NLT).

Reference to the wicked one, satan is put with a small letter 's' throughout this book. This is simply my way of reminding every believer that satan and demons of every kind, were defeated and disarmed by Jesus Christ on the cross and that in the name of Jesus Christ we have been given authority to resist him, rebuke him, bind him, paralyse his power, and overcome him, until the day he will be physically chained and thrown into the lake of fire for all eternity.

Introduction

Jesus Christ the Son of God was manifested to take away the sin of the world, to open the way of every man, woman, boy, or girl to experience His salvation, culminating in eternal life. This is accomplished through the process of forgiveness of sins through the blood that was shed on the cross. You need to believe on Jesus Christ, that He was God incarnate sent to take away your sin, you need to believe that he died, was buries and that on the third day God raised Him from the dead. You need to repent- which is agreeing with God as to what is wrong and what is right and then acknowledge and confess Jesus Christ as Lord of your life. In the process you become the righteousness of God in Jesus Christ, who was made to be sin for us. (2 Corinthians 5:21). Being the righteousness of God means Almighty God declares you are "not guilty of all charges" and shakes your right hand.

Your spirit which was dead is made alive and joined to the Spirit of Jesus Christ. In your spirit you become intermarried to Jesus Christ, in your spirit you become one with Jesus Christ. You become a new creature in your spirit (2 Corinthians 5:21).

That means, you become, a born-again child of God, an adopted child of God- adopted into the Family of God, into the heavenly Royal household (Romans 8:15, Ephesians 1:5).

You are three in one, have a spirit, with a soul (being the seat of your emotions, intellect, will and your conscience) in a physical body. (1 Thessalonians 5:23). As you acknowledge Jesus Christ as Lord, something very dramatic happens in your spirit you however need to be renewed in the thinking of your mind as you are taught the word of God to know the truth which will set you free. The truth is the correct understanding of the word of God.

While being born again is an event that happens in an instant, the renewal of your mind or the transformation of your mind is a process you need to commit to.

At this point you need to be filled with or immersed into the Holy Spirit or baptised with the Holy Spirit (Acts 1:8, Acts 2:38-39). The Holy Spirit brings upon the believer miracle working power and makes the word of God real in your life.

However, there is much more at stake. The full package of salvation encompasses Jesus Christ being beaten on His back and suffering pain-the scriptures declare that this was allowed to happen so that Jesus Christ would carry our sicknesses, disease and infirmity of every kind. The legal right for you to live in a healthy body was bought for you by Jesus Christ. (1 Peter 2:24, Isaiah 53:4-6, Matthew 8:16-17).

Further, the scriptures teach us that Jesus Christ was cursed by hanging on a tree so that the blessing of Abraham may come upon the gentiles through Jesus Christ and in the same breath He crucially opened the way for you to receive the Holy Spirit who is the Game Changer. The Holy Spirit is given in the name of Jesus Christ, we only have access to the Holy Spirit through Jesus Christ. The Holy Spirit is the Spirit of Jesus Christ. The Holy Spirit is our Helper, Comforter, Strengthner, Counsellor, Standby, Advocate and Intercessor. (John 14:16 AMP). The Holy Spirit gives us the experience of God the Father and of the Son Jesus Christ. (John 14:20-21).

The blessing of Abraham encompasses every positive outcome in your life (Galatians 3:13-14).

Jesus Christ experienced poverty and indignity, while on the earth. He was born in a manger as there was no room in the inn. He had no personal accommodation of His own (Matthew 8:20) and when He had to pay taxes, He had to ask a disciple to go fishing and get money from the mouth of the fish (Matthew 17:27). The scriptures then declare in 2 Corinthians 8:9 "For you know the grace of our Lord Jesus Christ, that though He was rich, yet for your sakes He became poor, that through His poverty might become rich." It is the will of Almighty God that every single person on Planet Earth lives above the poverty line and Jesus Christ released the grace to make that possible for every man, every woman and every boy and girl.

Jesus Christ also bought us peace and mental well-being by defeating and disarming publicly and openly the enemy satan. He undressed satan and made him march down a public highway in humiliation. In Colossians 2:14-15 the scriptures tell us: "Having wiped out the handwriting of requirements that was against us, which was contrary to us. And He has taken it out of the way, having nailed it to the cross. Having disarmed principalities and powers, He made a public spectacle of them triumphing over them in it (the cross). The scriptures record that the beating needful to bring us peace was upon Him (Isaiah 53:5).

Further the scriptures tell us that Jesus Christ was manifested to undo, destroy, loosen, and dissolve the works that the devil has done. (1 John 3:8). He was manifested and made visible to undo and destroy the damage done by the devil in people's lives- the hurt and mental trauma.

His word further tells us that Jesus Christ shared in having flesh and blood-so that through death He might destroy, bring to nought, and make of no effect, him who had the power of death, that is the devil and that he might deliver and completely set free all those who through the haunting fear of death were held in bondage throughout the course of their lives. (Hebrews 2:14-15). Jesus Christ was manifested to destroy the enemy satan and grant us not only physical but also mental well-being, a life free of anxiety, depression and giving us complete mental and character soundness.

In summary therefore Jesus Christ did not only come into the world a) to bring forgiveness of sin and the gift of eternal life, but He also b) bought you health in your body by the stripes on His back (that is by the pain He suffered), c) He bought you honour and dignity as well as providence through His suffering lack, He brought to you a full package of blessing and positive outcomes by being cursed for hanging on a tree and d) brought you mental well-being, by defeating and disarming satan and demons to bring you peace and set you free from fear, anxiety, depression and every other form of mental torment. This is the full package of salvation, and it is the desire of Almighty God that you experience this full package. This full package is the reason the Son of God Jesus Christ, the Messiah was made manifest.

This package however also opens a new door of the working of the abundance of grace of Almighty God, giving you abilities of heaven and making you an extension of Almighty God on the Earth. This puts purpose in your life, puts every single human being into the calling that Almighty God has for their lives. When you live your life in the purpose of God, it opens the way for joy, peace, and total fulfilment. This book is written to help anyone as a step-by-step guide to experiencing the transforming power of Jesus Christ, to help you experience this total package, the total aim of which is to make you a vessel of excellence. It is written as a guide for individuals as well as church leaders and pastors, taking one on a complete journey of transformation by the power of Jesus Christ.

Section 1:

Turning Your Situation Around
Making Change Happen

Chapter 1

Turning To God Calling Upon His Name

You have had a journey in your life. There are things you have seen, things you have done and situations you have experienced.

Some situations you encountered were a result of the circumstances in which you were born while others are the result of situations thrust at you and others still a result of the choices and decisions you made.

Whatever your experience please understand that the architect of all the good things you have experienced is the God of heaven who has loved mankind in Jesus Christ.

The scriptures declare:

"For God so loved the world that He gave His only begotten Son so that whosoever believes in Him should not perish but have eternal life."

John 3:16.

The thief does not come except to steal, and to kill, and to destroy. I have come that they may have life and that they may have it more abundantly.

John 10:10.

Every good gift and every perfect gift is from above, and comes down from the Father of lights, with whom there is no shadow of turning."

James 1:17.

"In Him (Jesus Christ) was life and the life was the light of men"

John 1:4

Likewise, the architect and author of all human misery and suffering is the enemy of God and mankind- satan. Which the scriptures also refer to as the evil one, the wicked one, the devil, the thief, murderer, destroyer, the old serpent, the deceiver of the whole world, a liar and father of all lying and the accuser of brethren.

He comes to steal, kill, and destroy. (John 10:10a).

You look at your life and see wounds from the past. You are in grief due to broken relationships, you are bitter, there are people you are struggling to forgive, maybe you have been driven into depression and anxiety and even despair.

All these being the result of the robber you encountered in the journey of your life. You may be wondering how do I deal with all this? Can I turn my life and situation around? The answer is-yes you can.

Others like you have done it and it has been done over and over again by different people-just like you.

Whatever situation you are facing, it can be turned around. This message will give you a step-by-step guide as to how you can engage the Almighty God in your life through Jesus Christ and how He can help you to turn your situation around and you will never be the same again. All scripture references are from the New King James Version (NKJV) unless stated otherwise.

The scriptures in 1 Chronicles 4:9-10 we read about a story of a man called Jabez, it says:

> *Now Jabez was more honourable than his brothers, and his mother called his name Jabez, saying "Because I bore him in sorrow".*
>
> *10 And Jabez called on the God of Israel saying, "Oh, that You would bless me indeed, and enlarge my territory, that Your hand may be with me, and that You would keep me from evil, that I may not cause pain!" So God granted him what he requested.*

Here we have the story of a man who was born in negative circumstances but was able to turn his situation around. His mother called him Jabez or sorrow maker. He was born into trouble, born in trouble, born for trouble.

If you like born in distressing circumstances, born surrounded by distressing circumstances and born into distressing circumstances.

The scriptures do not tell us exactly what distressing situation he was born in-we can imagine it was a combination of poverty and lack, disease and sickness, anxiety and depression, most likely difficult relationships etc.

Whatever situation you find yourself in, I am sure you can identify with Jabez. You will notice that in the preceding chapter and the preceding first eight verses of the chapter we have read, there is a list of names of people in the genealogy of Judah the patriarch. At Jabez however the flow of names pause to describe one guy more honourable than his brothers, distinguished from them in that he made some deluxe decisions which were life changing and by which he was able to turn his situation round.

Jabez had a different mind-set - he refused to accept the status quo, he rebelled against the status quo. He was completely persuaded that there was a better way and a better person to turn to in order to change his situation and circumstance. He knew differently, he believed differently, and he acted differently.

What did he know? What did he believe? What did he do? The answers to these three questions will be key to your turning your situation around too.

Let's look at each of these questions in turn.

First what did Jabez know? He knew that His predicament and that of his family was the result of the working of a robber in his life and the family's circumstances.

The robber is satan, the thief, the murderer, and destroyer of people's lives.

Jabez, crucially, also knew that there is God who loves and cares about him and who has the ability to turn his situation around completely.

He was fully persuaded about the God who has good outcomes in store for him. He knew God is good.

What did he believe? He believed that if he could repent and call on the name of this God, He would hear him and forgive him his past mistakes, heal his body, his mind, his relationships, give him back joy, peace, well-being- basically give him the full package he was yearning for.

What did he do? The scriptures record that Jabez called on the God of heaven. The call was an act of rebelling against the status quo. A lot of times we know what we ought to do but fail to do it. You might have habits you are struggling to overcome- maybe tobacco, alcohol, or excess weight killing you.

You might have other character attributes that are destroying your life, your relationships- maybe anger, impatience, and other manifestations of selfishness.

You know what you need to do but are struggling to do it. You need help to turn your situation around and you need this help desperately.

You may have tried everything you knew to no avail. You need the help of God. You need to call on Him. But we know that one cannot call on a God they have not believed in for the scriptures say in Isaiah 53:1-2

> *"Who has believed our report? And to whom has the arm of the Lord been revealed."*

So we know that when one believes a message of salvation as it is preached, then repents and calls on the name of the Lord Jesus Christ, the hand of God or the power of God is revealed to that person. Repentance is aligning one's way of thinking and acting with God. For the scriptures say in Isaiah 55:7

> *"Let the wicked forsake his way, and the unrighteous man his thoughts; Let him return to the Lord, and He will have mercy on him; and to our God and He will abundantly pardon."*

The Lord Jesus also said in Luke 13:3

> *"I tell you, no but unless you repent you will all likewise perish."*

The scriptures also say in Romans 10:14-15

"How then shall they call on Him in whom they have not believed? And how shall they believe in Him of whom they have not heard? And how shall they hear without a preacher?

15 And how shall they preach unless they are sent? As it is written: How beautiful are the feet of those who preach the gospel of peace, who bring glad tidings of good things!"

You are reading this message because I have been sent to you with a message of the gospel. This is not an accident or chance happening, it is your divine appointment with Almighty God. Here is your opportunity to turn your situation around.

To whom then do you need to call? You need to call on the name of the Lord Jesus Christ. He is the Son of Almighty God who was given to you so that He can forgive your sin and past mistakes, change you from the inside; make you a child of God and give you a new beginning in your life.

He is your neighbour on your journey. Before I invite you to do that, I need to explain it further.

In the gospel of Luke 10:29-37 we read a very revealing story:

29 But he, wanting to justify himself, said to Jesus, "And who is my neighbour?"

30 Then Jesus answered and said: "A certain man went down from Jerusalem to Jericho, and fell among thieves, who stripped him of his clothing, wounded him, and departed, leaving him half dead.

31 Now by chance a certain priest came down that road. And when he saw him, he passed by on the other side.

32 Likewise a Levite, when he arrived at the place, came and looked, and passed by on the other side.

33 But a certain Samaritan, as he journeyed, came where he was. And when he saw him, he had compassion.

34 So he went to him and bandaged his wounds, pouring on oil and wine; and he set him on his own animal, brought him to an inn, and took care of him.

35 On the next day, when he departed, he took out two denarii, gave them to the innkeeper, and said to him, 'Take care of him; whatever more you spend, when I come again, I will repay you.'

36 So which of these do you think was neighbour to him who fell among the thieves?

37 *And he said, "He who showed mercy on him." Then Jesus said, "Go and do likewise."*

Here the Lord Jesus described the situation of a man who was on a journey. He called him 'a certain man'. This could have been a certain woman, a certain young man or a certain young woman. Let's assume this person is you- hearing or reading this message today.

You are on a journey of this life. We shall call this your road to Jericho. I do not know what you have encountered. What I do know however is that you did meet a robber- called satan who attacked, robbed and stole from you leaving you half dead.

Take a moment to reflect on this robber and what he did to you and to your family. I do not know what this robber did to you personally. We know that this robber is in the business of destroying people's relationships, making people struggle with alcohol, tobacco and other illicit substances.

He is in the business of giving depression anxiety and helplessness. He is in the business of sowing divisions in families, giving disease and sickness of every description. He is in the business of deceiving people into sexual exploitation of every description leaving them with scars from the past. When you encountered this robber he left you half dead.

The scriptures describe three kind of people who came your way as you lay wounded on your road to Jericho.

The first person is a priest who found you lying and passed by the other side. This represents your encounter with false religion. You may have tried going to church or you have encountered religious people in the past but through them you never found God and you never found answers to your predicament.

The second person described is the Levite who came your way- this was your attempt to use human wisdom of various forms to get out of your predicament, legal systems, what the government offers-the doctor, the chemist – the full package of human wisdom in its various forms. They tried to help you with little success but your basic condition remained essentially the same.

At this point all hope is lost. You have tried everything you know. But you know what- there is another person to come your way and that is your good Samaritan.

The Good Samaritan is the Lord Jesus Christ, He is your true and un-failing, ever-present neighbour on your road to Jericho. This is what He wants to do for you. To bind your wounds of the past to give you healing, physical, emotional and spiritual healing. He wants to carry you to an inn- a church where you can be looked after and be taken care of. He wants you to be under a servant of God, a pastor given two denarii-an anointed servant of God, called by God to care for God's people, to guide and lead them in the way of eternal life. He wants you to be part of a church congregation where you attend regularly, have fellowship and be guided in the way of eternal life.

Let's summarise: You are in a situation which needs to be turned around. Jabez was born in such a situation, in distressing circumstances but he managed to turn his situation around. This was because he knew of a God who loved and cared for him, he believed that if he called on the name of that God, his situation and circumstances were going to change and he called and God intervened in his situation.

The Lord Jesus Christ is you good Samaritan. In the journey of your life, you met a robber, who wounded you and left you half dead.

Dead religion passed you by the other side, and did not help you to find God. Human wisdom of every kind passed you by the other side and could not get to the root of your problem.

But we thank God you do have a good Samaritan, who had compassion on you. His name is the Lord Jesus Christ.

He died and shed His own blood, so that your sin can be forgiven and on the third day, God raised Him from the dead and He is alive today. He wants you to believe on His name- that He died for you and rose again so that He can live in your heart.

He wants you to repent from your sin- that is stop arguing with God as to what is right and what is wrong, turn around and let your speech, thought process and actions align with the word of God.

Finally you need to call on the name of the Lord Jesus Christ and invite Him to come into your life and to be your Lord and Saviour. The scriptures say in Romans 10:9-10,13 :

> *That if you confess with your mouth the Lord Jesus and believe in your heart that God raised Him from the dead, you will be saved. For with the heart one believes unto righteousness, and with the mouth confession is made unto salvation...*
>
> *13 For whoever calls on the name of the Lord shall be saved.*

The scriptures also tell us:

> *For I delivered to you first of all that which I also received: that Christ died for our sins according to the Scriptures.* 1 Corinthians 15:3
>
> *Nor is there salvation in any other, for there is no other name under heaven given among men by which we must be saved* (**except the name of Jesus Christ**) Acts 4:12.

The following prayer will guide you to ask Jesus Christ to come into your life, to forgive your and past mistakes and to make you a child of God, if you pray it sincerely from your heart: Repeat after me:

Dear God in heaven, I thank you for sending your own Son Jesus Christ, to die for my sin, to shed His blood so that my sin may be forgiven, I believe that Jesus Christ rose again on the third day and He is alive today. I repent from all my sin today and I call on your name Lord Jesus, I ask you to come into my life, to forgive all my sin and to make me a child of God. Be my Lord from today. Thank you Lord Jesus for coming into my life, for forgiving my sin and making me your child. Thank you for giving me eternal life and for writing my name in the Book of Life. In Jesus's name I pray. Amen.

You may ask, how will I know that Jesus Christ has forgiven me and has indeed come into my life and given me eternal life? You can know and have assurance that yes indeed as you prayed sincerely from the heart you are now indeed forgiven and now a redeemed child of God because of the promises that he made. For Jesus Christ said in His word in John 6:37:

"All that the Father gives to Me will come to Me, and the one who comes to Me I will by no means cast out."

There is no possibility that He could ever say no, all He requires is your sincerity. His word also teaches us that God who promised us eternal life cannot lie. It says in Titus 1:2

"In hope of eternal life, which God, who cannot lie, promised before the world began".

His word also tells us that God wants you to know and have complete confidence and assurance that when you call on Jesus Christ and receive Him as Lord and Saviour, you have received eternal life. In John 5:11-13 His word says:

"And this is the testimony: that God has given us eternal life, and this life is in His Son.

12 He who has the Son has life and He who does not have the Son does not have life.

13 These things have I written to you who believe in the name of the Son of God that you may know that you have eternal life and that you may continue to believe in the name of the Son of God."

You may also ask: What do I do now?

You now need to 1. Be under a servant of God (see Chapter 2); 2. You need to learn to pray (see Chapter 3); 3. Learn to read the word of God (see Chapter 4); 4.To be baptised under water (see Chapter 5); 5 To grow into Jesus Christ and put off the old man (see Chapter 6); 6 You need to be filled with the Holy Spirit (see Chapter 7).

You will notice that being under a servant of God might look like an event- it is actually a process- as you need to belong to a congregation, and learn to be part of a team and learn to know and to be known by the key people in that team. The Pastors, Elders etc.

Learning how to pray is a process- as you will grow in your prayer life. Likewise learning to read the word of God is a process in which you will develop with time.

Being baptised under water is an event which ideally should happen as soon after you have believed on the Lord Jesus Christ as possible. In the Acts of the Apostles, on many occasions people were baptised on the same day that they repented and believed on the Lord Jesus Christ.

To grow into Jesus Christ and put off the old man is essentially a process. Giving up certain habits can sometimes happen so dramatically like an event however.

Being filled with the Holy Spirit is an event which is followed by a process of knowing the working of the Holy Spirit in your life- learning how to be led by the Holy Spirit, and how to receive counsel of the Holy Spirit.

It follows therefore that while some of these events will happen sequentially, a lot will be happening concurrently.

Chapter 2

Be Under A Servant Of God

Six Steps to Growing in Christ;

Being under a Servant of God:

You now need to belong to a church congregation where you attend regularly. As a new believer in Jesus Christ you need to find a Church with an anointed servant of God.

The word of God teaches us in Ephesians 4:7-16:

But to each one of us grace was given according to the measure of Christ's gift.

8 Therefore He says: "When He ascended on high, He led captivity captive, and gave gifts to men."

9 (Now this, "He ascended"- what does it mean but also that He also first descended into the lower parts of the earth?

10 He who descended is also the One who ascended far above all the heavens, that He might fill all things.)

11 And He Himself gave some to be apostles, some prophets, some evangelists, and some pastors and teachers,

12 For the equipping of the saints for the work of the ministry, for edifying the body of Christ,

13 Till we come to the unity of the faith and of the knowledge of the Son of God, to a perfect man, to the full measure of the stature of the fullness of Christ;

14 That we should no longer be children, tossed to and fro and carried about with every wind of doctrine, by the trickery of men, in the cunning craftiness of deceitful plotting,

15 But, speaking the truth in love, may grow up in all things into Him who is the head- Christ-

16 From whom the whole body, joined and knit together by what every joint supplies, according to the effective working by which every part does its share, causes growth of the body for the edifying of itself in love.

We notice here that God gave gifts to the church in the form of Apostles, Prophets, Evangelists, Pastors and Teachers, for the equipping of the saints for the work of the ministry, for edifying the body of Christ, till we all come to the unity of the faith and of the knowledge of the Son of God, to a perfect man, to the measure of the stature of the fullness of Christ. It is the will of God that children of God are not tossed to and fro by every wind of doctrine.

In the local church you will be taught and equipped and given guidance in the things of God. You need to meet regularly with other believers for fellowship, prayer and teaching of the word of God.

His word teaches us in Acts 2:42

"And they continued steadfastly in the apostles' doctrine and fellowship, in the breaking of bread, and in prayers."

His word also teaches us not to forsake assembling together on a regular basis in Hebrews 10:25

"Not forsaking the assembling of ourselves together, as is the manner of some, but exhorting one another, so much the more as you see the Day approaching."

Other believers will help, support and strengthen you as you leave behind old habits of bondage to the enemy satan.

You are three in one- with a spirit (the part of you that is eternal), a soul (your mind-being the seat of the emotions, intellect, will and conscience) and a body. When you receive Jesus Christ as Lord- it is your spirit which is regenerated, made alive and joined to the Spirit of Jesus Christ.

Hence His word says in 2 Corinthians 5:17

"Therefore, if anyone is in Christ, he is a new creation; old things have passed away; behold, all things have become new."

So, while you are a new creature in your spirit- you now need to embrace the process of being renewed in the thinking of your mind and being transformed to think, speak and act the way of a regenerated child of God. I will cover this in some detail in the chapters that follow.

In the local church you will also be able to find like-minded believers with whom you can establish close relationships. The two most important things to influence your life are what you hear/read and who are your close companions, who are the people from whom you take counsel. This does not mean you reject all non-believers, but it means you do not take counsel for life from them. They may be your teachers or colleagues in trade or school but not your role models for life.

From now on your strongest relationships must be with fellow believers. 2 Corinthians 6:14-18 speaks about not being un-equally yoked with non-believers. If you remain un-equally yoked, sooner or later that person will impact you negatively.

Proverbs 13:20 says:

He who walks with the wise shall be wise, but the companion of fools will be destroyed.

Psalms 1:1-3 also talks about the blessedness of a man who does not walk in the counsel of the un-godly nor sits in the seat of the scornful.

In summary therefore the benefits of belonging to a church congregation under an anointed servant of God includes:

1. You will have a place to nourish you spiritually as you get taught the word of God.
2. You will belong to brethren with whom you will have fellowship on a regular basis.
3. You will have sources of Godly counsel when you need it.
4. You will have positive role models as you grow in your faith.
5. It will be easier for you to let go of the bad habits you would have been involved with before you became a child of God.

There are a number of practical issues to consider here. In the era of technology where people receive messages on line, on television, internet chartrooms etc - it is still important to have physical fellowship. These technological innovations have made communication and teaching easier but cannot altogether replace human face to face fellowship, one on one counselling from a servant of God be it a pastor or an elder in the church.

Chapter 3:

You Need To Learn To Pray

Prayer is talking to God. It is important for a new believer to learn to pray to God every day. Talk to Him about your plans for every day. Talk to Him about your concerns, your anxieties. Talk to Him about your needs. As you do Almighty God also wants to talk back to you and reveal to you- your purpose and the plans He has for you.

The Lord Jesus Christ gave us a model prayer in Matthew 6:9-13

> *"In this manner, therefore, pray: Our Father in heaven, Hallowed be Your name.*
>
> *10 Your kingdom come. Your will be done on earth as it is in heaven.*
>
> *11 Give us this day our daily bread.*
>
> *12 And forgive us our debts, as we forgive our debtors.*
>
> *13 And do not lead us into temptation, but deliver us from the evil one. For yours is the kingdom and the power and the glory forever. Amen."*

In this model prayer the Lord Jesus Christ teaches us to start by addressing God as our Father and beginning your prayer with worship, hallowing His name or declaring that He is holy. At this point remember the names of God which declare His attributes in your life. It is easier to remember these names by their original Hebrew. These names of Jehovah or Jahweh declare what He wants to be to you, the attributes He desires to manifest in your life.

Hallowed be Your name Jahweh-Tsidkenu the Lord my Righteousness (He desires above all to manifest His righteousness in your life through the sacrifice of the Lord Jesus Christ on the cross. 2 Corinthians 5:21, Jeremiah 33:16).

Hallowed be Your name Jahweh-Jireh the Lord my Provider- He wants to be the source of all your provision (Genesis 22:14, Matthew 6:11).

Hallowed be Your name Jahweh-Shalom the Lord my Peace (He wants to be your giver of peace and total well-being Judges 6:24, John 14:27).

Hallowed be your name Jahweh-Nissi the Lord my Banner of Victory (He wants to be your source of victory, success and emotional satisfaction Exodus 17:15, 1Corinthians 15:57).

Hallowed be your name Jahweh-Rapha the Lord who is my Healer (He wants to be your healer and giver of good health and emotional well-being. (Exodus 15:26, Isaiah 53:5, 1Peter2:24).

Hallowed be Your name Jahweh-Shammar the Lord who is Present with me (He wants to manifest His presence in your life, this will manifest as His goodness and His glory upon your life Ezekiel 48:35, Matthew 28:20)

Hallowed be your name Jahweh-Rohi the Lord who is my Shepherd (The Lord wants to guide, shield and lead you as you make important decisions in your life every day, to lead you in the paths of righteousness. Psalms 23:1, John 10:11).

Hallowed be your name Jahweh-M'Kaddesh, the Lord who Sanctifies me, who concencrates me and sets me apart for His purpose and mission. Leviticus 20:8, John 17:17.

Then asking for His kingdom to come, to be manifested and to take root in your life, in your family, community, country and Planet Earth. The main attributes of the kingdom of God are eternal life, power, righteousness, peace and joy. His word says in Romans 14:17

"For the kingdom of God is not eating and drinking, but righteousness, peace and joy in the Holy Spirit."

It also says in 1 Corinthians 4:20

"For the kingdom of God is not in word but in power."

So as you pray ask for the manifestation of the attributes of the kingdom of God starting in your life and family and for the whole Planet Earth.

Pray for righteousness, that people may be saved, come to know Jesus Christ, cry for the out-pouring of the Holy Spirit who convicts the world of sin, righteousness and judgement (John16:8, Joel 2:28-32).

Pray for peace and well being in the same manner starting with your life and family – remember specifically those parts of the world with unrest, wars and strife, disease hunger and starvation. Ask for peace from the God who makes wars to cease (Psalms 46:9). Pray for God to move the hearts of those who have the substance of this life, to give liberally to those in need and who suffer lack.

Pray for the abolishing of poverty across Planet Earth through the manifestation of the love of God. (1 John 3:17).

Pray for the manifestation of the power of God in salvation of souls, deliverance from every manifestation of evil.

Pray for the will of God to be done in every facet of your life, family and ministry. This means you need to let go and let God accomplish His perfect will and purpose in your life.

Pray for His daily provision

Ask for forgiveness for the mistakes you have done and also for the things you should have done but did not do. Ask for the cleansing by the blood of Jesus Christ your Saviour. As you do that you need also to forgive and release those who have wronged you.

Ask God, not to lead you into temptation, to grant you grace for the hour of temptation, trials and testing and for deliverance from the wicked one satan.

Finally finish your prayer by worshipping Him- for His is the kingdom, the power and the glory forever and ever. Declare that He reigns in the earth, He reigns in your life, He is all powerful, the Lord of Hosts. Declare that all glory is due to Him who reigns forever and ever. Amen.

The model prayer was not meant really to be recited and repeated verbatim day in and day out-no. It was meant to give you a guide.

In summary:

a) Address God as your Father.
b) Take a moment to worship Him.
c) Address His names which declare what He wants to be to you and claim the promises they make to your life.
d) Pray for the manifestation of the kingdom of God- righteousness, power, peace and joy and for the will of God.
e) Forgive and ask for forgiveness
f) Ask for deliverance from the evil one and that you are not led into temptation
g) Close with worship and adoration.

You will notice that from day to day you can vary all items on this prayer outline depending on the needs you are facing, so that no two prayer sessions need to be the same.

Set apart time for prayer every day. Aim for spending an hour in prayer every day. This may be first thing on rising or last thing before retiring or at any other time during the day.

Our Lord Jesus Christ who set us an example prayed. Mark 1:35 says

"Now in the morning, having risen a long while before daylight, He went out and departed to a solitary place; and there He prayed".
Matthew 14:23 tells us:

"And when He had sent the multitudes away, He went up on the mountain by Himself to pray. Now when evening came, He was alone there."
In the garden of Gethsemane Matthew 26:39-41 tells us

"He went a little farther, fell on His face and prayed, saying 'Oh My Father, if it is possible, let this cup pass from Me, nevertheless, not as I will, but as You will.'

40 Then He came to the disciples and found them sleeping, and said to Peter, "What! Could you not watch with Me one hour?

41 Watch and pray, lest you enter into temptation. The spirit is willing, but the flesh is weak."

The Lord Jesus also taught us in Matthew 6:6

"But you when you pray, go into your room, and when you have shut your door, pray to your Father who is in secret place; and your Father who sees in secret will reward you openly."

We learn here that a) Prayer is individual b) God rewards prayer in various ways and openly. c)Prayer strengthens you for the hour of trials and testing. d) Prayer is preventative or prophylactic against temptation-that is, it stops you from being tempted in the first place. e) God answers prayer.

Also remember that prayer does not only give you the opportunity to talk to God, it also gives us the opportunity to hear back from our heavenly Father.

He says in Jeremiah 33:2-3 **"Thus says the Lord who made it, the Lord who formed it to establish it (the Lord is His name):**

3'Call to Me and I will answer you, and show you great and mighty things, which you do not know'".

Here the Lord says I made you for my purpose and I desire to establish you so that you can accomplish that purpose. Before you accomplish that purpose however, there are things I need to reveal to you, to make you understand. Before I do that however I need you to call to me.

As we pray, we should expect the Lord to speak back to us through His word, to reveal things to us through His Holy Spirit and as these things are revealed we get better understanding of His nature and character as well as His purposes and plans for us. In the process we grow in the knowledge of God and of the Lord Jesus Christ. Prayer therefore facilitates spiritual growth.

You came from God. You are a product of His thoughts, His planning. He has a purpose for your life. Before you entered your mother's womb He knew you and ordained you for a purpose.

In Jeremiah 1:4-5 His word says: **"Then the word of the Lord came to me saying:**

5 'Before I formed you in the womb I knew you; before you were born I sanctified you; I ordained you a prophet to the nations.'"

His word also says in Romans 8:28-30

"And we know that all things work together for good to those who love God, to those who the called according to His purpose.

29 For whom He foreknew he also predestined to be conformed to the image of His Son, that He might be the first born among many brethren.

30 Moreover whom He predestined He also called, whom he called he also justified, and whom He justified, these He also glorified."

He foreknew you- you are a product of His thoughts.

Then He predestined you- which means you already have a script written in heaven giving the details of the life you were ordained for, the purposes you were ordained to accomplish.

Now He is calling you- asking you to seek Him so that he can reveal to you the purpose He has called you for, the mission you need to accomplish in this life.

The beginning point, of that calling is repentance and acknowledging Jesus Christ as Lord. You are born again into the household of God, your sin is forgiven, you are made the righteousness of God in Jesus Christ. At this point you also need to set yourself apart or sanctify yourself for His purpose and will. The other word for this is consecration. (see Chapter 9, Understanding Holiness).

As you continue to seek His purpose you are justified by faith in Jesus Christ. That means if the enemy satan tries to throw mud at you- it will not stick because you are justified by the blood of His Son Jesus Christ.

Finally, He will glorify you or share with you His glory- make you experience His promises- make you experience His joy, peace and loving kindness, His mercies that are new every morning. You will experience His provision, health, victory, His presence, guidance and more.

Sadly, many people are living their lives outside Almighty God's purpose for them.

You need to seek Him in prayer so that He reveals His purposes to you and take you through the journey of foreknown, predestined, called, justified and glorified.

Chapter 4:

Reading And Meditating On The Word

You need to make reading and meditating on the word of God part of your everyday life.

2 Timothy 3:16 tells us

"All Scripture is given by inspiration of God and is profitable for doctrine, for reproof, for correction, for instruction in righteousness, that the man of God may be complete, thoroughly equipped for every good work."

1 Peter 2:1-2 tells us

"Therefore, laying aside all malice, all deceit, hypocrisy, envy, and all evil speaking, as newborn babes, desire the pure milk of the word, that you may grow thereby, if indeed you have tasted that the Lord is gracious."

When you have believed on the Lord Jesus Christ, repented of your sin and called on His name, you need to know that you have now become a child of God (see Ch. 10, Understanding Sonship), your sin has been forgiven, you have been made righteous before God and received eternal life (see Ch. 8, Understanding Righteousness), you have been redeemed (see Ch. 11, Understanding Redemption).

You need to live a holy life (see Ch. 9, Understanding Holiness).You now have responsibilities as a child of God. The first is to belong to a church congregation and meet with other believers regularly, the second to pray (as we have explained in Ch. 3 above) and the third to read the word of God.

We notice from the scripture in Second Timothy that all scripture are given, by God and profitable to a child of God to give instructions for living right with God- it is our instruction manual-for reproof (gentle rebuke, reprimand, admonition), to make the man or woman of God complete and equipped thoroughly for every good work. For this to happen one needs the correct understanding of scripture.

The correct understanding of scripture is called the truth. **It is the truth that sets people free.** (John 8:31-32).

The truth also sanctifies- it helps the believer to identify enemy lines, enemy lies and distortions of truth enabling you to set yourself apart for Almighty God or to consecrate yourself.

Jesus Christ said in John 17:17- "Sanctify them by your truth- your word is truth."

In other words- Your word correctly understood is the truth.

Understanding of the truth is critical for sanctifying yourself, consecrating yourself or setting yourself apart for Almighty God.

Setting yourself apart for Almighty God is in turn the beginning point for living a holy life, which in turn is critical for experiencing the workings of Almighty God in your life.

Correct understanding of scripture is in turn obtained when scripture is studied under guidance and supervision of the men and women given as gifts to the church.

Ephesians 4:7,8, 11-16:

But to each one of us grace was given according to the measure of Christ's gift.

8 Therefore He says: "When He ascended on high He led captivity captive, and gave gifts to men." ...

11 And He gave some to be apostles, some prophets, some evangelists, and some pastors and teachers.

12 For the equipping of the saints for the work of the ministry, for the edifying of the body of Christ,

13 till we all come to the unity of the faith and of the knowledge of the Son of God, to a perfect man, to the measure of the stature of the fullness of Christ;

14 that we should no longer be children, tossed to and fro and carried about with every wind of doctrine, the trickery of men, in the cunning craftiness of deceitful plotting,

15 but speaking the truth in love, may grow up in all things into Him who is the head-Christ-

16 from whom the whole body, joined and knit together by what every joint supplies, according to the effective working by which every part does its share, causes growth of the body for the edifying of itself in love.

So then, God gave gifts to the church in the form of

Apostles – special messengers,

Prophets – men with gifts to speak forth the mind of God at a given time,

Evangelists – men gifted to preach the gospel to cause conversion to Christ,

Pastors – shepherds of God's people and

Teachers – preachers with a special endowment to explain scriptures accurately.

Please note that Apostles will have gifts that pan across the five- fold ministry and will prophecy, evangelise, shepherd and teach.

The believer then needs to study the word of God under guidance of the five-fold ministry.

Please take note of the following:

a) As a new born babe desire the milk of the word of God- start with understanding the foundational doctrines of salvation (see Section 2- Critical Areas of Knowledge for the Child Of God) and move on to more solid food as you grow in your faith. Desire is key.

b) Be prepared to be corrected, to be given gentle rebuke or reproof.

c) Let your mind be renewed with the word of God.

Romans 12:2 says

"And do not be conformed to this world, but be transformed by the renewing of your mind, that you may prove what is that good, acceptable and perfect will of God."

The word transform used in the above scripture comes from the Greek word metamorphoo- which is the same word for metamorphosis - it is therefore referring to complete transformation like what happens to a caterpillar to become a butterfly. A caterpillar crawls at 4 mm per second whereas a butterfly flies 5 metres per second.

d) Get thoroughly equipped, thoroughly furnished for every good work by the correct understanding of the word of God; akin to a well decorated, well skilled and well-equipped soldier. This is a process- it takes time- allow yourself time to grow in the things of God.

e) Correct understanding of the word of God is called the truth-it sets you free to serve God, sets you free from the bondage of the enemy.

f) Correct understanding of the word sanctifies- enables you to set yourself apart for Almighty God, which is also called consecration- this enables you to co-operate with the Holy Spirit in the way you think, speak and act- which is holiness.

g) You need holiness to experience the workings of Almighty God in your life.

You need to read and study the word of God. I would recommend beginning from the Gospel according to St John, then the Acts of the Apostles and the epistles-then the rest of the Gospels and the entire Bible (in time). Get a version of the bible that you understand well. I would recommend the New King James Version.

Memorise key scriptures starting with John 3:16, Romans 10:9-10, John 1:12, Romans 3:23, Romans 6:23, 2 Corinthians 5:21.

Chapter 5

You Need To Be Baptised Under Water

Summary:

You are commanded to be baptized after you have believed in Jesus Christ.

Baptism makes you fulfil all righteousness.

Baptism symbolises the washing away of your sins.

Baptism symbolises your dying together and rising from the dead with Jesus Christ.

Baptism symbolises the dying of your old self, old habits, old ways of life.

Baptism symbolises a new beginning, a new way of life for you child of God.

The symbolism is best realised when you are baptised by complete immersion under water.

While baptism is not essential for you to be saved and to inherit internal life, it is powerful and immensely empowering to the child of God because it is a public declaration to satan and demons that your sins have been washed away by the blood of Jesus Christ, that you are identifying with the death and resurrection of the Lord Jesus Christ and you are now a child of God. It also helps you to fulfil all righteousness.

Notice the following:

a) The Lord Jesus Christ Himself came to the river Jordan to be baptized by John. **Matthew 3:13-15:**

Then Jesus came from Galilee to John at the Jordan to be baptized by him.

14And John tried to prevent Him, saying, "I need to be baptized by You, and are You coming to me?"

15 But Jesus answered and said to Him, "Permit it to be so now, for thus it is fitting for us to fulfil all righteousness." Then He allowed Him.

b) The word baptize comes from Greek baptizein -to immerse, to bathe or wash clean.

It is a symbolic outward and public expression of the washing away of our sins by the blood of our Lord and Saviour Jesus Christ. In Acts 22:16 when Saul of Tarsus was baptized we read:

And now why are you waiting? Arise and be baptised, and wash away your sins, calling on the name of the Lord.

1 Corinthians 6:11 we read of the sinful past of every believer and how the blood of Jesus forgave us and washed away our sin. Baptism is a symbolic expression of that.

And such were some of you. But you were washed, but you were sanctified, but you were justified in the name of the Lord Jesus and by the Spirit of our God.

It is also a symbolic outward and public expression of dying with Jesus Christ, you being buried together with Him and then rising from the dead, leaving in the grave the old habits, your former life, your former failures and entering a new life in Jesus Christ.

Romans 6:3-8, 11

Or do you not know that as many of us as were baptized into Christ were baptized into His death?

4 Therefore we were buried with Him through baptism into death, that just as Christ was raised from the dead by the glory of the Father, even so we also should walk in newness of life.

5 For if we have been united together in the likeness of His death, certainly we also shall be in the in the likeness of His resurrection,

6 knowing this, that our old man was crucified with Him, that the body of sin might be done away with, that we should no longer be slaves to sin.

7 For he who has died has been freed from sin.

8 Now if we died in with Christ, we believe that we shall also live with Him...

11 Likewise you also, reckon yourselves to be dead indeed to sin, but alive to God in Christ Jesus our Lord.

Colossians 2:12 reads: *Buried with Him in baptism, in which you also were raised with Him through faith in the working of God, who raised Him from the dead.*

c) You should be baptised after you have believed on the Lord Jesus and called on His name.

Mark 16:16 reads: **He who believes and is baptized shall be saved; but He who does not believe will be condemned.**

Earlier we saw how Paul the apostle was baptized after conversion, in Acts 10 in the house of Cornelius, believers were baptized after they heard the word and believed.

In Acts 16:33, the Philippian jailor believed and was baptized.

And he took them the same hour of the night and washed their stripes. And immediately he and all his family were baptized.

See also Acts 2:38: **"Then Peter said to them, repent and let every one of you be baptised in the name of Jesus…"** and Acts 2:41 **"Then those who gladly received the word were baptised…"**

d) The symbolic meaning of baptism is best fulfilled and demonstrated when baptism is done by total and complete immersion under water.

The Lord Jesus Christ was baptised at the river Jordan, the scriptures record that "Jesus came up immediately from the water". Matthew 3:16. Clearly, He went into the water and the assumption would be that he was immersed and completely covered with water.

In Acts 8 we read a story of how Philip the deacon, baptised an Ethiopian eunuch.

So he commanded the chariot to stand still. And both Philip and the eunuch went down into the water, and he baptised him.

39 Now when they came up out of the water, the Spirit of the Lord caught Philip away, so that the eunuch saw him no more; and he went on his way rejoicing. Acts 8:38-39

Here both Philip and the eunuch went into the water and came up out of the water. They did not need to go into the water if the intention would have been to sprinkle him with water on the forehead.

I'm certain the eunuch would have had some drinking water with him in the chariot. The assumption would be that he was completely covered under water.

We also notice that baptism happened as soon as possible after one believed in the Lord Jesus Christ and on many occasions on the same day as with the Philippian jailor and the Ethiopian eunuch.

Chapter 6

Grow Into Christ And Put Off The Old Man

Summary:

Experience the measure of the fullness of Christ.

Grow up in all things unto Him.

Be kind one to another, tender-hearted and forgive one another even as God in Christ also forgave you.

Let your communication impart grace to the hearers.

Put off the old man and put on the new man who was created after God in true holiness and righteousness.

You now need to grow into Christ and put off the old man.
Let the light of Christ permeate every facet of your life.
Let your life be flood-lit by the light of Christ.
Be renewed in the spirit of your mind.
Let the life of Christ permeate every aspect of your being.
Put on the new man who was created after God.
Live in righteousness and holiness.
Put to death the old man, old habits, and old way of thinking.

In Ephesians 4:17-32 the word of God teaches us:

This I say, therefore, and testify in the Lord, that you should no longer walk as the rest of the Gentiles walk, in the futility of their mind,

18 having their understanding darkened, being alienated from the life of God, because of the ignorance that is in them, because of the blindness of their heart;

19 who being past feeling, have given themselves over to lewdness, to work all uncleanliness with greediness.

20 But you have not so learned Christ,

21 if indeed you have heard Him and have been taught by Him, as the truth is in Jesus:

22 that you put off, concerning your former conduct, the old man

which grows corrupt according to deceitful lusts,

23 and be renewed in the spirit of your mind,

24 and that you put on the new man which was created according to God, in true righteousness and holiness.

25 Therefore putting away lying, "Let each of you speak truth with his neighbour", for we are members of one another.

26 "Be angry, and do not sin": Do not let the sun go down on your wrath,

27 nor give place to the devil.

28 Let him who stole, steal no longer, but rather let him labour, working with his own hands what is good, that he may have something to give to him who has need.

29 Let no corrupt word proceed out of your mouth, but what is good for necessary edification, that it may impart grace to the hearers.

30 And do not grieve the Holy Spirit of God, by whom you were sealed for the day of redemption.

31 Let all bitterness, wrath, anger, clamour, and evil speaking be put away from you, with all malice. 32 And be kind to one another, tender-hearted, forgiving one another, even as God in Christ forgave you.

So then as you pray to God and read the word of God which renews your mind, your way of thinking and then your way of acting.

Jesus Christ who is the Word of God is light, the light of God begins to shine into your life. (John 1:4-5). That light shines in the dark areas of your life and the darkness flees.

In Jesus Christ is also the life of God. You then begin to grow in the knowledge of Jesus Christ or the attributes of Jesus Christ begin to manifest in you more and more.

You then need to make a conscious effort to put away former conduct, habits of the past- which are driven by lust- these may include sexual immorality, substance misuse/abuse (including tobacco, alcohol, illicit drugs), lying, wrath, unsavoury communication or inappropriate language including swearing.

You should develop a language or manner of speech that imparts grace to the hearers.

You should put away bitterness, clamour, evil speaking and malice.

You should put on tender-heartedness, kindness, a forgiving spirit and attitude as you have also been forgiven by Jesus Christ.

Putting away some of the attributes of the "old man" may sometimes need time, intense counselling, guidance and support.

This is necessary for the believer to realise "the measure of the stature of the fullness of Christ" and "grow up in all things into Him who is the head- Christ" (see Ephesians 4:13 and 15 above).

Chapter 7

You Need To Be Filled With The Holy Spirit

Summary:

The Holy Spirit is the game changer.

You need the total in-filling of the Holy Spirit.

The Lord Jesus Christ Himself needed to be filled with the Holy Spirit.

The Lord Jesus Christ Himself only started preaching and demonstrating the power of God after being filled with the Holy Spirit.

The disciples of Jesus Christ exhibited qualities of being fearful, powerless, timid, weak, immature, carnal minded, full of strife and impotent, despite having been with Jesus Christ for three and half years.

When filled with the Holy Spirit- that all changed- they became bold, fearless, powerful witnesses of Jesus Christ who demonstrated His power with undeniable miracles.

Even ordinary disciples like Stephen, Philip and others demonstrated the power of God after being filled with the Holy Spirit.

There were visible external signs of being filled with the Holy Spirit- situations, people etc never remained the same.

You need to have a passionate desire to be filled with the Holy Spirit.

2 Corinthians 5:21 declares: **Therefore if anyone is in Christ, he is a new creation; old things have passed away; behold, all things have become new.**

You need to be filled with the Holy Spirit to live a victorious life as a child of God.

Remember even the Lord Jesus had to be filled with the Holy Spirit- we read in Matthew 3:16-17:

When He had been baptized, Jesus came up immediately from the water; and behold, the heavens opened to Him, and He saw the Spirit of God descending like a dove and alighting upon Him.

17 And suddenly a voice came from heaven, saying, "This is My beloved Son, in Whom I am well pleased."

The Lord was able to declare after that:

"The Spirit of the Lord is upon Me, because He has anointed Me to preach the gospel to the poor;

He has sent Me to heal the broken-hearted, to proclaim liberty to the captives and recovery of sight to the blind,

to set at liberty those who are oppressed;

to proclaim the acceptable year of the Lord." *Luke 4:18-19.*

Even the Lord Jesus started preaching and demonstrating the power of God after He had been filled with the Holy Spirit.

The disciples of the Lord Jesus Christ needed to be filled with the Holy Spirit.

Remember even Simon Peter denied the Lord Jesus three times just before the crucifixion.

The scriptures records how a servant girl came to Peter and said **"You also were with Jesus of Galilee."** Peter denied with an oath **"I do not know the Man"** and he even began to curse and to swear **"I do not know the Man"**.

When Peter realised His mistake, he went out and wept bitterly. Matthew 26:69-75

The same Peter on the day of Pentecost after being filled with the Holy Spirit, stood up and boldly proclaimed the gospel in Acts 2:1-46.

Three thousand people were added to the church on one day.

The difference was that the same disciples who often exhibited qualities of being fearful, powerless, timid, weak, immature, carnal minded, full of strife and impotent despite having lived with the Lord Jesus Christ for three and half years, being taught by Him and seeing the miracles He performed, when filled with the Holy Spirit became bold and fiery preachers who could demonstrate the power of God openly without fear or compromise.

We read in the Scriptures about the men chosen to serve tables were full of Holy Spirit and wisdom, among them was Stephen who even as he was being stoned by the Jews, continued to declare to them the word of God with power- to the point of death. Acts 6:1-15, 7:1-60.

We also read of Philip the deacon, who went and preached in Samaria, demonstrating the power of God. Acts 8:5-8. He was not one of the 12 apostles, but he was filled with the Holy Spirit.

You also need to be filled with the Holy Spirit with outward manifestation of the power of God.

In Acts 1:4-5 and verses 7- 8 the scriptures tell us how the Lord Jesus commanded His disciples not to leave Jerusalem as He was ascending to heaven, but to wait in Jerusalem until they were baptised with or immersed into and filled with the Holy Spirit.

"For John truly baptized with water, but you shall be baptized with the Holy Spirit not many days from now." Acts 1:5

And He said to them, **"It is not for you to know the times or seasons which the Father has put in His own authority.**

But you shall receive power when the Holy Spirit has come upon you; and you shall be witnesses to Me in Jerusalem, and in all Judea and Samaria, and to the end of the earth. Acts 1:7-8.

The word "power" here is from the Greek word dynamis- miracle working power, mighty power, power that works mighty deeds and wonderful works, ability giving power.

So child of God understand that your Father knows that you desperately need the Holy Spirit- for your benefit, for victory over the enemy satan, for a victorious walk with Almighty God.

His word says in Luke that we can ask for the Holy Spirit in faith and receive baptism with the Holy Spirit. You need to have a desire for Him, for His working and for His manifestations in your life.

His word says in Matthew 5:6: **Blessed are those who hunger and thirst for righteousness, for they shall be filled.**

You need to hunger and thirst after the Holy Spirit.

His word also says in Psalms 42:1: As the deer pants for the water brooks, so pants my soul for You, O God.

You need to thirst after the Holy Spirit.

Your heavenly Father knows you need the Holy Spirit

We read:

If a son asks for bread from any father among you, will he give him a stone?

Or if he asks for a fish, will he give him a serpent instead of a fish? Or if he asks for an egg, will he give him a scorpion?

If you then, being evil, know how to give good gifts to your children, how much more will your heavenly Father give the Holy Spirit to those who ask Him! Luke 11:11-13.

So if we humans, evil as we are can give good gifts to our children for their benefit, how much more will the heavenly Father who is holy, righteous, kind, loving, faithful and whose mercies for us are new every morning- how much more will He give you the Holy Spirit -for your benefit- when you ask Him for the Holy Spirit. I believe the answer is a zillion times!

You can receive the baptism of the Holy Spirit through being prayed for with laying of hands by church elders.

Now when the apostles who were at Jerusalem heard that Samaria had received the word of God, they sent Peter and John to them,

who when they had come down, prayed for them that they might receive the Holy Spirit.

For as yet He had not fallen upon none of them.

They had only been baptised in the name of the Lord Jesus.

Then they laid hands on them, and they received the Holy Spirit. Acts 8:14-17

Here we notice that being baptized with and being filled with the Holy Spirit is a distinct experience from believing and calling on the Lord Jesus Christ for you to be saved. We also notice that when people were baptized and filled with the Holy Spirit, there were some outward manifestations which people observing saw and were convinced that something had happened.

In the same portion of scripture, a certain Simon, "saw" that through laying of the apostles hands the Holy Spirit was given, and he offered money to the apostles to buy the gift from them. Peter the apostle, rebuked him and asked him to repent. (Acts 8:18-24).

The point is that when true in filling or baptism with the Holy Spirit happens, there will always be outward manifestations.

The most common outward manifestation of the in filling of the Holy Spirit described in scripture is speaking with other tongues.

This was the case on the day of Pentecost (Acts 2:1-11).

In Acts 10 we read a fascinating story about Cornelius, a highly decorated and high ranking soldier in the Roman Army, but one who feared God.

An angel of God appeared to him and asked him to go and look for Apostle Simon Peter who was two days journey away. When Simon Peter arrived and preached Jesus Christ to them, the Holy Spirit fell on them:

While Peter was still speaking these words, the Holy Spirit fell upon all those who heard the word.

And those of the circumcision who believed were astonished, as many as came with Peter, because the gift of the Holy Spirit had been poured out on the Gentiles also.

For they heard them speak with tongues and glorifying God.

Acts 10:44-46.

Here we notice that Peter preached the gospel and people believed and there was an outpouring of the Holy Spirit upon them with outward manifestations-one of which was – people were heard speaking with other tongues.

Mark 16:17-18 declares:

And these signs shall follow those who believe: In my name they will cast out demons; they will speak with new tongues;

18 they will take up serpents; and if they drink anything deadly, it shall not hurt them; they will lay hands on the sick, and they will recover.

We notice therefore that every believer needs to be filled with or baptized with the Holy Spirit.

Without being in filled and baptized the Holy Spirit a believer is weak, impotent, fearful, powerless, timid, immature, carnal-minded and full of strife.

The Holy Spirit gives you power, boldness, effectiveness, authority and might as a witness of Jesus Christ.

The Holy Spirit makes the word of God real in the life of the believer.

The Holy Spirit enables you to manifest the power of God in healing, deliverance and the manifestation of other gifts. (1 Corinthians Ch. 12, 13 and 14)

You must desire to be filled and baptized with the Holy Spirit. (1 Corinthians 14:1)

The Holy Spirit is received by faith on the promises of God.

To receive the Holy Spirit you must ask God to fill and baptize you with the Holy Spirit.

You will in most instances need to be laid hands by the elders in the church.

When you are filled and baptized with the Holy Spirit there will be outward manifestations including speaking in new tongues.

There are benefits of speaking in new tongues.

In Summary: When you believe on the Lord Jesus Christ and the sacrifice He did for you when He suffered and died on the cross and rose again from the dead on the third day, you need to repent from your sins, that is align with the word of God in the way you think, speak and act. You then need to call on the name of the Lord Jesus Christ and invite Him to be Lord of your life.

When you do this you receive salvation, you are given the gift of eternal life, you become an adopted child of God, your sin is forgiven, you become a new creation, you are born again, you are redeemed from eternal damnation, you receive redemption from the power of satan, redemption from poverty and lack, you receive the blessing of Abraham through Jesus Christ.

You need to have assurance of your salvation, by believing God's promises and His promises alone.

You need to belong to a church congregation where you meet regularly with fellow believers.

You need to develop a relationship with Jesus Christ through prayer (talking to God) and reading the word of God regularly. The word renews your mind to think and act like the Lord Jesus Christ.

You need to put on and grow up in Christ as you manifest more and more of the attributes of Jesus Christ and put away the "old man". Rebel from and leave your former way of life, former conducts, behaviours, attitudes and way of talking.

Be baptized under water which symbolises, the washing away of your sins by the blood of Jesus Christ, the putting away and burying of your " old man" and the resurrection of the new man. It is a declaration of your new life with Jesus Christ.

Be filled and be baptized with the Holy Spirit who will give you power, boldness, effectiveness, authority and might as a witness of Jesus Christ.

Section 2:

What You Need To Know And Understand

Critical Areas Of Knowledge For The Child Of God.

Summary of Section 2

In this section I will go through critical things a child of God needs to know and understand to enable a productive relationship with God the Father, Jesus Christ the Son and the Holy Spirit.

An understanding of these five needs will result in one experiencing God in their lives and living in the victory of Jesus Christ.

The five needs one needs to know and understand are:

1. **Righteousness** – you are the righteousness of God in Jesus Christ. You need to understand your legal position after believing on Jesus Christ, you receive the gift of righteousness as an undeserved favour from Almighty God because of what Jesus Christ did for you when He shed His own blood, died and rose again. This is not because of what you did – none of us would qualify for righteousness if it was a result of our works.

2. **Holiness** – our Almighty God is holy, which means He is pure. Holiness is a central attribute of God. The opposite of holiness is being evil – which is the nature of satan, the devil. For you to experience God in your life you need to be holy too.

3. **Sonship** – when you acknowledge the risen Jesus Christ as Lord, something very dramatic happens in your spirit. (You are three in one with a spirit – the part of you made in the image of God and which is eternal, with a soul – the seat of the intellect, the will, emotions and conscience, in a physical body). When you acknowledge Jesus Christ as Lord, your dead spirit is made alive and joined to the Spirit of Jesus Christ. You become intermarried to Jesus Christ and become an adopted member of the household of God. You become an heir of the Father and a joint heir with Jesus Christ. You are adopted by Almighty God to become a member of the household of God with the authority and privileges that it bestows upon you.

4. **Redemption** – the sin of Adam and Eve sold out mankind to death – spiritual death which is eternal separation from God. When God appeared on the scene He pronounced judgement upon the serpent, the man and the woman. The result of the judgement is disease and sickness; poverty, lack and toil; and enmity between mankind and satan. Jesus Christ the Son of God was made manifest to suffer and die so as to reverse that package in its entirety. He paid the ransom price to buy us back the privileges lost as a result of the fall of man and the ensuing judgement.

He redeemed us from sin, disease and sickness, poverty and lack and defeated, disarmed satan and his demons and gave the believer authority over satan and demons.

5. **Continuous positive attitude in His presence** – as you live in the presence of Almighty God you need a continuous positive attitude under every circumstance you may face. Your cup needs to be half full not half empty- always approach life from a positive angle knowing that the final say for your situation will always come from heaven and the final outcome will always be victory for you.

I will go into these subjects in turn in this section.

Chapter 8

Understanding Righteousness

Summary:

Righteousness is right standing with God.

You cannot enter God's presence without it.

One needs to know- Sin separates us from God.

Sin is giving your back to God and living for yourself.

By default your agenda will then be engineered by the enemy of God and mankind satan.

God wants you to turn back to Him. He loves you as you are.

You need to understand that Jesus died to buy us righteousness.

One needs to believe – He died for me and rose from the dead on third day and He is alive today.

One needs to repent- align with God, agree with God's word as regards what is right and what is wrong.

One needs to call- on the name of the Lord Jesus,

acknowledge Him as Lord of your life and invite Him to come into your heart

"For behold I stand at the door and knock,
if anyone hears My voice and opens the door (of their heart)
I will come into him and dine with him and he with Me"
Revelations 3:20.

With righteousness you also receive eternal life, forgiveness of sin,

you are born again (regenerated), you receive sonship and you receive redemption.

This full package is called **salvation**.

Covered in this chapter (All quotations from New Kings James Version unless otherwise stated).

8.1. Understanding Righteousness

8.2. The prayer for righteousness and salvation

8.3. How do I know I have received salvation

8.4. With salvation comes eternal life

8.5. With salvation comes forgiveness of sin

8.6. Salvation is a gift from God to you- it is for free- receive it.

8.7. The package of salvation

8.1 Understanding Righteousness

Sin separates you from God. Sin is giving your back to God and living for yourself. By default your agenda will be engineered by the enemy of God and mankind satan.

God wants you to turn back to Him.

He loves you as you are.

You need to understand that Jesus died to buy us righteousness.

You will need to understand that when Jesus died on the cross and shed His blood, He did so, so that you may gain access into the presence of the Almighty God.

For the scriptures say

"He made Him who knew no sin (Jesus Christ) to be sin for us so that we may become the righteousness of God in Him." (2 Corinthians 5:21 NKJV)

"For if you confess with your mouth that Jesus is Lord and believe in your heart that God raised Him from the dead you will be saved." (Romans 10:9)

"For God so loved the world that he gave His only begotten Son so that whosoever believes in Him should not perish, come to destruction but have everlasting, eternal life" (John 3:16).

"Nor is there salvation in any other for there is no other name under heaven given among men by which we must be saved" (except the name of Jesus Christ) (Acts 4:12).

"For Christ died for our sins according to the scriptures" (I Corinthians 15:3).

So then righteousness means being in right standing with God, or having His approval.

This comes by knowing and believing the sacrifice that His Son Jesus Christ gave when He suffered and died on the Cross of Calvary.

One then needs to repent (That is to agree with God as to what is right and wrong, to align oneself with His word).

For the Scripture says **"Unless you repent you will likewise perish"** Luke **13:3.**

Then call on the name of the Lord for the scriptures say:

"Whosoever calls on the name of the Lord shall be saved" Romans 10:13.

8.2 The Prayer for Salvation

The following prayer will guide you if you pray it sincerely from your heart:

Father in heaven I thank you that you sent your Son Jesus Christ

to die for me on the cross and to shed His blood that my sin may be forgiven.

I believe that Jesus Christ is the Son of God and that He died and rose again on the third day.

I repent from all my sin today.

I open my heart to you Lord Jesus and I ask you today to come into my life,

to forgive my sin and to make me a child of God.

From today I acknowledge you Jesus as Lord of my life.

Thank you Lord for hearing my prayer.

Thank you Lord for forgiving my sin.

Thank you Lord Jesus for coming into my life and making me a child of God.

From today I will live for you. In Jesus' name I pray Amen.

This prayer when prayed sincerely from your heart ushers you into the presence of God, all your past mistakes are forgiven and you receive eternal life.

8.3 How will I know I have received salvation?

You may ask – how do I know I have received salvation, that my sin is forgiven, that I have been received into His presence, that I have received eternal life?

You will know by faith, that is by believing His promises – because He made a promise that anyone who comes to Him He will never say no.

John 6:37 says

"All that the Father gives Me will come to Me and the one who comes to me I will by no means cast out."

He also says in 1 John 5: 13

"These things I have written to you who believe in the name of the Son of God,
that you may know that you have eternal life,
and that you may continue to believe in the name of the Son of God."

Finally understand that God cannot lie for the scriptures say in Titus 1:2

"In hope of eternal life which God, who cannot lie promised before time began."

In other words when you believe in the name of Jesus you need to have assurance that you have eternal life. That assurance is from faith alone – by believing His promises.

Almighty God wants you to know that you have eternal life after you have believed on Jesus Christ-

these things have I written to you who believe- that you may know you have eternal life. (1 John 5:13).

8.4 With Salvation Comes Eternal Life

Righteousness or right standing with God or receiving God's approval, brings with it other important benefits. These include:

Eternal life
Forgiveness of sin
Regeneration or being born again
Sonship (see also Chapter 10)
Redemption (see also Chapter 11).

When you believe on the Lord Jesus and the sacrifice He made for you on the cross, repent from your sin and call upon His name to invite the Lord Jesus Christ to become Lord of your life, you also receive eternal life.

In Matthew 25:46 the Lord Jesus said:

"And these will go into everlasting punishment, but the righteous into eternal life."

John 3:16 above tells us that when we believe in Jesus we receive eternal life. In Romans 5:21 we read:

"So that as sin reigned in death, even so grace might reign through righteousness to eternal life through Jesus Christ our Lord."

In the Lord Jesus Christ therefore we receive righteousness which leads to eternal life.

Romans 6:23 also tells us **"For the wages of sin is death, but the gift of God is eternal life in Jesus Christ our Lord."**

In 1 John 5:11-13 His word says:

"And this is the testimony: that God has given us eternal life, and this life is in His Son.

12 He who has the Son has life and he who does not have the Son does not have life.

13 These things have I written to you who believe in the name of the Son of God,

that you may know that you have eternal life,

and that you may continue to believe in the name of the Son of God".

It is important to understand that eternal life does not begin after one dies; it begins here on earth after receiving salvation through Jesus Christ, and it is in the Lord Jesus Christ.

Jesus Christ said in John 17:3

And this is life eternal, that they may know You,
the only true God and Jesus Christ whom You have sent.

Eternal life is therefore the knowledge and experience of God.
To know God you need to experience His power –
the power of the resurrection of Jesus Christ (Phillipians 3:10),
His peace which surpasses all understanding (Phillipians 4:7),
His joy inexpressible (1Peter 1:8)
and His love which passes all knowledge (Ephesians 3:19).

8.5 With Salvation Comes Forgiveness Of Sin.

When one believes on the Lord Jesus Christ and the sacrifice He made on the cross for mankind when He died and rose again from the dead, repents from sin and calls on the name of the Lord their past mistakes or wrong doing before God are cancelled. In other words all their sins are forgiven.

Whatever those sins might have been.

Luke 24:46-47 says

"Then He (Lord Jesus Christ) said to them,
"Thus it is written and thus it was necessary for the Christ to suffer and rise from the dead the third day,
47 and that repentance and remission of sins should be preached in His name to all nations,
beginning at Jerusalem.

In Ephesians 1:7 the word also says:

"In Him (Lord Jesus Christ) we have redemption through His blood,
the forgiveness of sins, according to the riches of His grace.

In Isaiah 1:18 His word also says:

"Come now, let us reason together", says the Lord,
"Though your sins are like scarlet, they shall be as white as snow;
though they are red like crimson, they shall be as wool".

It is the desire of God to forgive the sins of His people who turn to Him in repentance and in faith.

8.6 Salvation Is A Gift Of Almighty God To You – It Is For Free – Receive It By Faith Alone.

The word of God teaches us that God has given us eternal life and this life is in His Son.

1 John 5:11-12 (NKJV): **And this is the testimony: that God has given us eternal life,**

and this life is in His Son. He who has the Son has life, he who does not have the Son of God does not have life.

Therefore if God has given, we need to know how to receive it by believing in Jesus Christ.

Ephesians 2:8-9 (NKJV) tells us: **For by grace you have been saved through faith, and that not of yourselves; it is a gift of God, not of works, lest anyone should boast.**

Romans 6:23 (NKJV) tells us: **For the wages of sin is death, but the gift of God is eternal life in Jesus Christ our Lord.**

When you work for something, it is a wage/salary. A gift is given for free. We are saved by grace- it's a free gift of God.

Grace is an unmerited, undeserved favour, grace is activity on the side of God that gives us advantage.

You are saved by believing on the sacrifice which Jesus Christ did for you when He suffered, shed His blood and died on the cross.

You also need to believe that God raised Him from the dead.

8.7 The Package Of Salvation

The Oxford dictionary defines salvation as:

"Deliverance from sin and its consequences and admission to heaven".

The word of God says in **1Timothy 1:15:**
"This is a faithful saying and worthy of all acceptance,
that Christ Jesus came into the world to save sinners, of whom I am chief".
We have also already seen above Romans 10:9:
"For if you confess with your mouth that Jesus is Lord and
believe in your heart that God raised Him from the dead you will be saved."
And also **John 3:16:**
"For God so loved the world that he gave His only begotten Son so

that whosoever believes in Him should not perish,
come to destruction but have everlasting, eternal life."

Also, **Acts 4:12 "Nor is there salvation in any other for there is no other name under heaven given to man by which we must be saved (except the name of Jesus Christ)."**

Salvation then is to be made complete in spirit, soul and body.

In spirit by being regenerated, being made alive again by the Spirit of God in your spirit.

In your soul- which is the mind and the seat of the intellect, emotions, the will and conscience. This is made complete as you become a person of sound character, sound intellectually, sound emotionally and having the correct moral sense of right and wrong.

You are made complete in your body as you receive healing and deliverance from sickness, disease and every form of infirmity.

Salvation also includes deliverance from the consequences of judgement which includes poverty and lack.

It includes as well deliverance from demon spirits and bondage imposed on us by the enemy. These include:

anxiety, depression, any other form of mental illness, personality disorders, substance misuse alcoholism, tobacco and illicit drugs, deliverance from familiar spirits and spirits of witchcraft, horoscopes and every form of satanism. *(see also Chapter 11)*

Chapter 9

Understanding Holiness

Summary:

Holiness is co-operating with the Holy Spirit in the way you think, the way you speak and in the things you do.

Holiness is refusing to co-operate with satan the enemy of God and the enemy of mankind in the way we think, the way we speak and the things we do.

Holiness is separating yourself to worship God alone, to serve God alone and to live for God alone.

The Holy Spirit is the standard for holiness.

Holiness is a pre-requisite for living life in the presence of God and experiencing God in one's life.

Knowledge of the word of God is critical for living a holy life.

Living a holy life is saying no to sin.

Covered in this chapter:

9.1 Definition of holiness.

9.2 Understanding the necessity for holiness.

9.3 Holiness is a central attribute of Almighty God.

9.4 The Holy Spirit is the standard for holiness.

9.5 Knowledge of the word of God is critical for holiness.

9.6 He wants to write His laws in your heart.

9.1 Definition Of Holiness

Once one enters the presence of the Almighty God, one needs to understand how to remain in the presence of God. You need to understand holiness.

I define holiness as co-operating with the Holy Spirit in thought, in word and in deeds (actions).

The corollary of this (the other side of the same coin) is that Holiness can also be defined as refusing to co-operate with satan (The enemy of God and

Mankind) in thought, in word and in deed.

Holiness is therefore about how we think, how we talk and how we act.

Holiness can also be defined as thinking, talking and acting in the manner God would think, talk and act.

The Lord Jesus Christ was God in every respect and at the same time human and while on earth was in a human body.

He experienced the same human weaknesses and frailties as we do.

If one asked "In this situation how would Jesus have spoken and acted?" To answer that question one needs to know the word of God, the Scriptures.

9.2 Understanding The Necessity For Holiness

You need holiness to experience Almighty God in your day to day life.

> **Hebrews 12:14 says "Follow peace with all men, and holiness, without which no man shall see the Lord".**

The seeing the Lord being referred to here is not just about heaven it is about seeing and experiencing the working of God in one's life right here on earth. Without holiness one cannot remain in His presence.

Matthew 5:8 tells us **"Blessed are the pure in heart, for they shall see God".**

Again here- purity in heart is being holy. Seeing God here is about experiencing the workings of Almighty God in this life.

In Leviticus 11:44, His word says: **"For I am the Lord your God. You shall therefore consecrate yourselves and be holy, for I am holy.."** To consecrate is to set yourself apart for Him and for Him alone.

In Leviticus 11:45 the Word goes on to says: **"For I am the Lord who brings you up out of the land of Egypt to be your God. You shall therefore be holy, for I am holy".**

Being brought up out of the land of Egypt, a land of bondage, signifies the deliverance from bondage of satan, the attaining of righteousness, through believing in Jesus Christ.

He says the reason for doing this is so that the Lord may be your God, that we give our total allegiance to Him, and in return He will be our God- that is our everything (our Righteousness, our Provider (our source of every provision), our Healer, our Banner of Victory, our Peace, our Guide and Shepherd, our Omnipresent One).

For God to manifest His attributes or rather for one to have access and experience His attributes in one's life, one needs to be holy. Our God is a jealous God.

Exodus 20:5 says: **"You shall not bow down to them nor serve them. For I, the Lord your God, am a jealous God visiting the iniquities of the fathers upon the children to the third and fourth generations of those who hate Me, 6 but showing mercy to thousands, to those who love Me and keep my commandments."**

The best way of understanding the jealousy, which God feels when His people worship or bow down to the enemy is to compare it to how a husband or wife feels about sharing their spouse with another man or woman.

The beginning point for holiness after acknowledging Jesus Christ as Lord for salvation, and being filled with the Holy Spirit is consecrating yourself, setting yourself apart for Almighty God- this is a declaration you make after making up your mind and in sincerity:

I am yours Lord with all that I am and with all that I am not, I give my life to you, have your way in my life, do what you want with me, I will serve you and you alone.

You also need to make a declaration to the enemy satan:

satan and demons, I reject you and command you in the name of Jesus Christ to let me go and serve my God, you have nothing in me and I have nothing in you.

Holiness is to do with allegiance to Almighty God.

Critically and principally holiness is about your thought process as your speech and actions follow your thoughts.

There is an attack on the word of God in the world today- it is critical for the children of God and the church to be aware and alert to this.

When the truth is lost, there can be no sanctification or consecration, there can be no holiness and there can be no experience of God.

That is why it is critical to fight for the truth- which is the correct understanding of the word of God. The truth helps us to identify the enemy satan and his workings in the lives of people on the earth.

9.3 Holiness Is A Central Attribute Of Almighty God

Please understand this: holiness is a central attribute of Almighty God whom we serve. It means He is pure, He does not make a mistake, He is never late and does all things well.

Exodus 15:11 says **"Who is like You, O Lord among the gods? Who is like You, glorious in holiness, fearful in praises, doing wonders?"**

The central attribute of God is holiness, He does all things including His wars and judgements in holiness.

1 Chronicles 16:29 says **"Give to the Lord glory due to His name; bring an offering, and come before Him. Oh worship the Lord in the beauty of holiness!"**

Psalms 29:2 also says **"Give unto the Lord glory due to His name; worship the Lord in the beauty of holiness"**.

Psalms 96:9 **"Oh worship the Lord in the beauty of holiness! Tremble before Him, all the earth."**

In Psalms 89:35 He says **" Once I have sworn by my holiness I will not lie to David"**.

The Lord our God is holy and to have fellowship with Him in His presence we need to be holy too. The standard bearer for holiness is the Holy Spirit.

9.4 The Holy Spirit Is The Standard For Holiness

The Holy Spirit is the standard for holiness- you therefore need to know the word of God as it reveals the character and personality of the Holy Spirit.

In John 14:15-17 the Lord Jesus says

"If you love me keep my commandments.

16 And I will pray the Father, and He will give you another Helper, (Comforter, Advocate, Standby, Counsellor, Intercessor, Strengthener) that He may abide with you forever-

17 the Spirit of truth, whom the world cannot receive because it neither sees Him nor knows Him, but you know Him, for He dwells with you and will be in you." (AMP).

The Holy Spirit is the standard for holiness.

When you receive the Lord Jesus to be Lord of your life, He comes into your life by His Spirit and you receive a measure of the Holy Spirit who regenerates (brings to live) your spirit and make you "Born again",.

Following this you will also need to be filled, immersed, or baptised with the Holy Spirit.

Sin occurs when one co-operates with the enemy of God and mankind who is satan, whereas holiness is co-operating with the Holy Spirit. Between the two is the process of repentance which really is changing allegiance.

9.5 Knowledge Of The Word Of God Is Critical For Holiness

Jesus Christ said in **John 17:17 "Sanctify them by your truth: your word is truth".**

So, sanctification, or being set apart for Almighty God, or consecration comes through the correct understanding of the word of God. This leads to holiness-

The word of God is a critical component in this as it reveals the way God thinks and the way He acts it is therefore the instruction manual.

Ephesians 4:23 says **"And be renewed in the in the spirit of your mind".**

The word of God as we read and meditate on it is a weapon for renewing our way of thinking aligning it with the way God thinks.

Whereas righteousness is a legal position in the eyes of God (being in right standing with God) which brings one into His presence, holiness is to do with maintaining the privileges of that position and is to do with actions of daily living compatible with that position.

The Psalmist says in Psalms 119:**11 "your word I have hidden in my heart that I may not sin against you."**

In Psalms 119:105 the word says **"Your word is a lamp to my feet and a light to my path."**

9.6 He Wants To Write His Laws In Your Heart

In Hebrews 8:7-12 His word says:

"For if that first covenant had been faultless, then no place would have been sought for a second.

8 Because finding fault with them, He says 'Behold the days are coming says the Lord, when I will make a new covenant with the house of Israel and with the house of Judah-

9 not according to the covenant that I made with their fathers in the day when I took them by the hand to lead them out of the land of Egypt; and I disregarded them, says the Lord.

10 For this is the covenant that I will make with the house of Israel after those days, says the Lord: I will put My law in their mind, and write it in their hearts; and I will be their God, and they shall be My people.

11 None of them shall teach his neighbour, and none his brother, saying, 'Know the Lord,' for all shall know me, from the least of them to the greatest of them.

12 For I will be merciful to their unrighteousness, and their sins and lawless deeds I will remember no more."

The new covenant referred to is the covenant in the blood of our Lord Jesus Christ.

We activate that covenant when we repent, believe in the Lord Jesus Christ, call upon Him to receive Him as Lord and Saviour.

When we do that God deposits His Spirit in our hearts- the Holy Spirit which regenerates us.

We then need to be filled with the Holy Spirit. It is the Holy Spirit who writes the laws of God in our hearts.

When we co-operate with the Holy Spirit in our thoughts, the words we speak and the actions we do- we live a holy life that is pleasing to God, we experience God's working in our everyday life and live a victorious Christian life.

Living a holy life is saying no to sin.

How to be filled with the Holy Spirit is covered in Chapter 7.

Chapter 10

Understanding Sonship

Summary:

When you believe on the Lord Jesus Christ, that He died to deliver you from sin and eternal damnation, that He rose again and is alive today, and you repent from sin (agree with God as to what is right and wrong, align yourself with His word) and then call on His name and ask Him to come into your life and to become your Lord you become righteous before God. *(see Chapter 8)*.

You receive forgiveness of sin, you receive eternal life, you are regenerated (born again, made alive again in your spirit) you are redeemed. *(see Chapter 11)*.

You are adopted to become a child of God and a son of God (whether male or female).

You now have the rights of a child of God.

You become a member of God's own household. You have the authority of a son of God.

You have the inheritance of a son of God, the most important of the inheritance is eternal life. You become an heir to the throne of God and joint heir with Jesus Christ.

Covered in this chapter: *(All quotations from the New Kings James Version unless otherwise stated)*.

10.1 You received the right, power and privilege to be a child of God.

10.2 You were adopted to be a child of God.

10.3 You are heir of God and joint heir with the Lord Jesus Christ.

10.4 You are God's own special person, a chosen generation and belong to the royalty of heaven.

10.5 When you pray address God as Father.

10.1 You Received The Right, Power And Privilege To Be A Child Of God

When you receive Jesus as Lord of your life, understand the sacrifice He made for you when He died, shed His blood for you and rose again from the dead on the third day you also need to understand that you became an adopted child of God.

You became a member of God's household, an heir to the throne of God and joint heir with Jesus Christ the Son of God.

You therefore have received an inheritance in God's household the most important of which is eternal, everlasting life.

God is now your Father and you have the rights of a son (whether male or female).

John 1:12 says **"But as many as received Him (Jesus Christ), to them He gave the right, the power and the privilege to become children of God, to those who believe in His name."(AMP).**

10.2 You Were Adopted To Be A Child Of God

Romans 8:15 says :**For you did not receive the spirit of bondage again to fear, but you received the Spirit of adoption by whom we cry out 'Abba, Father'".**

Galatians 4:4-7 tells us: **But when the fulness of time had come, God sent forth His Son, born of a woman, born under the law,**

5 to redeem those who were under the law, that we might receive the adoption as sons.

6 And because you are sons, God has sent forth the Spirit of His Son into your hearts, crying out, "Abba, Father!"

7 Therefore you are no longer a slave but a son, and if a son, then an heir of God through Christ.

Fear is one of the greatest weapons satan uses against mankind, but when you realise God is your Father who has unlimited abilities all your fears should flee.

10.3 You Are Heir Of God And Joint Heir With The Lord Jesus Christ

Romans 8:16-17 says **"The Spirit Himself bears witness with our spirit that we are children of God, and if children, then heirs- heirs of God and joint heirs with Christ, if indeed we suffer with Him, that we may also be glorified together." (NKJV)**

An heir of God and joint heir with Christ – that speaks of authority and rulership.

Authority over every negative circumstance in your life and authority over every demon spirit of the enemy.

You have the authority to speak to command situations to change.

In Luke 17:6 the Lord said **"If you have faith as a mustard seed, you can say to this mulberry tree, 'Be pulled up by the roots and be planted in the sea' and it would obey you".**

In Matthew 17:20 the word says: So Jesus said to them **"Because of your unbelief; for assuredly, I say to you if you have faith as a mustard seed, you will say to this mountain, 'Move from here to there' and it will move; and nothing shall be impossible for you".**

You have been given the power and authority to change every negative situation you could face.

10.4 You Are God's Own Special Person, A Chosen Generation And Belong To The Royalty Of Heaven

1 Peter 2:9-10 says **"But you are a chosen generation, a royal priesthood, a holy nation, His own special people, that you may proclaim the praises of Him who called you out of darkness into His marvellous light,**

10 who once were not a people but are now the people of God, who had not obtained mercy but now have obtained mercy."

This is special and you should rejoice and celebrate this every day of your life.

Ephesians 2:19 says **"Now, therefore, you are no longer strangers and foreigners, but fellow citizens with the saints and members of the household of God."**

10.5 When You Pray Address God As Father

In Matthew 6:9 the Lord Jesus Christ taught us to address God as our Father
"Pray therefore like this: Our Father who is in heaven, hallowed be Your name".

Knowing and understanding son-ship is critical as it gives you the expectation to receive from God what a child would expect from a loving Father.

This also enables you to command the enemy of God and mankind, satan to let you go and to let go the things you are entitled to have as the right of a son in God's household.

Chapter 11

Understanding Redemption

Summary:

Understanding redemption is critical for every child of God.

When the Lord Jesus suffered and died for mankind he restored back to mankind the rights which were taken away from mankind when man sinned against God and fell in the Garden of Eden as described in the third chapter of the bible Book of Genesis.

The fall of man had consequences resulting from sin and consequences resulting from the judgement that followed.

It is important to understand the differences between the two.

The disobedience or sin of Adam and Eve resulted in death- the spirit of man became separated from God.

When God appeared on the scene He pronounced judgement upon satan and upon mankind.

The result of that judgement to mankind manifests in three main areas a) enmity with satan resulting in mental oppression b) physical pain, disease and suffering and c) poverty, lack, barrenness and toil.

The Lord Jesus died to redeem us from death that resulted from sin and suffered to redeem us from pain, suffering and the poverty that had resulted from judgement.

He also defeated and disarmed satan on the cross to give us victory and authority over the enemy satan.

Covered in this chapter: *(all scriptures are quoted from the New King James Version NKJV unless otherwise stated.)*

11.1 Understanding the origins of sin and the redemption from sin.

11.2 Understanding the consequences of judgement and our redemption from the consequences of judgement.

11.3 Understanding redemption from disease and sickness.

11.4 Understanding redemption from poverty, lack, toil and barren-ness.

11.1 Understanding The Origins Of Sin And The Redemption From Sin

Let's start by looking at the scriptures. As stated before the big bang theory does not help us understand the fundamental principles we need to grasp here.

Genesis 3:1-9

1"Now the serpent was more cunning than any other beast of the field which the Lord God had made. And he said to the woman, "Has God indeed said, 'you shall not eat of every tree of the garden'?"

2 And the woman said to the serpent, "We may eat the fruit of the trees of the garden;

3 but of the fruit of the tree which is in the midst of the garden, God has said, 'You shall not eat it, nor shall you touch it, lest you die."

4 Then the serpent said to the woman, "You shall not surely die,

5 for God knows that in the day you eat of it your eyes will be opened, and you will be like God, knowing good and evil".

6 So the woman saw that the tree was good for food, and that it was pleasant to the eyes, and a tree desirable to make one wise, she took of its fruit and ate. She also gave to her husband with her, and he ate.

7 Then the eyes of both of them were opened, and they knew that they were naked; and they sewed fig leaves together and made themselves coverings.

8 And they heard the sound of the Lord God walking in the garden in the cool of the day, and Adam and his wife hid themselves from the presence of the Lord God among the trees of the garden.

9 Then the Lord God called to Adam and said to him, "Where are you?

10 So he said, "I have heard your voice in the garden, and I was afraid because I was naked; and I hid myself."

11 And He said, "Who told you that you were naked? Have you eaten from the tree of which I commanded you that you should not eat?"

12 Then the man said, "The woman whom You gave to be with me, she gave me of the tree, and I ate."

13 And the Lord God said to the woman, "What is this that you have done?" The woman said, "The serpent deceived me, and I ate."

14 So the Lord God said to the serpent: Because you have done this,

You are cursed more than all cattle, And more than every beast of the field; On your belly you shall go, And you shall eat dust all the days of your life.

15 And I will put enmity Between you and the woman and between your seed and her Seed He shall bruise your head, And you shall bruise his heel".

16 To the woman He said: I will greatly multiply your sorrow and your conception; In pain you shall bring forth children; Your desire shall be for your husband, And he shall rule over you."

17 Then to Adam He said, "Because you have heeded the voice of your wife, and have eaten from the tree of which I commanded you saying, 'You shall not eat of it': Cursed is the ground for your sake; In toil you shall eat of it. All the days of your life.

18 Both thorns and thistles it shall bring forth for you, And you shall eat the herb of the field.

19 In the sweat of your face you shall eat bread till you return to the ground For out of it you were taken; For dust you are, And to dust you shall return".

Romans 5:12 says

"Therefore as through one man sin entered the world, and death through sin, and thus death spread to all men, because all have sinned".

Romans 3:23 says

"For all have sinned and fall short of the glory of God".

The sin of Adam and Eve resulted in spiritual death. Mankind could no longer have fellowship or communion with God. The result of this is eternal separation from God. This would result in perishing in hell for all eternity.

In Matthew 20:28 the Lord Jesus said

"Just as the Son of Man did not come to be served but to serve, and to give His life as a ransom for many."

In Mark 10:45 He said the same. The Lord Jesus Christ was the ransom price paid so that we could be set free from the bondage resulting from sin. His resurrection meant we can be resurrected from spiritual death.

In 1 Corinthians 15:3 the apostle Paul says:

"For I delivered to you first of all that which I also received: that Christ died for our sins according to the scriptures".

Romans 5:18 then says

> "Therefore as through one man's offense judgement came to all men, resulting in condemnation, even so through one Man's righteous act the free gift came to all men, resulting in justification for life".

While in Adam all mankind were condemned in Christ we receive justification. Romans 5:8 says

> "But God demonstrates His own love toward us, in that while we were still sinners, Christ died for us."

Ephesians 1:7 says

> "In Him (Jesus Christ) we have redemption through His blood, the forgiveness of sins according to the riches of His grace."

John 3:16 says

> "For God so loved the world that He gave His only begotten Son, that whosoever believes in (trusts in, relies on, clings to) Him should not perish (come to destruction) but have eternal (everlasting) life (AMP).

In Christ the rights of mankind which were sold out in the sin of Adam are bought back and reclaimed. Jesus paid the stipulated payment required to bring back the rights of mankind. He bought us back from eternal damnation and eternal separation from God. He bought us back from bondage of every kind that the enemy want to subject mankind.

11.2 Understanding The Consequences Of Judgement And Our Redemption From The Consequences Of Judgement

Following the sin and fall of man, God appeared on the scene and pronounced judgement on mankind.

The judgement resulted in firstly a declaration of war between mankind and satan (Genesis 3:15).

These results in mental oppression by satan of various forms including depression, anxiety, negative relationships, hate, substance dependency and misuse including alcohol, tobacco and illicit drugs.

Secondly the judgement resulted in all forms of physical pain, disease and suffering including the pain of childbirth (Genesis 3:16) Finally the judgement resulted in poverty and lack, barrenness and toil (Genesis 3:17-19).

11.2.1 Understanding Redemption From Mental Oppression

The sin of Adam and Eve resulted in judgement from God upon mankind, the result was a package of negative things including sin, disease and sickness of every kind, lack and poverty, selfishness, mental turmoil and distress, fear, anxiety and depression, bondage to substance and substance misuse, hate and negative relationships to name a few- Jesus Christ the Son of God was manifested to reverse this package in its entirety.

1 John 3:8 **says "[But] he who commits sin [who practices evildoing] is of the devil [takes his character from the evil one], for the devil has sinned (violated the law) from the beginning. The reason the Son of God was made manifest (visible) was to undo (destroy, loosen, and dissolve) the works the devil [had done] (AMP).**

On the cross not only did the Lord Jesus pay the purchase price to buy us back, to buy back our rights which had been taken over by satan when Adam sinned, He also defeated and disarmed satan on the cross and publicly.

Colossians 2:15 says **"Having disarmed principalities and powers, He made a public spectacle of them, triumphing over them in it (the cross)".**

Hebrews 2:14 and 15 says **"Inasmuch as the children have partaken of flesh and blood, He himself (Jesus Christ) likewise shared (partook) in the same, that through death He might destroy him who had the power of death, that is the devil,**

15 and release those who through fear of death were all their lifetime subject to bondage."

The Lord Jesus partook of flesh and blood, He became human like us and when He died on the cross he destroyed the power of satan over our lives so that we no longer live our lives in bondage to fear of death.

We overcome every form of oppression by satan including, rage, and hate, negative relationships, anxiety, and depression, dependency on substances like tobacco, alcohol and illicit drugs.

In the Name of Jesus you are given the authority to say to satan "Let me go", "you have no rights over me anymore", Jesus paid by His own blood the price for my freedom from fear and from every bondage you want to subject my life.

Please note that the Lord Jesus Christ redeemed us from sin and reversed every negative statement of judgement that resulted from it.

Not only that, but He also defeated, disarmed and destroyed the orchestrator of sin and judgement that is satan.

11.2.2 Understanding Redemption From Disease And Sickness

The Lord Jesus Christ redeemed us from the judgement of pain disease and sickness.

In Matthew 8:16-17 the word of God says

"When the evening had come, they brought to Him (Lord Jesus Christ) many who were demon-possessed. And He cast out the spirits with a word and healed all who were sick,

17 that it might be fulfilled which was spoken by Isaiah the prophet, saying: 'He Himself took our infirmities and bore our sicknesses'".

The scripture in the Book of the prophet Isaiah referred to was Isaiah 53:1-6 which reads:

1 Who has believed our report? And to whom has the arm of the Lord been revealed?

2 For He shall grow up before Him as a tender plant. And as a root out of dry ground. He has no form or comeliness; and when we see Him, there is no beauty that we should desire Him.

3 He is despised and rejected by men, a Man of sorrows and acquainted with grief. And we hid as it were our faces from Him.

4 Surely He has borne our griefs and carried our sorrows; Yet we esteemed Him striken, smitten by God and afflicted.

5 But He was wounded foe our transgressions, He was bruised for our iniquities; the chastisement of our peace was upon Him, and by His stripes we are healed.

6 All we like sheep have gone astray; and the Lord has laid on Him the iniquity of us all.

This chapter in Isaiah refers to the suffering of the Lord Jesus Christ and how He redeemed us from sin as well as from anxiety, depression and mental illness as well as from physical disease.

In verse 5 He was bruised for our iniquities, the beating (chastisement) that was needful to bring us peace, mental and physical well being was upon Him and by His stripes, the scourging stripes on His back, we are healed.

Notice this healing is in present tense not in past tense.

In verse 4 again surely He bore or carried our griefs and carried our anxiety, depression and every other form of mental illness (sorrows). He, Lord Jesus before He was taken to the cross was scourged.

Matthew 27:26-35 says referring to Governor Pontius Pilate

"Then he released Barabbas to them; and when He had scourged Jesus, he delivered Him to be crucified.

27 Then the soldiers of the governor took Jesus into the Praetorium and gathered the whole garrison around Him.

28 And they stripped Him and put a scarlet robe on Him.

29 When they had twisted a crown of thorns, they put it on His head, and a reed in His right hand. And they bowed the knee before Him and mocked Him, saying 'Hail, King of the Jews'.

30 Then they spat on Him and took the reed and struck Him on the head.

31 And when they had mocked Him, they took the robe off Him, put His own clothes on Him, and led Him away to be crucified.

32 Now when they came out, they found a man of Cyrene, Simon by name. Him they compelled to bear His cross.

33 And when they had come to a place called Golgotha, that is to say, Place of a Skull, they gave Him sour wine mingled with gall to drink. But when He had tasted it, He would not drink.

35 Then they crucified Him, and divided His garments, casting lots, that it may be fulfilled which was spoken by the prophet: They divided My garments among them, and for My clothing they cast lots".

From this passage of scripture, we notice that the Lord Jesus suffered pain, anguish, humiliation, mockings, was spat on – every kind of abuse imaginable.

He was made to carry a heavy cross; He was made to drink sour wine mixed with gall nothing could taste worse that. Every negative thing He suffered was for the purpose of redeeming us from that so that we can experience the opposite.

A big mistake of religious people is to feel pity for the plight the Lord Jesus was in during His passion- they forget He was the Son of God suffering for us for our redemption- what He was going through is what we were in, what we were going through- He chose to suffer it to get us out of it.

When you are drowning in the middle of a sea or river you do not pity people risking their lives to rescue you, after they have rescued you – you appreciate them.

He suffered pain to redeem us from disease and sickness so that we can live a life of health and well-being, He was humiliated so that we may be lifted up and honoured, He was made to drink the bitter and sour so that we can drink the sweet and savoury.

1 Peter 2:24 says **"Who Himself (Lord Jesus Christ) bore our sins on His own body on the tree, that we, having died to sin, might live for righteousness- by whose stripes you were healed."**

Psalms 103:2-3 says, **"Bless the Lord, O my soul, and forget not His benefits, who forgives all your iniquities, who heals all your diseases".**

In Exodus 15:26 the word says **"And said if you diligently heed the voice of the Lord your God and do what is right in His sight, give ear to His commandments and keep all His statutes, I will put none of the diseases on you which I have brought on the Egyptians. For I am the Lord who heals you."**

In Hebrew the term used here was Jehovah –Rapha which means *"The Lord Who Heals"*. The Lord Jesus Christ is our Jehovah-Rapha because He redeemed us from disease and sickness for by His stripes we are healed and made whole.

11.2.3 Understanding Redemption From Poverty, Lack, Toil, And Barrenness.

Following the fall of man, one of the judgements which God pronounced on mankind was poverty and lack, barrenness, and toil.

Let's recap what it says Genesis 3:17-19:

17 Then to Adam He said, "Because you have heeded the voice of your wife and have eaten from the tree of which I commanded you saying, 'You shall not eat of it': Cursed is the ground for your sake; In toil you shall eat of it. All the days of your life.

18 Both thorns and thistles it shall bring forth for you, and you shall eat the herb of the field. 19 In the sweat of your face you shall eat bread till you return to the ground for out of it you were taken; For dust you are, and to dust you shall return".

You see here that the ground was cursed to bring forth thorns and briars, in toil you shall eat of it all the days of your life, in sweat of your face you shall eat bread. The Lord Jesus redeemed you from the curse of poverty, lack and sweat and toil.

In Matthew 27:29 above, the Roman soldiers put a crown of thorns upon His head, the purpose for this was to break the curse of barrenness and poverty upon your life.

In 2 Corinthians 8:9 the word of God says **"For you know the grace of our Lord Jesus Christ, that though He was rich, yet for your sakes He became poor, that you through His poverty might become rich."**

The Lord Jesus became poor for our sake and experienced poverty or mean circumstances. For example, He was born in most lowly place, in a stable, most humble circumstances because there was no room for Him in places of dignity, comfort and honour.

In Luke 2:1-7 the word of God says

"And it came to pass in those days that a decree went out from Caesar Augustus that all the world should be registered.

2 This census first took place while Quirinius was governing Syria.

3 So all went to be registered, everyone to his own city.

4 Joseph also went up from Galilee, out of the city of Nazareth, into Judea, to the city of David, which is called Bethlehem, because he was of the house and lineage of David,

5 to be registered with Mary, his betrothed wife, who was with child.

6 So it was, that while they were there, the days were completed for her to be delivered.

7 And she brought forth her firstborn Son, and wrapped Him in swaddling cloths, and laid Him in a manger, because there was no room for them in the inn."

Yes, there was no room for the Son of the Most High God who owns the heaven and earth and everything in them to be delivered. The reason was to redeem mankind- He took our place in poverty, humility and lack so that we may have room and have dignity, comfort and honour.

In Matthew 8:19-20 the word of God says: **"Then a certain scribe came and said to Him, 'Teacher, I will follow You wherever You go'. And Jesus said to him, 'Foxes have holes and birds of the air have nests, but the Son of Man has nowhere to lay His head."**

Put simply the Lord of Lords, had no accommodation. He could have afforded to hire the best hotels of His time every night but HE CHOSE TO BEAR OUR HOMELESSNESS.

11.2.4 Redemption Means Jesus Christ Opened The Door For Receiving The Holy Spirit And Through Him The Blessing Of Abraham

The word of God further says in Galatians 3:13-14 **"Christ has redeemed us from the curse of the law, having become a curse for us (for it is written, 'cursed is everyone who hangs on a tree')**

14 that the blessing of Abraham might come upon the Gentiles in Christ Jesus, that we might receive the promise of the Spirit through faith."

The curse of the law spoke negative things to those who disobeyed the law. The curse brought every negative situation imaginable from poverty to disease, slavery and bondage, fear and anxiety but the Lord Jesus became a curse for us and redeemed us from the curse of the law so that we may experience the blessings of Abraham and also that we might receive the promise of the Holy Spirit through faith.

Let's look at these two aspects separately. Let's look at the blessing of Abraham.

In Genesis 12:1-3

"Now the Lord had said to Abram, 'Get out of your country, from your family, and from your father's house to a land that I will show you.

2 I will make you a great nation; I will bless you and make your name great; and you shall be a blessing.

3 I will bless those who bless you and I will curse him who curses you; and in you all the families of the earth shall be blessed."

The grace of our Lord Jesus Christ means we can enjoy work and derive satisfaction from it rather than it being a chore.

We can claim back health in our bodies as well as healing from disease because of the suffering of the Lord Jesus who carried our griefs, sorrows and pains.

The Lord Jesus Christ redeemed us from sin and from the consequences of judgement.

We need to claim redemption by faith – believing the sacrifice of the Christ.

Chapter 12

Understanding The Power Of A Continuous Positive Attitude

Summary:

To walk and live in the presence of the almighty God one needs to have and maintain a positive attitude.

This is critical. You need to see your cup as half-full and not half-empty.

You need to always be grateful for who you are, what you are, what you have received and to celebrate that every day of your life as you strife for better and for more. We have each been given different talents and to each according to our abilities.

We need to see the giver in positive light all the time and appreciate the positive intentions of the giver.

A positive attitude brings down barriers. A positive attitude is critical in overcoming adversity. A positive attitude releases the delivering power of God. Remember God feels your pain.

The underlying principle is that ultimately the positive will prevail over every negative.

It is like watching a game such as a football match when you already know that the final result is that your team won!

Another term for a continuous positive attitude is faith.

A continuous positive attitude therefore means you do not lose trust in God under any circumstances.

Covered in this chapter: *(all scriptures are quoted from the New King James Version NKJV unless otherwise stated.)*

12.1 Understanding a positive attitude.
12.2 Celebrating life in a positive attitude.
12.3 A positive attitude is not easily offended and brings down barriers.
12.4 A Positive attitude overcomes adversity.
12.5 A positive attitude releases the delivering power of God.

12.1 Understanding a positive attitude.

In Matthew 25:14-30 the Lord Jesus Christ spoke a parable saying:

"For the kingdom of heaven is like a man travelling to a far country, who called his own servants and delivered his goods to them.

15 And to one he gave five talents, to another two, and to another one, to each according to his own ability; and immediately he went on a journey.

16 Then he who had received the five talents went and traded with them, and made another five talents.

17 And likewise he who had received two gained two more also.

18 But he who had received one went and dug in the ground and hid his lord's money.

19 After a long time the lord of those servants came and settled accounts with them.

20 So he who had received five talents came and brought five other talents, saying "Lord, you delivered to me five talents; look, I have gained five more talents besides them."

21 His lord said to him, "Well done good and faithful servant, you were faithful over a few things, I will make you ruler over many things. Enter into the joy of your lord."

22 He also who had received two talents came and said "Lord, you delivered to me two talents; look I have gained two more talents besides them."

23 His lord said to him "Well done good and faithful servant, you were faithful over a few things, I will make you ruler over many things. Enter into the joy of your lord."

24 Then he who had received the one talent came and said, "Lord, I knew you to be a hard man, reaping where you have not sown, and gathering where you had not scattered seed.

25 And I was afraid and went and hid your talent in the ground. Look there you have what is yours.

26 But his lord answered and said to him, 'You wicked and lazy servant, you knew that I reap where I have not sown, and gather where I have not scattered seed.

27 So you ought to have deposited my money with the bankers, and at

my coming I would have received back my own with interest.

28 Therefore take the talent from him and give to him who has ten talents.

29 For to everyone who has, more will be given, and he will have abundance; but from him who does not have, even what he has will be taken away.

30 And cast the unprofitable servant into the outer darkness. There will be weeping and gnashing of teeth."

Notice here that the talents were given to each servant according to their abilities.

We all have different abilities, gifts, capabilities but we have each been given something to work with.

The difference between the first two servants and the third was attitude.

The first two had a positive attitude to their task and to their master.

The first could have asked why he was given so many responsibilities that would have meant waking up early on more morning doing more miles of trading and more work.

The second did not ask why he had been given two and not five.

He celebrated his two talents, with a positive spirit he went and worked with them.

One of the critical requirements for experiencing and enjoying the presence of God is having a positive attitude.

A positive attitude sees one's cup as half-full rather than half empty, it sees, celebrates, embraces and rejoices in what is there without perpetually mourning about what could be there.

It appreciates what has been given, it appreciates each day, it gives thanks continually, it is full of contentment for each step achieved, it sees the giver positively, it acknowledges the good intentions, it thinks positively, talks positively and acts positively even in a negative situation, it sees through the negative and sees the ultimate positive outcome.

The underlying principle is that ultimately the positive will prevail over the negative. Whether there is a challenging situation you are going through and whatever it may be, always remember to be positive and thankful.

12.2 Celebrating life in a positive attitude.

The psalmist says **"This is the day that the Lord has made, we will rejoice and be glad in it"** Psalm 118:24.

In Psalms 100:4 the word of God says "**Enter into gates with thanksgiving and into His courts with praise: be thankful unto Him and bless His name.**"

Psalms 32:11 says "**Be glad in the Lord and rejoice you righteous and shout for joy, you all that are upright in heart.**"

Isaiah 61:10 says "**I will greatly rejoice in the Lord, my soul shall be joyful in my God; for He has clothed me with the garments of salvation, He has covered me with the robe of righteousness, as a bridegroom decks himself with ornaments, and as a bride adorns herself with her jewels.**"

12.3 A positive attitude is not easily offended and brings down barriers.

A positive attitude is a persevering attitude and does not easily get offended. It is also a winning attitude. The word of God gives a good illustration of this in Matthew 15:22-28.

It reads:

"**And behold, a woman of Canaan came from that region and cried out to Him (Lord Jesus Christ) saying, 'Have mercy on me, O Lord, Son of David! My daughter is severely demon-possessed.**"

23 But He answered her not a word. And His disciples came and urged Him, saying, 'Send her away, for she cries out after us.'

24 But He answered and said, 'I was not sent except to the lost sheep of Israel.'

25 Then she came and worshipped Him, saying, 'Lord help me!'

26 But He answered and said, 'It is not good to take the children's bread and throw it to the little dogs.'

27 And she answered and said, 'Yes, Lord, yet even the little dogs eat the crumbs which fall from their master's table.'

28 Then Jesus answered and said to her, 'O woman, great is your faith! Let it be to you as you desire.' And her daughter was healed from that very hour."

Here we see a remarkable story of a woman whose attitude and determination was so positive that she passed every test that was thrown at her.

She came to the Lord Jesus with a petition and at first He appeared as if He was ignoring her, as if He was not taking any notice.

The Lord Jesus had taken notice, and was in fact deeply compassionate to the plight of this woman's daughter.

The whole exercise was a test of the woman's positive attitude and her faith and determination. This woman carried own putting forward her petition.

Then the disciples came and asked the Lord to send her away! I am sure that this lady heard it and must have been thinking –the Master ignored me now His disciples are saying send her away!

The Lord Jesus then in another test to her faith answered her and said I was not sent to you Cannanites- she read through this came forward and started worshipping the Lord Jesus.

Then He answered and called her a little dog in a further test to her faith and attitude and she answered further – it is alright Lord – I will be happy with crumps that fall from your table Lord- at that point she got her miracle and the Lord marvelled at her faith, determination, and positive attitude.

Remarkable story, most would have left at the first or second hurdle but for this lady was ignored- apparently- her response -no problem I will continue to ask.

Disciples say send her away- her response- no problem He is about to hear me.

The Lord Jesus says woman I was not sent to you- her answer-let me worship Him.

The Lord says you are a little dog woman- her answer- thank you I will do with the crumbs.

Her positive attitude broke every barrier in front of her till she got her breakthrough.

12.4 A positive attitude overcomes adversity – Lessons from the Book of Job Summary:

Notable quotations from the Book of Job:

"Naked I came from my mother's womb and naked shall I return there."

"The Lord gave, and the Lord has taken away; Blessed be the name of the Lord."

"In all this Job did not sin nor charge God with wrong."

"You speak as one of the foolish women speaks. Shall we indeed accept good from God, and shall we not accept adversity?'

"In all this Job did not sin with his lips."

"But as for me, I would seek God, and to God I would commit my cause- Who does great things, and unsearchable, marvellous things without number."

"For I know that my Redeemer lives, and He shall stand at last on the earth."

"And after my skin is destroyed, this I know, that in my flesh I shall see God, whom I shall see for myself, and my eyes shall behold, and not another. How my heart yearns within me!"

"But He knows the way I take; when He has tested me, I shall come forth as gold."

The story of Job is illustrative and instructive. In Job 1:6-20 we read

"Now there was a day when the sons of God came to present themselves before the Lord, and satan also came among them.

7 And the Lord said to satan, 'From where do you come?' So satan answered the Lord and said, 'From going to and fro on the earth, and from walking back and forth on it.'

8 Then the Lord said to satan, 'Have you considered My servant Job, that there is none like him on the earth, a blameless and upright man, one who fears God and shuns evil?'

9 So satan answered the Lord and said, 'Does Job fear God for nothing?

10 Have You not made a hedge around him, around his household, and around all that he has on every side? You have blessed the work of his hands, and his possessions have increased in the land.

11 But now, stretch out Your hand and touch all that he has, and he will surely curse You to your face!'

12 And the Lord said to satan, 'Behold all that he has is in your power; only do not lay a hand on his person.' So satan went out from the presence of the Lord.

13 Now there was a day when his sons and daughters were eating and drinking wine in their oldest brother's house;

14 and a messenger came to Job and said, 'The oxen were ploughing and the donkeys feeding besides them,

15 when the Sabeans raided them and took them away- indeed they have killed the servants with the edge of the sword; and I alone have escaped to tell you.

16 While he was still speaking, another also came and said, 'The fire of God fell from heaven and burnt up the sheep and the servants, and consumed them; and I alone have escaped to tell you!

17 While he was still speaking, another also came and said, 'The Chaldeans formed three bands, raided the camels and took them

away, yes, and killed the servants with the edge of the sword; and I alone have escaped to tell you!

18 While he was still speaking, another also came and said, 'Your sons and daughters were eating and drinking wine in their oldest brother's house,

19 and suddenly a great wind came from across the wilderness and struck the four corners of the house, and it fell on the young people, and they are dead; and I alone have escaped to tell you!'

20 Then Job arose, tore his robe, and shaved his head; and he fell to the ground and worshipped.

21 And he said: 'Naked I came from my mother's womb and naked shall I return there. The Lord gave, and the Lord has taken away; Blessed be the name of the Lord.'

22 In all this Job did not sin nor charge God with wrong."

When calamity came upon Job he fell to the ground and worshipped and the word of God says in all this Job did not charge God with wrong. He continued with a positive attitude.

In Chapter 2:9-10 after God had given satan permission to struck Job with painful boils from the sole of his feet to the crown of his head.

The word of God says

"Then the wife said to him, 'Do you still hold fast to your integrity? Curse God and die!'

10 But he said to her, 'You speak as one of the foolish women speaks. Shall we indeed accept good from God, and shall we not accept adversity?' In all this Job did not sin with his lips."

We see Job in the most testing of circumstances, He did not become bitter with God, but he maintained a positive attitude.

While still distressed with sickness and calamity on his household in Job 5:8-9 he said

"But as for me, I would seek God, and to God I would commit my cause- 9 Who does great things, and unsearchable, marvellous things without number."

In verse Job 5:17-19 he said

"Behold happy is the man whom God corrects; therefore do not despise the chastening of the Almighty.

18 For He bruises, but He binds up; He wounds, but His hands make whole.

19 He shall deliver you in six troubles; Yes in seven no evil shall touch you."

In Job 19:25-27 he said

"For I know that my Redeemer lives, and He shall stand at last on the earth;

26 And after my skin is destroyed, this I know, that in my flesh I shall see God, whom I shall see for myself, and my eyes shall behold, and not another. How my heart yearns within me!

In Job 23:10 he said **"But He knows the way I take; when He has tested me, I shall come forth as gold."**

In Job 42:12-17 the word says

"Now the Lord blessed the latter days of Job more than his beginning; for he had fourteen thousand sheep, six thousand camels, one thousand yoke of oxen, and one thousand female donkeys.

13 He also had seven sons and three daughters.

14 He called the name of the first Jemimah, the name of the second Keziah, and the name of the third Keren-Happuch.

15 In all the land were found no women so beautiful as the daughters of Job; and their father gave them an inheritance among their brothers.

16 After this Job lived one hundred and forty years, and saw his children and grandchildren for four generations.

17 So Job died, old and full of days."

We see that Job finally overcame adversity by maintaining a positive attitude towards God. In all this Job did not sin nor charge God with wrong. In all this Job did not sin with his lips.

12.5 A positive attitude releases the delivering power of God.

In Acts 16:16-30 we read

"Now it happened, as we went for prayer, that a certain slave girl possessed with a spirit of divination met us, who brought her masters much profit by fortune-telling.

17 This girl followed Paul and us, and cried out, saying, 'These men

are servants of the Most High God, who proclaim to us the way of salvation.'

18 And this she did for many days. But Paul, greatly annoyed, turned and said to the spirit, 'I command you in the name of Jesus Christ to come out of her.' And he came out that very hour.

19 But when her masters saw that their hope of profit was gone, they seized Paul and Silas and dragged them into the market place to the authorities.

20 And they brought them to the magistrates, and said, 'These man, being Jews, exceedingly trouble our city;

21 and they teach customs which are not lawful for us, being Romans, to receive or observe.'

22 Then the multitude rose up together against them; and the magistrates tore off their clothes and commanded them to be beaten with rods.

23 And when they had laid many stripes on them, they threw them into prison, commanding the jailer to keep them securely.

24 Having received such a charge, he put them into the inner prison and fastened their feet in the stocks.

25 But at midnight Paul and Silas were praying and singing hymns to God, and the prisoners were listening to them.

26 Suddenly there was a great earthquake, so that the foundations of the prison were shaken; and immediately all the doors were opened and everyone's chains were loosed.

27 And the keeper of the prison, awaking from sleep and seeing the prison doors open, supposing the prisoners had fled, drew his sword and was about to kill himself.

28 But Paul called with a loud voice, saying, 'Do yourself no harm, for we are all here.'

29 Then he called for a light. Ran in, and fell down trembling before Paul and Silas.

30 And he brought them out and said, 'Sirs, what must I do to be saved?'"

Here we see the story of an Apostle and his companion, being falsely accused for what they had not done, being beaten, humiliated and then cast into, not just a prison but the inner prison, the equivalent of a maximum security prison.

As if that was not enough, their feet were fastened in stocks.

At their midnight hour they did something amazing- they started praising God, celebrating His goodness, singing hymns and praises to God.

The most natural thing to do would have been to be asking God why allow us to be humiliated, beaten, fastened in stocks, put into inner prison for no cause- they did not do that, they instead maintained a positive attitude to their God, celebrated His goodness in the midst of such adversity- and you know what – He responded with force, an earthquake, shaking the foundations of the prison, stokes were broken.

After midnight Paul and Silas found themselves out of jail and preaching to the household of the prison keeper. If they had mourned, pity partied, etc it is likely they would have spent the night in jail and woke up with an unsaved jailor.

Section 3:

Almighty God's Promises To You

Summary of Section 3

In this section I will explain to you the five principal benefits of walking and living your life in the presence of Almighty God. These are promises which Almighty God makes to the person who believes in Jesus Christ and walks in obedience to Almighty God. These promises are summarised to us from Genesis 17 verses 1-8 and fulfilled in Jesus Christ.

They are:

a) **Almighty God promises to give to you His "Promised Land"** as you walk and live your life in His presence and in obedience to Him. You will experience the love of God- His mercies that are new every morning, His goodness, His peace, His joy, His hope and you will experience His love which will in turn give you the capacity to love others unconditionally.

b) **Almighty God promises to make you a person of "Character, Stature and Achievement".** For this to happen you need to understand the qualities which Abraham our father in the faith possessed- he was a man of faith. You also need to know God and His essential attributes, you need to have a knowledge of His word, to have a strong conviction (to have a high degree of persuadedness concerning His word); you also need to understand how to overcome the wicked one satan.

c) **Almighty God promises "To be your God",** to be your defining attribute through Jesus Christ- to be your everything-your giver of righteousness; your provider of every need; your healer and giver of healing and well being – spiritual, physical and mental; your giver of victory in every situation you face; your giver of peace and emotional wellbeing; to be present with you always- your ever present one; to guide you as you make important decisions in your life.

d) **Almighty God promises "To multiply you exceedingly"** as you live and walk in His presence. He promises to shield you, fortify you, lift you up, increase and multiply you exceedingly in every area of your life; to make you a person who is satisfied with his own life and achievements; to make you a kind- the God-kind and reproduce you after that kind; to make you a person of impact; to make you a witness of Jesus Christ who declares His word with power and conviction, to multiply His grace and peace upon your life.

e) **Almighty God promises to make you "Exceedingly fruitful"** as you live and walk in His presence. You need to understand the context in which you will bear fruit for Almighty God; to understand that the source of your fruitfulness is abiding in Jesus Christ, in obedience to His word; that we bear fruit for God as we give a Godly flavour to society in as much as salt and condiments give flavour to food; to understand that we bear fruit for Almighty God as we let the light of Jesus Christ shine through us to the world.

In this section I will do through these promises of Almighty God to you in turn in the chapters that follow.

Chapter 13

The Promised Land

When you live and walk in my presence-God says I will give to you the Promised Land, an experience of God's love and kindness.

Summary:

When one gives one's life to God and accepts the Lord God's invitation to walk before Him to live with Him and in His presence through repentance, accepting and acknowledging the sacrifice that the Lord Jesus Christ gave when He suffered, died and rose again from the dead, the Lord God promises to make all His goodness to pass before us, to have us taste His goodness, to show us that He is good.

The Lord wants us to experience every day of our lives His goodness, His compassion, mercy and loving kindness, His peace, His joy, as we trust in Him He wants to give us hope and the capacity to love and care for others unconditionally through Jesus Christ.

Covered in this chapter: *(all scriptures are quoted from the New King James Version NKJV unless otherwise stated.)*

13.1 He wants us to experience His goodness.
13.2 The Lord God wants us to experience His compassion, mercy and loving kindness every day of our lives.
13.3 God wants you to experience His peace.
13.4 He wants you to experience His joy.
13.5 As we trust in the Lord He gives us hope with which we can face every situation.
13.6 The Lord God wants to give us capacity to love and care for others **unconditionally**.

13.1 He wants us to experience His goodness

In Exodus 33:19 the word of the Lord says **"I will make all my goodness to pass before you…"**

In Psalms 34:8 His word says **"Oh taste and see that the Lord is good; blessed is the man who trusts in Him"**.

Psalms 136:1 says **"Oh give thanks to the Lord, for He is good! For His mercy endures forever"**.

When one gives one's life to God and accepts the Lord God's invitation to walk before Him to live with Him and in His presence through repentance, accepting and acknowledging the sacrifice that the Lord Jesus Christ gave when He suffered, died and rose again from the dead, the Lord God promises to make all His goodness to pass before us, to have us taste His goodness, to show us that He is good.

The way He does this best is by giving to us His joy (the joy brought to us by His presence in our lives) and His peace (the assurance and sense of well-being that His presence brings to us) and by making us experience for ourselves His grace (favours), His love and care on a daily basis.

When one experiences His goodness and His love, you are able to love others unconditionally.

13.2 The Lord God wants us to experience His compassion, mercy and loving kindness every day of our lives.

God is love and love is kind.

In Titus 3:4-5 His word says **"But when the goodness and loving kindness of God our Saviour appeared, He saved us, not because of works done by us in righteousness but according to His own mercy, by the washing of regeneration and renewal of the Holy Spirit"**(ESV).

Psalms 136:1 Says **"Oh give thanks to the Lord for He is good for His mercy and loving kindness endures forever"** (AMP).

In 2 Chronicles 7:6 **"The priests stood at their posts, and the Levites also with instruments of music to the Lord, which King David had made to praise and give thanks to the Lord- for His mercy and loving kindness endure forever…"**

Lamentations 3:22-23 says **"Through the Lord's mercies we are not consumed, because His compassions fail not. They are new every morning; great is Your faithfulness"**.

In Psalms 36:7-8 the Psalmist says **"How excellent is thy loving kindness, O God! Therefore the children of men put their trust under the shadow of thy wings.**

8 They shall be abundantly satisfied with the fatness of thy house; and thou shall make them drink from the rivers of thy pleasures" (KJV).

In Psalms 63:3-4 the Psalmist says **"Because Your loving kindness is better than life, my lips shall praise You. Thus I will bless You while I live".**

13.3 God wants you to experience His peace The Lord God also wants us to experience His peace.

In Isaiah 53: 4-5 referring to the Lord Jesus Christ says **"Surely He has borne our griefs and carried our sorrows; Yet we esteemed Him striken, smitten of God and afflicted.**

5 But He was wounded for our transgressions, He was bruised for our iniquities; the chastisement of our peace was upon Him and by His stripes we are healed".

The amplified Bible puts it this way **"Surely He has borne our griefs (sicknesses, weaknesses, and distresses) and carried our sorrows and pains [of punishment], yet we [ignorantly] considered Him stricken, smitten, and afflicted by God [as if with leprosy].**

5 But He was wounded for our transgressions, He was bruised for our guilt and iniquities; the chastisement [needful to obtain] peace and well-being was upon Him, and with the stripes [that wounded] Him we are healed and made whole."

Here the scriptures declare that the Lord Jesus Christ suffered pain, distress and anguish and in so doing carried our sicknesses, weaknesses and distresses to buy back peace, healing and well-being.

In John 14:27 the Lord Jesus Christ says **"Peace I leave with you, My peace I give to you; not as the world gives do I give to you. Let not your heart be troubled, neither let it be afraid".**

After the resurrection of the Lord Jesus Christ He appeared to His disciples and Luke 24:36 says **"Now as they said these things, Jesus Himself stood in the midst of them, and said to them, 'Peace to you'.**

In the epistles written by the Apostle Peter, he begins by declaring **"...Grace to you and peace be multiplied".** (1Peter 1:2).

The same also in His second epistle **"Grace and peace be multiplied to you in the knowledge of God and of Jesus Christ our Lord"** (2 Peter 1:2).

In Romans 15:13 the Apostle Paul wrote **"Now may the God of hope fill you with all joy and peace in believing, that you may abound in hope by the power of the Holy Spirit".**

In Ephesians 2:14, the word says referring to the Lord Jesus Christ **"For He Himself is our peace, who made both one, and has broken down the middle wall of separation, having abolished in His flesh the enmity, that is, the law of commandments contained in ordinances, so as to create in Himself one new man from the two, thus making peace".**

13.4: He wants you to experience His joy.

In Psalms 4:7-8 His word says **"You have put more joy in my heart than they have when their grain and wine abound.**

8 In peace I will both lie down and sleep; for you alone Lord, make me dwell in safety."

In Nehemiah 8:10 the word says **"Then he said to them, 'Go your way, eat the fat, drink the sweet, and send portions to those for whom nothing is prepared; for this day is holy to our Lord. Do not sorrow, for the joy of the Lord is your strength.'"**

In Psalms 126:2 the word says **"Then our mouth was filled with laughter, and our tongue with singing. And they said among the nations, 'The Lord has done great things for them".**

In Psalms 35:9, the psalmist says **"And my soul shall be joyful in the Lord; it shall rejoice in His salvation'.**

Psalms 36:8 **"They are abundantly satisfied with the fullness of Your house, and You give them drink from the rivers of your pleasures".**

In Psalms 105:43, the psalmist says **"He brought out His people with joy, His chosen ones with gladness."**

In Isaiah 55:12 the word also says **"For you shall go out with joy, and be led out with peace; The mountains and the hills shall break forth into singing before you, and all the trees of the field shall clap their hands."**

In Luke 2:10 **"Then the angel said to them, 'Do not be afraid for behold I bring you good tidings of great joy which shall be to all people.'"**

In John 15:11 The Lord Jesus said to His disciples **"These things I have spoken to you, that My joy may remain in you, and that your joy may be full".**

In Romans 14; 17, the word says **"For the kingdom of God is not eating and drinking, but righteousness and peace and joy in the Holy Spirit".**

In 1Peter1:8 His word says **"Whom having not seen you love. Though now you do not see Him, yet believing, you rejoice with joy inexpressible** and full of glory".

The joy here is described as **inexpressible.** The Amplified bible describes it as **inexpressible** and **glorious, triumphant, heavenly joy.** The Good News bible describes this joy as **"great and glorious joy which words cannot express".** The King James Bible describes it as **"joy unspeakable".**

13.5: As we trust in the Lord He gives us hope with which we can face every situation.

The Lord gives us hope.

The word of God in Jeremiah 17:7 says **"Blessed is the man that trusts in the Lord, and whose hope is the Lord. For he shall be as a tree planted by the waters, which spreads out its roots by the river, and will not fear when heat comes; but its leaf will be green, and will not be anxious in the year of drought, nor will cease from yielding fruit".**

The Lord God is a fountain of living waters to those who trust in Him.

Jeremiah 17:13 goes on to say **"O Lord the hope of Israel, all who forsake You shall be ashamed. 'Those who depart from Me shall be written in the earth, because they have forsaken the Lord, the fountain of living waters'".**

Jeremiah 17: 17 goes further to say **"Do not be a terror to me; You are my hope in the day of doom".**

Romans 5:5 says **"Now hope does not disappoint, because the love of God has been poured out in our hearts by the Holy Spirit who was given to us".**

I Corinthians 13:13 says **"And now abide faith, hope, love, these three; but the greatest is love".** Here Paul the Apostle by the Holy Spirit declares that the qualities that will endure and cause endurance in the hearts and minds of mankind are faith, hope and love.

In Hebrews 11:1 the word defines faith –**"Now faith is the substance of things hoped for, the evidence of things not seen".**

There can be no faith without hope for faith is the substance of hope, when we hope in the Lord God and trust in Him, then we have faith in Him.

13.6: The love of God gives us capacity to love and care for others unconditionally.

When the Lord God makes all His goodness to pass before us and we experience His loving kindness, His joy, His peace and we hope and trust in Him.

That experience comes to us through believing in the Lord Jesus and the sacrifice He made on the cross when He shed His own blood and died for our for-giveness and our redemption.

That experience of the fullness of His grace and goodness gives us the capaci-ty to love and care for others unconditionally.

In 1 Corinthians 13 1-8, 13 the Apostle Paul writing by the Holy Spirit says

"Though I speak with the tongues of men and of angels, but have not love, I have become sounding brass or a clanging cymbal.

2 And though I have the gift of prophecy, and understand all mysteries and all knowledge, and though I have all faith, so that I could remove mountains, but have not love, I am nothing.

3 And though I bestow all my goods to feed the poor. And though I give my body to be burned, but have not love, it profits me nothing.

4 Love suffers long and is kind; love does not envy; love does not parade itself, is not puffed up;

5 does not behave rudely, does not seek its own, is not provoked, thinks no evil;

6 does not rejoice in iniquity, but rejoices in the truth;

7 bears all things, believes all things, hopes all things, endures all things.

8 Love never fails. ...

13 And now abide faith, hope, love, these three; but the greatest of these is love".

Verses 4 to 8 list the qualities of true love of God-it is kind, it suffers long, it does not seek the welfare of self at the expense of the welfare of others, it is not easily provoked but gives others room to make mistakes without feeling imme-diately offended, does not envy, does not rejoice in sin but rejoices in the truth, love is not cynical, but gives others the benefit of the doubt, looks at situations positively and it does not fail. Love is in action and not just in talking.

Chapter 14

Character, Stature And Achievement

God said if you walk and live in my presence I will make you a person of character, stature and achievements.

Summary:

God promises to make you fathers and mothers, young men and young women, boys and girls of character, stature and achievements.

God promises to make you a person who builds stable, healthy and enduring relationships between spouses, parents and children, brethren, neighbours, colleagues and society at large.

God promises to make you a person of stature and achievement in the affairs of this life through the knowledge and wisdom of Jesus Christ.

This will be possible through

1. The knowledge of God and His essential attributes,
2. The knowledge of His word,
3. A strong conviction of His word and
4. Overcoming the wicked one (satan).

Covered in this chapter: *(all scriptures are quoted from the New King James Version NKJV unless otherwise stated.)*

14.1 Learning from Abraham the father of those who believe-the qualities he possessed.

14.2 To receive His promises you need to understand the need to know God and His essential attributes.

14.3 To receive His promises you need to understand the need to have the knowledge of the word of God.

14.4 To receive His promise you need to understand the need to have a strong conviction, a high degree of persuadedness concerning His promises.

14.5 To receive His promises you need to understand how to overcome the wicked one.

14.5.1 To overcome the wicked one you need to understand the nature of satan.

14.5.2 To overcome the wicked one you need to understand the origins of satan.

14.6 Understanding the believer's victory over satan.

14.6.1 Understanding the authority of the believer to bind and rebuke satan in the name of The Lord Jesus Christ.

14.6.2 Understanding the victory over satan through the confession of the blood of the Lord Jesus Christ.

14.1 Learning from Abraham the father of those who believe – the qualities he possessed.

The main qualities in Abraham that qualifies him to be the father of those who believe is that he believed the word of God in an unwavering way.

He was fully persuaded about what God had spoken. He had a strong conviction on which he was able to act and obey.

He also knew God and some of the critical qualities that He possesses that is that God raises the dead and speaks of non-existent things that he has foretold as if they already exist.

Abraham staggered not at the promises of God through unbelief, considered not his own body as good as dead nor the deadness of Sarah his wife's womb.

When human reason for hope had gone he believed in a God who raises the dead and calls things that do not exist as if they already existed.

We read in **Genesis 15:1-6**:

1 "After these things, the word of the Lord came to Abram in a vision, saying, 'Do not be afraid, Abram, I am your shield, your exceeding great reward'.

2 But Abram said 'Lord God, what will You give me, seeing I go childless, and the heir of my house is Eliezer of Damascus?'

3 Then Abram said, 'Look you have given me no offspring; indeed one born in my house is my heir!'

4 And behold the word of the Lord came to him saying 'This one shall not be your heir, but one who will come from your own body shall be your heir.'

5 Then He brought him outside and said, 'Look now towards heaven, and count the stars if you are able to number them.' And He said to him, 'So shall your descendants be'.

6 And he believed in the Lord and He accounted it to him for righteousness."

In Genesis 17:1-5 the word of God says

1 "When Abram was ninety-nine years old, the Lord appeared to Abram and said to him, 'I am Almighty God; walk before me and be blameless.

2 And I will make My covenant between Me and you and will multiply you exceedingly.'

3 Then Abram fell on his face and God talked with him, saying

4 As for Me, behold, My covenant is with you, and you shall be a father of many nations.

5 No longer shall your name be Abram, but your name shall be Abraham; for I have made you a father of many nations."

In Isaiah 51:1-2 the word says

"Listen to me you who follow after righteousness, you who seek the Lord:

Look to the rock from whom you were hewn, and to the hole from which you were dug.

2 Look to Abraham your father and to Sarah who bore you; for I called him alone and blessed him and increased him."

Here the word of the Lord declares that Abraham is the father of those who believe, and Sarah is the mother of the women who believe.

The word declares here that God called him alone and blessed him and increased him.

If you look further to Romans 4:16-22 says

"Therefore [inheriting] the promise is the outcome of faith and depends [entirely] on faith, in order that it might be given as an act of grace [unmerited favour], to make it stable and valid and guaranteed to all his descendants—not only to the devotees and adherents of the law, but also to those who share the faith of Abraham, who is [thus] the father of us all.

17 As it is written, I have made you the father of many nations. [He was appointed our father] in the sight of God in Whom he believed, Who gives life to the dead and speaks of the non-existent things that [He has foretold and promised] as if they [already] existed.

18 [For Abraham human reason for] hope being gone, hoped in faith

that he should become the father of many nations as he had been promised, so [numberless] shall your descendants be.

19 He did not weaken in faith when he considered the [utter] impotence of his own body, which was as good as dead because he was about a hundred years old, or [when he considered] the barrenness of Sarah's [deadened]womb.

20 No unbelief or distrust made him waver (doubtingly question) concerning the promise of God, but he grew strong and was empowered by faith as he gave glory to God,

21fully satisfied and assured that God was able and mighty to keep His word and to do what He had promised.

22 That it why his faith was credited to him as righteousness (right standing with God)." (AMP)

The main qualities in Abraham that qualifies him to be the father of those who believe is that he believed the word of God in an unwavering way.

He was fully persuaded about what God had spoken. He had a strong conviction on which he was able to act and obey.

He also knew God and some of the critical qualities that He possesses that is that God raises the dead and speaks of non-existent things that he has foretold as if they already exist.

14.2 To receive His promises you need to have the knowledge of God and His essential attributes.

In 1 John 2;12-14 His word says,

12 "I write to you, little children, because your sins are forgiven you for His name's sake.

13 I write to you, fathers, because you have known Him who is from the beginning. I write to you, young men because you have overcome the wicked one. I write to you, little children because you have known the Father.

14 I have written to you, young men, because you are strong and the word of God abides in you and you have overcome the wicked one."

Here the word of God summarises the critical components in a believer which give stature, character, and achievement.

The first of these is the knowledge of God -this is separate from knowing His word – this refers to knowing Him in operation, His acts, His ways and His character as experienced by a believer.

This occurs when there is a personal relationship with Him enhanced by a repeated cycle of prayer and answered prayer.

Psalms 103:7 says

"He made known His ways to Moses, His acts to the children of Israel."

Knowing His acts or works alone is not sufficient. The children of Israel continued to murmur with unbelief in the wilderness despite having seen the works of God repeatedly, they did not know the ways of God. Moses on the other hand both knew the ways of God and saw the acts of God.

He says here I write to you fathers because you have **known** Him who was from the beginning. Knowledge of God is critical for God to manifest His character through you. For this to happen you need to engage with Him in prayer and reading His word. This results in spiritual growth.

14.3 To receive His promises you need to understand the need to seek the knowledge of the word of God.

In 1 John 2 where we have read His word says

"I have written to you, young men, because you are strong and the word of God abides in you".

In Joshua 1:8 The word says

"This Book of the Law shall not depart from your mouth, but you shall meditate in it day and night, that you may observe to do according to what is written in it. For then you will make your way prosperous, and then you shall have good success."

In Psalms 119:105 His word says

"Your word is a lamp to my feet and a light to my path."

Colossians 3:16 says

"Let the word of Christ dwell in you richly in all wisdom, teaching and admonishing one another in psalms and hymns and spiritual songs, singing with grace in your hearts to the Lord."

Acts 17:11 describes the Jews at Berea

"These were more fair-minded than those at Thessalonica, in that they received the word with all readiness, and searched the Scriptures daily to find out whether these things were so."

In Ephesian 6:17 the Apostle Paul describing the armour of God says **"And take the helmet of salvation, and the sword of the Spirit, which is the word of God."**

The apostle was describing the armour of the Roman soldier who was guarding him. In today's terminology I believe he would not have used the term 'sword' but rather terms like the nuclear missile, the laser guided missile, the machine gun, the bazooka, or the hand grenade of the Spirit which is the word of God. In Spiritual warfare therefore, the word of God is an offensive weapon against the enemy which the child of God needs to possess richly to the point where you can speak as well as act upon that word.

14.4: To receive His promise you need to understand the need to have a strong conviction, a high degree of persuadedness concerning His promises.

In Joshua 1:1-9 after the death of Moses God needed to raise another leader of character, stature and achievement to take the children of Israel into the Land of Promise, we read

> **"After the death of Moses the servant of the Lord, it came to pass that the Lord spoke to Joshua the son of Nun, Moses' assistant saying:**
>
> **2 'Moses My servant is dead. Now therefore, arise, go over this Jordan, you and all this people, to the land which I am giving to them- the children of Israel.**
>
> **3 Every place that the sole of your foot will tread upon I have given you, as I said to Moses.**
>
> **4 From the wilderness and this Lebanon as far as the great river, the River Euphrates, all the land of the Hittites, and to the Great Sea towards the going down of the sun, shall be your territory.**
>
> **5 No man shall be able to stand before you all the days of your life; as I was with Moses, so I will be with you. I will not leave you nor forsake you.**
>
> **6 Be strong and of good courage, for to this people you shall divide as an inheritance the land which I swore to their fathers to give them.**
>
> **7 Only be strong and very courageous, that you may observe to do according to all the law which Moses My servant commanded you; do not turn from it to the right hand or to the left, that you may proper wherever you go.**

8 This Book of the Law shall not depart from your mouth, but you shall meditate in it day and night, that you may observe to do according to all that is written in it. For then you will make your way prosperous, and then you will have good success.

9 Have I not commanded you? Be strong and of good courage; do not be afraid, nor be dismayed, for the Lord your God is with you wherever you go.'"

We see here that verse 6 says "Be strong and of good courage" and in verse 7 "Only be strong and very courageous" and in verse 9 "Be strong and of good courage, do not be afraid nor be dismayed".

The strength referred to here is strength of conviction and courage to act on the instruction of God. Fear and dismay would hinder strength of conviction and courage.

In 1 Chronicles28:20 we read

"And David said to his son Solomon, 'Be strong and of good courage, and do it; do not fear nor be dismayed, for the Lord God- my God- will be with you. He will not leave you nor forsake you, until you have finished all the work for the service of the house of the Lord'".

Again here David admonishes his son Solomon to be strong in conviction and of good courage and to act and do what God has commanded-not to be fearful or dismayed as fear and dismay paralyse God's people so that they are not able to act on the word of the Lord.

In Ephesians 6:10 the word says **"Finally my brethren, be strong in the Lord and in the power of His might".**

Strength of conviction to act on His word, conviction that the word which God speaks is backed by His power, not being fearful or dismayed are critical components for receiving the promises of God.

14.5 To receive His promises you need to understand how to overcome the wicked one.

I will dwell on overcoming the wicked one AS IT IS CRITICAL for every child of God to know the enemy we are dealing with, his nature, his origins, the weapons he uses and above all how he was defeated openly and publicly by the Lord Jesus Christ on the cross. In no other area of walking with God is the acquiring of KNOWLEDGE more critical.

14.5.1 To overcome the wicked one you need to understand the nature of satan.

The devil, satan, the wicked one (Ephesians 6:16, 1 John 5:19), is described in the word of God as a thief, a murderer, a destroyer (John 10:10), a liar and the father of lies (John 10:44), the accuser of brethren (Revelations 12:10), the deceiver of the whole world, the old serpent, the great dragon (Revelations 12:9), the adversary (1 Peter 5:8).

The devil is the architect and orchestrator of all sin, all wrong doing and all evil.

In John 10:10 the Lord Jesus says **"The thief does not come except to steal and to kill and to destroy. I have come that they may have life and that they may have it more abundantly".**

In John 8:44 the Lord Jesus spoke to people seeking to kill Him and said **"You are of your father the devil, and the desires of your father you want to do. He was a murderer from the beginning, and does not stand in the truth, because he has no truth in him. When he speaks a lie, he speaks from his own resources, for he is a liar and the father of it".**

1 John 3:8 says, **"[But] he who commits sin [who practices evildoing] is of the devil [takes his character from the evil one], for the devil has sinned [violated the divine law] from the beginning. The reason the Son of God was made manifest (visible) was to undo (destroy, loosen, and dissolve) the works the devil [has done] (AMP)".**

In 1 Peter 5:8-9 the word of God says **"Be sober, be vigilant, because your adversary the devil walks about like a roaring lion, seeking whom he may devour. Resist him steadfast in the faith, knowing that the same sufferings are experienced by your brotherhood in the world."**

14.5.2 To overcome the wicked one you need to understand the origins of satan.

Satan was created by God and was once a highly decorated angel called Lucifer. Due to pride, he rebelled against God, taking with him a third of the angels of God and was thrown out of heaven and 'fell' to the earth. The other angels who fell with him became demons. His aim is to frustrate every plan and purpose of God on the earth and in mankind.

Isaiah 14:12-17 describes the fall of Lucifer:

"How are you fallen from heaven, O Lucifer, son of the morning! How are you cut down to the ground, you who weakened the nations!

13 For you have said in your heart: 'I will ascend into heaven, I will exalt my throne above the stars of God; I will also sit on the mount of the congregation on the farthest side of the north;

14 I will ascend above the heights of the clouds, I will be like the Most High'.

15 Yet you shall be brought down to Sheol, to the lowest depth of the Pit,

16 those who see you will gaze at you and consider you, saying:

'Is this the man who made the earth tremble, who shook kingdoms,

17 who made the world as a wilderness and destroyed its cities, who did not open the house of his prisoners.'"

Revelations 12:3-4

"And another sign appeared in heaven: behold a great, fiery red dragon having seven heads and ten horns, and seven diadems on his heads.

4 His tail drew a third of the stars of heaven and threw them on the earth."

Revelations 12:7-9 says

"And war broke out in heaven: Michael and his angels fought with the dragon; and the dragon and his angels fought,

8 but they did not prevail, nor was a place found for them in heaven any longer.

9 So the great dragon was cast out, that serpent of old, called the devil and satan, who deceives the whole world; he was cast to the earth, and his angels were cast out with him."

Ezekiel 28:12-19 describes the beauty and splendour of Lucifer before he fell:

"Son of man, take up a lamentation for the king of Tyre and say to him, 'Thus says the Lord God: You were the seal of perfection, full of wisdom and perfect in beauty.

13 You were in Eden, the garden of God; every precious stone was your covering: the sardius, topaz, and diamond, beryl, onyx, and jasper, sapphire, turquoise, and emerald with gold.

The workmanship of your timbrels and pipes was prepared for you on the day you were created.

14 You were the anointed cherub who covers; I established you; you were on the holy mountain of God; you walked back and forth in the

midst of fiery stones.

15 You were perfect in your ways from the day you were created, till iniquity was found in you.

16 By the abundance of your trading, you became filled with violence within, and you sinned; therefore I cast you as a profane thing out of the mountain of God; and I destroyed you, O covering cherub, from the midst of the fiery stones.

17 Your heart was lifted up because of your beauty; you corrupted your wisdom for the sake of your splendour; I cast you to the ground, I laid you before kings, that they may gaze at you.

18 You defiled your sanctuaries by the multitude of your iniquities, by the iniquity of your trading; therefore I brought fire from your midst; it devoured you. And I turned you to ashes upon the earth in the sight of all who saw you.

19 All who knew you among the peoples are astonished at you; you have become a horror, and shall be no more forever."'

The Lord Jesus Christ witnessed this fall of Lucifer. In Luke 10:18 "And He (Lord Jesus Christ) said to them, 'I saw satan fall like lightning from heaven'.

14.6 Understanding the believer's victory over satan.

Our victory over satan is in believing on the Lord Jesus Christ, the sacrifice He made on the cross when He died for us and rose again from the dead.

In John 10:10 **"The thief comes (referring to satan) only in order to steal and kill and destroy. I came that they may have and enjoy life, and have it in abundance"** (to the full, till it overflows) (AMP).

In John 3:16 **"For God so greatly loved and dearly prized the world that He (even) gave up His only begotten (unique) Son, so that whosoever believes in (trusts in, clings to, relies on) Him shall not perish (come to destruction, be lost) but have eternal (everlasting) life"**(AMP).

In John 14:6: Jesus said to him **'I am the Way, and the Truth and the Life; no one comes to the Father except through me."**

The Lord Jesus's agenda was and is to undo the devil's agenda in every person – He came to give life and in abundance, He is the Way the Truth and the Life, He was the essence of God's love to the world so that whosoever (anyone of every colour, creed, even religion) believes in Him should not come to destruction (eternal) but have everlasting life.

1 John 4:4 also says **"You are of God, little children, and have overcome them, because He who is in you is greater than He who is in the world."**

When one believes in the Lord Jesus Christ, calls on His name and receives Him as Lord of his life, one gets saved, receives eternal life and is delivered from the devil's principal agenda which is to lead people to eternal separation with God, eternal death and eternal damnation.

The believer also needs to have an understanding and a revelation of the victory that was won for them when the Lord Jesus died on the cross.

That satan was disarmed, defeated and made to march down the road naked and was humiliated publicly.

Colossians 2:15 says **"[God] disarmed the principalities and powers that were ranged against us and made a bold display and public example of them, in triumphing over them in Him and in it [the cross]"** (AMP).

In Hebrews 2:14-15 His word also says **"Since, therefore, [these His] children share in flesh and blood [in the physical nature of human beings], He [Himself] in a similar manner partook of the same [nature], that by [going through] death He might bring to nought and make of no effect him who had the power of death—that is, the devil—**

15 And also that He might deliver and completely set free all those who through the [haunting]fear of death were held in bondage throughout the whole course of their lives."

The Lord Jesus Christ therefore by dying on the cross nullified, brought to nought, destroyed, him who had the power of death and set free those who were subjected to bondage all their lives through the fear of death- people who have been living petrified by fear of death are set free when they acknowledge the Lordship of Jesus Christ because He conquered death.

Therefore He says in Luke 10:19-20 **"Behold I give you authority and power to trample upon serpents and scorpions, and [physical and mental strength and ability] over all the power that the enemy [possesses];and nothing shall in any way hurt you.**

20 Nevertheless, do not rejoice at this, that the spirits are subject to you, but rejoice that your names are enrolled in heaven"(AMP).

14.6.1 Understanding the authority of the believer to bind and rebuke satan in the name of the Lord Jesus Christ.

In Matthew 12:29 The Lord Jesus referring to satan said **"Or how can one enter a strong man's house and plunder his goods, unless he first binds the strong man? And then he will plunder his house."**

In Zechariah 3:1-2 the word says **"Then he showed me Joshua the high priest standing before the Angel of the Lord, and satan standing at his right hand to oppose him.**

2 And the Lord said to satan, 'The Lord rebukes you, satan! The Lord who has chosen Jerusalem rebuke you! Is this not a brand plucked from the fire?'"

The authority that the Lord Jesus Christ gives to the believer gives authority and power to trample or over-run satan and his strategies over one's life or situation, to bind satan and stop him from hindering or interfering in the affairs of one's life and to rebuke satan in the name of and by the authority of the Lord Jesus Christ.

It is important for the believer to remember to use this authority often.

14.6.2 Understanding the victory over satan through the confession of the blood of the Lord Jesus Christ.

The believer also needs to know and understand the power of the blood of the Lord Jesus Christ.

In Exodus 12:7 and 13 says **"And they shall take some of the blood and put it on the two doorposts and on the lintel of the houses where they shall eat it...**

13 Now the blood shall be a sign for you on the houses where you are. And when I see the blood, I will pass over you; and the plague shall not be on you to destroy you when I strike the land of Egypt."

The blood of the sheep or goats symbolised the blood of the Lord Jesus Christ which was shed on the cross, it is the blood of the Passover. That blood was the purchase price for our redemption from the bondage and all the rights which satan had over mankind as a result of the sin of Adam and Eve in the Garden of Eden.

1 Peter 1:18-19 says **"Knowing that you were not redeemed with corruptible things, like gold and silver, from your aimless conduct received by tradition from your fathers,**

19 but with the precious blood of Christ, as of a lamb without blemish and without spot."

In Revelations 12:10-11 the word says **"Then I heard a loud voice saying in heaven, 'Now salvation, and strength, and the kingdom of our God, and the power of His Christ have come, for the accuser of our brethren, who accused them day and night, has been cast down.**

11 And they overcame him (satan) by the blood of the Lamb (Jesus Christ) and by the word of their testimony, and they did not love their loves to the death.'"

The confession of the blood of the Lord Jesus Christ gives the believer victory and deliverance from the bondage of satan when confessed in faith. The believer has the authority to sprinkle the blood of Lord Jesus Christ over their lives, their loved ones, their possessions etc and make a declaration of victory over satan.

In Matthew 26:27-28 the word of God reads **"Then He took the cup, and gave thanks, and gave it to them saying, 'Drink from it, all of you. 28 For this is My blood of the new covenant, which is shed for many for the remission of sins.'"**

The blood of the Lord Jesus that was shed is therefore the seal of the New Covenant. And the confession of that blood gives the believer victory over satan.

Chapter 15

I Will Be God To You

Almighty God promises: When you live and walk in My presence, I will be God to you.

Summary:

Being God to you means:

He promises to manifest His nature to you and manifest His presence to you.
It means He would like to be your everything in the Lord Jesus Christ.
He promises to be your giver of righteousness and right standing with Him.
He promises to be the ultimate source of all your provision.
He promises to guide you as you make the important decisions in your life regarding carrier choice, long term relationships, investments and every other important decision you make in your life.
He promises to be your ultimate source of health and well-being.
He promises to be your source of victory and emotional satisfaction.
He promises to be your giver of peace and emotional wellbeing.
All these promises are fulfilled to you through our Lord Jesus Christ.

Covered in this chapter: *(all scriptures are quoted from the New King James Version NKJV unless otherwise stated.)*

When you live and walk in His presence, God promises

15:1 : To be your everything- He says when I am in relationship with you, you have everything you need through Jesus Christ.
15:2 : To be your guide as you make important decision of your life, career and relationships including marriage through Jesus Christ.
15.3 : To be your healer and source of well-being, through Jesus Christ.
15.4 : To be your giver of righteousness through Jesus Christ.
15.5 : To give you victory in every situation you face through Jesus Christ.
15.6 : To be present with you in every situation you face through Jesus Christ.

15.7 :To give you His kingdom – His righteousness, peace and joy in your life through Jesus Christ.

15.8 :To be your ultimate source and provider through Jesus Christ.

15:1 He promises to be your everything – when I am in relationship with you, you have everything you need.

In the book of Exodus when The Lord appeared to Moses he asked His name.

Exodus 3:13-14 -Then Moses said to God, "Indeed, when I come to the children of Israel and say to them, The God of your fathers has sent me to you and they say to me, 'What is His name?' What shall I say to them?"

14 And God said to Moses, I AM WHO I AM." And He said "Thus you shall say to the children of Israel, 'I AM has sent me to you.'"

The Hebrew word used here was Yahweh which means I AM WHO I AM and I WILL BE WHO I WILL BE or "If I am in relationship with you, you have everything you need."

He therefore wants to be your all. To be to you what you need at your point of need.

A number of names of God depict the different ways in which He would like to manifest Himself in the lives of His people.

Some of these names are:

Jehovah-Tsidkenu "The Lord Our Righteousness" Jeremiah 23:6, 2 Corinthians 5:21
Jehovah-Jireh which means "The Lord will Provide" Genesis 22:12-14, 2 Corinthians 8:9
Jehovah–Nissi which means "The Lord My Banner of Victory" Exodus 17:15, 1 Corinthians 15:57
Jehovah –Rapha which means "The Lord Who Heals" Exodus 15:26, 1 Peter2:24, Matthew 8:16-17
Jehovah-shalom "The Lord is Peace" Judges 6:22-24, John 14:27
Jehovah- Shammah "The Lord is There" Ezekiel 48:35, Matthew 28:20
Jehovah-Sabaoth "The Lord of Hosts" 1 Samuel 1:11, 1 Samuel 17:45-47, Luke 2:13
Jehovah-Mekoddishkem "The Lord Who Sanctifies You" Ezekiel 20:12; John 17:17
Jehovah- Raah "The Lord is My Shepherd" Psalms 23:1, John 10:11.

Every person needs God to manifest Himself in their lives as their Righteousness, their Provider, their Banner of victory, their Healer, the giver of their Peace, the One Who is always present with them, their deliverer, their Sanctifier as well as their Shepherd (to guide and shield).

All these manifestations of God are reality to us through the sacrifice that the Lord Jesus made during His suffering for us and His death on the cross.

15.2 God promises to be your guide as you make important decision of your life, career and relationships.

Let's look first at **Psalms 23:1-6 (AMP)**

> **"The Lord is my Shepherd (to feed, guide and shield me), I shall not lack.**
>
> **2 He makes me to lie down in (fresh, tender) green pastures; He leads me besides the still and restful waters.**
>
> **3 He refreshes and restores my life (my self); He leads me in the paths of righteousness (uprightness and right standing with Him- not for my earning it, but) for His name's sake.**
>
> **4 Yes though I walk through the (deep, sunless) valley of the shadow of death, I will fear or dread no evil, for You are with me; Your rod (to protect) and Your staff (to guide), they comfort me.**
>
> **5 You prepare a table before me in the presence of my enemies. You anoint my head with oil; my (brimming) cup runs over.**
>
> **6 Surely or only goodness, mercy and unfailing love shall follow me all the days of my life, and through the length of my days the house of the Lord (and His presence) shall be my dwelling place."**

This psalm summarises what the Lord means when He says I will be to you God.

It is important however to note that all the manifestations of God in our lives are reality to us in Jesus Christ for in John 10:11

He said "I am the good Shepherd. The good shepherd lays down His life for the sheep." (KJV).

The Lord Jesus wants to leads and guides us by His Spirit. Jesus is our Jehovah-Raah our Shepherd.

15.3 God promises to be your healer and source of well-being your Jehovah-Rapha

1 Peter 2:24 says

> "Who Himself bore our sins in His body on the tree, that we, having died to sins, might live for righteousness- by whose stripes you were healed".

Isaiah 4:4-5 referring to the Lord Jesus says

> "Surely He has borne our griefs and carried our sorrows; yet we esteemed Him striken, smitten by God, and afflicted.
>
> 5 But He was wounded for our transgressions, He was bruised for our iniquities; the chastisement of our peace was upon Him and by His stripes we are healed."

So then when the Lord Jesus was in sorrow during His suffering He carried our sorrows, when He was in grief in the garden of Gethsemane, and during the carrying of the cross and on the cross itself, He was carrying our griefs, when they chastised Him, He was buying us peace, when they whipped Him on the whipping post He was buying us health.

Matthew 8:16-17 says

> "When the evening had come, they brought to Him many who were demon-possessed. And He cast out the spirits with a word, and healed all who were sick,
>
> 17 that it might be fulfilled which was spoken by Isaiah the prophet, saying: 'He Himself took our infirmities and bore our sicknesses'".

The Lord Jesus is our Jehovah-Rapha.

15.4 God promises to be your giver of righteousness through Jesus Christ- He is our Jehovah-Tsidkenu

2 Corinthians 5:21 referring to the Lord Jesus says

> "For He made Him who knew no sin to be sin for us, that we might become the righteousness of God in Him".

So we are the righteousness of God in Jesus Christ – He is our Jehovah-Tsidkenu.

15.5 When you live and walk in His presence God promises you victory in every situation you face

In Exodus 17:8-16 we read

> "Now Amalek came and fought with Israel in Rephidim.
>
> 9 And Moses said to Joshua, 'Choose us some men and go out, fight with Amalek. Tomorrow I will stand on the top of the hill with the rod of God in my hand.'
>
> 10 So Joshua did as Moses said to him, and fought with Amalek. And Moses, Aaron and Hur went up to the top of the hill.
>
> 11 And so it was, when Moses held up His hand, that Israel prevailed, and when he let down his hand, Amalek prevailed.
>
> 12 But Moses' hands became heavy; so they took a stone and put it under him, and he sat on it. And Aaron and Hur supported his hands, one on one side, and the other on the other side; and his hands were steady until the going down of the sun.
>
> 13 So Joshua defeated Amalek and his people with the edge of the sword.
>
> 14 Then the Lord said to Moses, ' Write this for a memorial in the book and recount it in the hearing of Joshua, that I will utterly blot out the remembrance of Amalek from under heaven.'
>
> 15 And Moses built an alter and called its name, The- Lord- is –My-Banner;
>
> 16 for he said, 'Because the Lord have sworn: the Lord will have war with Amalek from generation to generation.'"

Notice here that the spirit of Amalek is the spirit that fights against God, His people and His purposes upon the earth.

This is the spirit of the wicked one, the evil one or satan.

Moses went up a hill just as the Lord Jesus Christ was crucified on a hill called Calvary.

When Moses lifted up his hands there was victory on the ground but when he put his hands down, Amalek prevailed against Joshua and Israel until Aaron and Hur held Moses hands on each side creating an image of the Lord Jesus dying on the cross of Calvary.

After the defeat of Amalek God asked Moses to write it down as a memorial in a book, to recount it in the hearing of Joshua and the generations to come, and declared that He God will utterly blot out remembrance of Amalek from under heaven.

Moses built an alter and called it its name Jehovah Nissi, the Lord is my Banner of victory because theirs is a hand against the throne of the Lord and the Lord will have war with Amalek from generation to generation.

Amalek is an image of satan. The victory against satan was won on the cross.

Colossians 2:15 says referring to the Lord Jesus **"Having disarmed principalities and powers, He made a public spectacle of them, triumphing over them in it (the cross)."**

The Lord Jesus is our Jehovah-Nissi.

1 Corinthians 15:57 says **"But thanks be to God, who gives us the victory through our Lord Jesus Christ."**

Hebrews 2:14 and 15 says **"Inasmuch as the children have partaken of flesh and blood, He himself (Jesus Christ) likewise shared (partook) in the same, that through death He might destroy him who had the power of death, that is the devil,**

15 and release those who through fear of death were all their lifetime subject to bondage." See also Chapter 11 Understanding Redemption.

15.6 The Lord Jesus promised to be present with you in every situation you face, to be to you Jehovah-Shammah.

He also says in Mathew 28:20 **"Teaching them to observe all things that I have commanded you; and lo I am with you always, even to the end of the age".**

The Lord Jesus also said in John 14:19-23

"A little while longer and the world will see Me no more, but you will see Me. Because I live, you will live also.

20 At that day you will know that I am in my Father, and you in Me and I in you.

21 He who has My commandments and keeps them, it is he who loves Me. And he who loves Me shall be loved by My Father, and I will love HIM AND MANIFEST Myself to him.

22 Judas (not Iscariot) said to Him, 'Lord, how is it that You will manifest Yourself to us, and not to the world?'

23 Jesus answered and said to him, 'If anyone loves Me, he will keep my word; and My Father will love him and We will come to him and make Our home with him.'"

The Lord Jesus and the Father wants to dwell in your heart by the Holy Spirit.

He wants to be present in you and to manifest in you- when there is a manifestation of the God-kind in your life there is no argument.

You will know He is in your life and those around you will know as well.

The Lord Jesus is your Jehovah-Shammah.

15.7 God promises you His kingdom-His righteousness, His peace and His joy in your life.

When the Lord Jesus taught His disciples to pray in **Matthew 6:9-13 He said**

"In this manner, therefore, pray: Our Father in heaven, hallowed be Your name.

10 Your kingdom come. Your will be done on earth as in heaven.

11 Give us this day our daily bread

12 and forgive us our debts as we forgive debtors.

13 And lead us not into temptation but deliver us from the evil one. For yours is the kingdom, the power and the glory forever. Amen."

When you pray- Your kingdom come in my life, family, country and the whole earth- what are you really asking for?

Romans 14:17 says **"[after all] the kingdom of God is not a matter of [getting the] food and drink [one likes] but instead it is righteousness [that state that makes a person acceptable to God] and [heart] peace and joy in the Holy Spirit AMP)".**

Here the critical elements of the kingdom of God are described as righteousness, peace and joy in the Holy Spirit.

1 Corinthians 4:20 says **"For the kingdom of God is not in word but in power".**

In Mark 10:15 the Lord Jesus **said "Assuredly, I say to you, whoever does not receive the kingdom of God as a little child will by no means enter into it."**

So then the important components of the kingdom of God are righteousness, peace of the heart, joy in the Holy Spirit, and manifestations of power.

The attitude for receiving the kingdom of God has to be that of a child which means accepting things at face value, shunning vain analysis, seeking to know and understand in meekness, reverence and fear. Acknowledging the limitations of the human mind.

15.8 The Lord Jesus promises to be your ultimate source and provider-your Jehovah-Jireh.

He also wants to be your Provider. The model prayer given by the Lord Jesus in Matthew 6 as above is an outline of how we should pray. "Give us this day our daily bread" signifies our acknowledgement that He is our source of supply for everything we need.

In 3 John verse 2 His word says **"Beloved I pray that you may prosper and be in health, just as your soul prospers".**

2 Corinthians 8:9 says **" For you know the grace of our Lord Jesus Christ, that though He was rich, yet for your sake He became poor, that you through His poverty might become rich".**

Deuteronomy 8:18 says **"But you shall remember the Lord your God for it is He who gives you power to get wealth, that He may establish His covenant which He swore to your fathers as it is this day".**

Matthew 27:29 says **"When they had twisted a crown of thorns, they put it on His head, and a reed in His right hand. And they bowed the knee before Him and mocked Him saying 'Hail, King of the Jews!'"**

This crown of thorns signified the breaking of the curse of poverty in the judgement of Genesis 3:18. Remember that the exact opposite of a crown of gold is a crown of thorns.

Whereas gold represents prosperity, honour and glory, thorns stand for barrenness, poverty, dishonour, and pain. The Lord Jesus is our Jehovah-Jireh, the provider and source of our daily bread.

Chapter 16

I Will Multiply You Exceedingly

Almighty God promises -as you live and walk in my presence, I will multiply you exceedingly. He needs first of all to make you feel secure- to uplift you and fortify you. Then He needs to make you a type- the Jesus Christ type or a kind called the God-kind- He will then multiply the God kind in you after its kind. These three steps often happen concurrently.

Summary:

It is the desire of Almighty God to transform you and make you a kind, the God kind and then to multiply, increase and fortify you as you walk and live in His presence.

As you walk in His presence God desires that you produce after your kind- the God kind.

God has a principle that every living creature produces after its kind.

He desires to shield you and fortify you from every attack of the enemy, to lift you up and fortify you in every area of your life.

Pray for His increase, multiplication, uplift, fortification and shielding in every area of your life.

He then desires you to reproduce after your kind in the knowledge of God.

Almighty God has declared that the earth shall be filled with the knowledge of glory of God as the waters cover the sea.

He desires to use you to be a worker together with God as He accomplishes this.

Therefore, bear witness to what the Lord Jesus Christ has done in your life.

A witness speaks what he/she has seen, heard, touched and experienced.

God desires to multiply grace (His favour and goodness upon your life) and peace as you walk and live in His presence.

Pray and cry for the multiplication of grace and peace upon your life, family and ministry.

Covered in this chapter: *(all scriptures are quoted from the New King James Version NKJV unless otherwise stated.)*

16.1 As you walk in His presence God has promised to shield you, fortify you, lift you up, increase and multiply you exceedingly and in every area of your life.

16.2 As you walk in His presence God desires that you produce after your kind- the God kind. God has a principle that every living creature produces after its kind.

16.3 As you walk and live in His presence His word will prevail and grow as you share and speak that word to your family, friends, colleagues and community. His word accomplishes the mission for which it is sent and does not return back void.

16.4 As you walk and live in His presence He declares that righteousness and praise shall spring forth before the nations until the earth is filled with the knowledge of the glory of God as the waters cover the sea.

16.5 Bear witness to what the Lord Jesus Christ has done in your life. A witness speaks what he/she has seen, heard, touched and experienced.

16.6 As you walk and live in His presence, He desires to multiply grace and peace upon your life.

16.1 As you walk in His presence God has promised to shield you, fortify you, lift you up, increase and multiply you exceedingly and in every area of your life.

In Genesis 15:1-6 we read:

> "After these things the word of the Lord came to Abram in a vision, saying, 'Do not be afraid, Abram, I am your shield, your exceeding great reward'.
>
> 2 But Abram said, 'Lord God, what will You give me, seeing I go childless, and the heir of my house is Eliezer of Damascus?'
>
> 3 Then Abram said, 'Look You have given me no offspring; indeed one born in my house is my heir!'
>
> 4 And behold, the word of the Lord came to him, saying, 'This one shall not be your heir, but one who will come out of your own body shall be your heir'.

5 Then He brought him outside and said, 'Look now towards heaven, and count the stars if you are able to number them.' And He said to him, 'So shall your descendants be.'
6 And he believed in the Lord, and He counted it to him to be righteousness."

Notice here that the Lord God begins by addressing fundamental needs in Abram- fear and insecurity by stating do not fear and further stating I am your defence, I am your shield.

The Lord God then states another fundamental truth- I am your exceeding great reward. Put simply God promises to shield you from the attacks of the enemy and to reward you for seeking Him diligently and co-operating with Him in the plan for your life.

He then promises to lift you up in every area of your life and to fortify you. Please note God has made a promise to lift you up, to fortify you and to multiply everything in your life that can be multiplied. Notice that Abram had an open and candid discussion with God about his concerns, areas of his deficiencies and needs.

We notice that Abram did not hide his griefs or weaknesses from God. He opened a dialogue with God concerning that which bothered him the most- being childless- he did not beat about the bush. You need to be open and candid with God about your situation and then to believe His word.

After Abram had stated to God his needs God took him outside and asked Abram to look at the stars and count them. God was giving Abram a visual image in his mind of what He could do for him. Something then happened in Abraham's heart- the word says "He believed in the Lord" or put differently he was convinced that God was able to do it, and that He was going to do it, he was fully persuaded that what God Had spoken, He was able to perform.

His word says it was accounted to him as righteousness. In our foundational text: Genesis 17: 1-2:

"When Abram was ninety-nine years old, the Lord appeared to Abram and said to him, 'I am Almighty God; walk before me and be blameless.
2 And I will make my covenant between Me and you, and will multiply you exceedingly".

God here begins by declaring His credentials- I am Almighty God- then He said I am proposing a special contract with you- if you agree to walk and live in my presence I will fortify you, lift you up, and multiply you in every area of your life.

In Romans 4:16-22 we read:

> **"Therefore it is of faith that it might be according to grace, so that the promise might be sure to all the seed, not only to those who are of the law, but also to those who are of the faith of Abraham, who is the father of us all**
>
> **17 (as it is written, 'I have made you a father of many nations') in the presence of Him whom he believed- God, who gives life to the dead and calls those things which do not exist as though they did;**
>
> **18 who, contrary to hope, in hope believed, so that he became the father of many nations, according to what was spoken, 'So shall your descendants be.'**
>
> **19 And not being weak in faith, he did not consider his own body, already dead (since he was about a hundred years old), and the deadness of Sarah's womb.**
>
> **20 He did not waver at the promise of God through unbelief, but was strengthened in faith, giving glory to God, and being fully convinced that what He had promised He was also able to perform.**
>
> **22 And therefore 'it was counted to him for righteousness.'"**

Hebrews 11:6 says

> **"But without faith it is impossible to please Him, for He who comes to God must believe that He is, and that He is a rewarder of those who diligently seek Him."**

So then the Almighty God promised as you walk and live in His presence to shield you, to reward you, to lift you up, to fortify you, to increase you, and multiply you in every area of your life.

You need to open an agenda with Him and to believe His word and His promises. As you pray, you need to claim His promises until they become a reality in your life.

Notice what Abraham did: He was strong in faith giving glory to God.

He was fully convinced, fully persuaded that God was able to do what He had spoken.

He by his faith gave glory to God.

Believed God's word contrary to natural hope and natural logic.

Believed God gives life to dead situations.

Believed God calls things which do not exist as if they did.

Notice also what Abraham did not do: Considered not the deadness of his body- because He who had promised raises the dead.

Considered not the deadness of Sarah's womb-because He who had promised raises the dead.

Wavered not/staggered not at the promise of God – He said God has spoken it, God is able to do it, period.

16.2 As you walk and live in His presence God desires that you produce after your kind- the God kind.

God has a principle that every living creature produces after its kind.

As the Lord God shields you, rewards you, lifts you up, fortifies you, increases and multiplies you in every area of your life, He also wants you to reproduce and multiply your experience in others.

He wants you to bear children, spiritual children through your witness of what God has done for you. In Genesis 1:11-12 we learn a principle of the working of God which He used in creation and still uses as He creates, the word of God says:

11"Then God said, 'Let the earth bring forth grass, the herb that yield seed, and the fruit tree that yields fruit according to its kind, whose seed is in itself, on the earth' and it was so.

12 And the earth brought forth grass, the herb that yield seed according to its kind, and the tree that yields fruit, whose seed is in itself according to its kind. And God saw that it was good."

You notice here that every plant, every animal including humans were created with capacity to produce seed that reproduces after its own kind. That is the principle of multiplication.

Whatever God produces in you spiritually, He has given you capacity and seed of the word of God which is capable of reproducing after your spiritual kind. God Himself sowed a spiritual Seed in Jesus Christ. In Genesis 3:15 the word says

"And I will put enmity between you (satan) and the woman, and between your seed and her Seed;

He shall bruise your head, and you shall bruise His heel."

The Seed of the woman referred to here is the Lord Jesus Christ.

In Genesis 26:4-5 the word says

"And I will make your descendants multiply as the stars of heaven; I will give to your descendants all these lands; and in your seed all the nations of the earth shall be blessed,

5 because Abraham obeyed My voice and kept my charge, My commandments, My statutes, and My laws."

In Galatians 3:16 the word says

"Now to Abraham and his seed were the promises made. He does not say, 'And to seeds' as of many, but as of one, 'And to your Seed' who is Christ."

Remember also that the seed is the word of God for when the Lord Jesus told a parable of the sower in Mark 4:3-8 it reads

"Listen! Behold, a sower went out to sow.

4 And it happened, as he sowed, that some seed fell by the wayside, and the birds of the air came and devoured it.

5 Some fell on stony ground, where it did not have much earth; and immediately it sprung up because it had no depth of earth.

6 But when the sun was up it was scorched, and because it had no root it withered away.

7 And some seed fell among thorns; and the thorns grew up and choked it, and it yielded no crop.

8 But other seed fell on good ground and yielded a crop that sprung up, increased and produced: some thirtyfold, some sixty, and some a hundred.'

9 And He said to them, ' He who has ears to hear, let him hear!'

10 But when He was alone, those around Him with the twelve asked Him about the parable.

11 And He said to them, To you it has been given to know the mystery of the kingdom of God; but to those who are outside, all things come in parables,

12 so that 'Seeing they may see and not perceive, And hearing they may hear and not understand; Lest they should turn, and their sins be forgiven them'.

The same parable is given in the gospel according to Luke in chapter 8:4-8. He explained the parable in Mark 4:14- 20:

"The sower sows the word.

15 And these are the ones by the wayside where the word is sawn. When they hear, satan comes immediately and takes away the word that was sown in their hearts.

16 These likewise are the ones sawn on stony ground who, when they

hear the word, immediately receive it with gladness;

17 and they have no root in themselves, and so endure only for a time. Afterward, when tribulation or persecution arises for the word's sake, immediately they stumble.

18 Now these are the ones sown among thorns; they are the ones that hear the word,

19 and the cares of this world, the deceitfulness of riches, and the desires for other things entering choke the word, and it becomes unfruitful.

20 But these are the ones sown on good ground, those who hear the word, accept it, and bear fruit: some thirtyfold, some sixty, and some a hundred".

We notice here that the seed is the word of God, it has capacity to bear fruit if sown in the right type of ground where it is allowed to take root, is watered and shielded.

Notice here the threats to the word of God accomplishing its purpose in your life are:

Word sown by wayside-people hear the word but immediately- satan snatches away the word before it has even gone deep- therefore child of God desire to hear the word of God, read it and protect, guard and cherish the word of God. Use all the means at your disposal to daily hear the word of God. Read your bible, go to church, use all other available channels to hear the word of God- the internet, television etc. Ultimately you need to belong to a church congregation under a servant of God called and anointed by God, to lead, guide you, counsel and pray for you.

Notice verse 11 And He said to them: 'To you it has been given to know the mystery of the kingdom of God'.

Understanding the mysteries of the kingdom of God is by grace- a favour given to us by God which we do not merit.

It is important that you do not take it for granted, but with thanksgiving and a degree of reverence.

Giving thanks to God always for revealing the secrets of the Kingdom of Heaven to us.

Word fell among rocks- word received with gladness but not allowed to take root- endures for a short time- then comes persecution and tribulation and the recipient stumbles and falters- guard the word you have received- allow it to take root, embed yourself among supportive brethren who can shield and support you during persecution and tribulation as a young Christian.

Sown among thorns- receive the word of God- but the cares of this world, the deceitfulness of riches, and the desires for other things choke the word- this is the main stumbling block for the celebrities who receive the word of God- the desire for fame and lime light, deceived by riches- child of God rebel against these- set yourself free to serve God – put Him at the centre of all you do. Obey His word in your financial dealings- remember to bring your tithes and offerings in obedience to Him.

Remember 1 Timothy 6:17 the word says

"Command those who are rich in this present age not to be haughty, not to trust in uncertain riches but in the living God, who gives us all things richly to enjoy".

Remember also that Jesus Christ is the word of God for John 1:1-14 says:

"In the beginning was the Word, and the Word was with God and the Word was God.

2 He was in the beginning with God.

3 All things were made through Him, and without Him was nothing made that was made.

4 In Him was life and the life was the light of men.

5 And the light shines in the darkness, and the darkness did not comprehend it.

6 There was a man sent from God, whose name was John.

7 This man came for a witness, to bear witness of the Light, that all through him might believe.

8 He was not that Light, but was sent to bear witness of that Light.

9 That was the true Light which gives light to every man coming into the world.

10 He was in the world, and the world was mad through Him, and the world did not know Him.

11 He came to His own, and His own did not receive Him.

12 But as many as received Him, to them He gave the right to become children Of God, to those who believe in His name:

13 who were born, not of blood, nor of the will of the flesh, nor of the will of man, but of God.

14 And the word became flesh and dwelt among us, and we beheld His glory, the glory as of the only begotten of the Father, full of grace and truth."

So then the seed is the word of God and the word of God is the Lord Jesus Christ.

In Revelations19:11-16 we read

"Now I saw heaven opened, and behold, a white horse. And He who sat on him was called Faithful and True, and in righteousness He judges and makes war.

12 His eyes were like a flame of fire, and on His head were many crowns. He had a name written that no one knew except Himself.

13 He was clothed with a robe dipped in blood, and His name is called The Word of God.

14 And the armies in heaven, clothed in fine linen, white and clean, followed Him on white horses.

15 Now out of His mouth goes a sharp sword, that with it He should strike the nations. And He Himself will rule them with a rod of iron. He Himself treads the winepress of the fierceness and wrath of Almighty God.

16 And He has on His robe and on His thigh a name written: KING OF KINGS AND LORD OF LORDS."

Here again we notice that the Lord Jesus Christ is referred to as the Word of God.

So then, God has established a principle on the earth that works in the natural as well as in the spirit- that every living thing has within itself seed with a capacity to reproduce after its own kind.

After God has worked in your life, He will give you capacity to produce after your own kind naturally (natural children) and more importantly spiritually (spiritual children).

Jesus Christ is called The Word of God, He also is the Seed, when The Word is sawn it has capacity to reproduce after its own kind.

Lets put it another way- when you walk and live in the presence of the Almighty God, He has an agenda to lift you up, to shield you, rewards you, fortifies you, increase and multiply you in every area of your life.

He does all this through His word. This will produce in you a type or a kind -called the God-kind of person or the Jesus Christ type.

You then have the capacity as you share the word of God and what God has done for you, the capacity to influence others to follow you and to be like you. You will be producing after your kind. The critical activities on your part is living the word and sharing the word which is the seed of God.

16.3 As you walk and live in His presence His word will prevail and grow as you share and speak that word to your family, friends, colleagues and community.

Let's look at the early Christian church and see the capacity of the seed called the word of God.

In Acts 6:1 the word says :

"Now in those days, when the number of the disciples were multiplying..."

and in Acts 6:7 we read further **"Then the word of God spread, and the number of the disciples multiplied greatly in Jerusalem, and a great many of the priests were obedient to the faith.**

8 And Stephen, full of faith and power, did great wonders and signs among the people."

In Acts 19:11-20 we read :

"Now God worked unusual miracles by the hands of Paul,

12 so that even handkerchiefs or aprons were brought from His body to the sick, and the diseases left them and evil spirits went out of them.

13 Then some of the itinerant Jewish exorcists took it upon themselves to call the name of the Lord Jesus over those who had evil spirits, saying ' We exorcise you by the Jesus whom Paul preaches.'

14 Also there were seven sons of Sceva, a Jewish chief priest, who did so.

15 And the evil spirit answered and said, 'Jesus I know, and Paul I know; but who are you?

16 Then the man in whom the evil spirit was leaped on them, overpowering them, and prevailed against them, so that they fled out of that house naked and wounded.

17 This became known both to all Jews and Greeks dwelling in Ephesus; and fear fell on them all, and the name of the Lord Jesus was magnified.

18 And many who had believed came confessing and telling their deeds.

19 Also, many of those who had practiced magic brought their books together and burned them in the sight of all. And they counted up the value of them, and it totalled fifty thousand pieces of silver.

20 So the word of the Lord grew mightily and prevailed."

The word of God when spoken has power to prevail, cause growth and multiplication.

In Hebrews4:12 the word says:

"For the word of God is living and powerful, and sharper than any two-edged sword, piercing even to the division of soul and spirit, and of joints and marrow, and is a discerner of the thoughts and intents of the heart."

Isaiah 55:10-11 says:

"For as the rain comes down and the snow from heaven, and do not return there, but water the earth, and make it bring forth and bud, that it may give seed to the sower and bread to the eater,

11 so shall My word be that goes forth from My mouth; it shall not return to Me void, but it shall accomplish what I please, and it shall prosper in the thing for which I sent it."

The scriptures here compare the word of God's effectiveness with rain which causes plants to grow to effect a harvest and declared that the word of God is the same.

It is sent on a mission and accomplishes its mission effectively, consistently and without fail.

The critical action here is the sharing of the word of God.

So then, as you live the word of God, it lifts you up and as you share and speak it to others it causes growth and multiplication. It has the capacity to do it. All you need to do is to obey and act upon it.

16.4 As you walk and live in His presence, He desires that righteousness and praise to spring forth before the nations until the earth is filled with the knowledge of the glory of God as the waters cover the sea.

In Isaiah 61:11 the word says

"For as the earth brings forth its bud, as the garden causes the things that are sown in it to spring forth, so the Lord God will cause righteousness and praise to spring forth before all the nations."

In Isaiah 45:8 The word of God says

"Rain down, you heavens, from above, and let the skies pour down righteousness; let the earth open, let them bring forth salvation, and let righteousness spring up together. I the Lord have created it."

In Isaiah 11:9 the word says

"They shall not hurt nor destroy in all My holy mountain, for the earth

shall be full of the knowledge of the Lord as the waters cover the sea".

Habakkuk 2:14 says

"For the earth will be filled with the knowledge of the glory of the Lord, as the waters cover the sea."

You will notice here it is the desire of the Almighty God that the whole Planet Earth be filled with righteousness, salvation and the knowledge of the glory of God as the waters cover the sea. You are a partner with the Almighty God as you play your part to make this happen.

16.5 Bear witness to what the Lord Jesus Christ has done in your life. A witness speaks what he/she has seen, heard, touched and experienced.

In Luke 24:44-49 the word of God says:

"Then He (the Lord Jesus Christ) said to them 'These are the words which I spoke to you while I was still with you, that all things must be fulfilled which were written in the Law of Moses and the Prophets and the Psalms concerning Me.'

45 And He opened their understanding, that they might comprehend the Scriptures.

46 Then He said to them, 'Thus it is written, and thus it was necessary for the Christ to suffer and to rise from the dead the third day,

47 and that repentance and remission of sins should be preached in His name to all nations, beginning at Jerusalem.

48 And you are witnesses to these things.

49 Behold I send the Promise of My Father upon you; but tarry in the city of Jerusalem until you be endued with power from on high."

Notice here in verse 45 He opened their minds so that they could understand the scriptures.

Also note that the Lord Jesus Christ Himself stated that it was necessary for Him to suffer and die and to rise again the third day and that in verse 47 repentance and remission of sins should be preached in His name to all nations.

Then He said in verse 48 YOU ARE WITNESSES TO THESE THINGS.

A witness speaks what they have seen, heard or experienced.

When Jesus Christ touches and changes your life, be a witness of what He has done for you.

In Matthew 28:18-20 the word says:

"And Jesus came and spoke to them, saying, 'All authority has been given to Me in heaven and on earth.

19 Go therefore and make disciples of all nations, baptizing them in the name of the Father and of the Son and of the Holy Spirit,

20 teaching them to observe all things that I have commanded you; and lo I am with you always, even to the end of the age' Amen.

Notice that as you go and witness Jesus Christ you are backed by the entire forces of heaven, all powers of rule and powers of force in heaven and on earth have been given to Jesus Christ by the Father. Jesus is the Commander in Chief and Executive President of the forces and authority of the Kingdom of Heaven.

Go therefore with boldness and backed by that authority and declare what He has done for you.

In Acts 1:4-8 the word of God says:

"And being assembled together with them, He commanded them not to depart from Jerusalem, but to wait for the Promise of the Father, 'which,' He said, ' you have heard from me,

5 for John truly Baptised with water, but you shall be baptised with the Holy Spirit not many days from now.'

6 Therefore, when they had come together, they asked Him, saying, ' Lord will You at this time restore the kingdom to Israel?'

7 And He said to them, 'It is not for you to know times or seasons which the Father has put in His own authority.

8 But you shall receive power when the Holy Spirit has come upon you; and you shall be witnesses to Me in Jerusalem, and in all Judea and Samaria, and to the end of the earth.'"

Here the Lord Jesus tells disciples, do not begin preaching or witnessing His power, until they are baptised, filled or immersed into the Holy Spirit. After they had received the power of the Holy Spirit, they were empowered to be witnesses of Jesus Christ starting from where they were, going to all Planet Earth.

You will also need to be filled with the Holy Spirit to be empowered to be a witness for Jesus Christ starting where you are.

In 1 John1:1-4 The word says:

"That which was from the beginning, which we have heard, which we have seen with our eyes, which we have looked upon, and our hands have handled, concerning the Word of life-

2 the life was manifested, and we have seen, and bear witness, and declare to you that eternal life which was with the Father and was manifested to us-

3 that which we have seen and heard we declare to you, that you also may have fellowship with us; and truly our fellowship is with the Father and with His Son Jesus Christ.

4 And these things we write to you that your joy may be full."

Here the Apostle John declares that as witnesses we speak and declare what we have heard, what we have seen with our eyes, what we have handled and touched with our hands and what was manifested to us and in us.

He also declares the result or end point of this witness statement is that those who hear our testimony may also have fellowship with Father and His Son Jesus Christ.

In other words our witness statement results in salvation of souls.

16.6 As you walk and live in His presence, He desires to multiply grace and peace upon your life.

In Luke 1:26-33 the word of God says:

"Now in the sixth month the angel Gabriel was sent by God to a city of Galilee named Nazareth,

27 to a virgin betrothed to a man whose name was Joseph, of the house of David. The virgin's name was Mary.

28 And having come in, the angel said to her, 'Rejoice, highly favoured one, the Lord is with you; blessed are you among women!'

29 But when she saw him, she was troubled at his saying, and considered what manner of greeting this was.

30 Then the angel said to her, 'Do not be afraid Mary, for you have found favour with God.

31 And behold, you will conceive in your womb and bring forth a Son, and shall call His name Jesus.

32 He shall be great, and will be called the Son of the Highest; and the Lord God will give Him the throne of His father David.

33 And He will reign over the house of Jacob forever, and of His kingdom there will be no end.'"

Notice the words of the angel to Mary, 'highly favoured or full of grace' in verse 28 and in verse 30 'you have found favour with God'.

The word grace means an active working of God in one's life which confers favour, good and blessing upon that life.

Grace always results in advantage or favourable outcome to the one who receives it.

Always pray for and cry for grace upon your life. Salvation comes to us by grace, for the word says in Ephesians 2:8

"For by grace you have been saved through faith, and that not of yourselves; it is the gift of God".

Acts 11:22-23 says:

"Then news of these things came to the ears of the church in Jerusalem, and they sent out Barnabas to go as far as Antioch.

23 When He came and had seen the grace of God, he was glad, and encouraged them all that with purpose of heart they should continue with the Lord."

Here the word of God says Barnabas arrived at the church at Antioch and saw the grace of God- nowhere else in scriptures do we read of grace being seen except at Antioch. Such must have been the manifestation of the favour and working of God in the church that anyone visiting saw a whole manifestation of the working of God that equalled seeing grace. Not surprising Acts 11:26 finishes by saying:

"And the disciples were first called Christians in Antioch."

Wow the word Christians was first used to refer to followers of the Lord Jesus Christ not in Jerusalem, or Nazareth, or Galilee ... or anywhere else but at Antioch, the same place where the grace of God was seen!

The Apostle Peter in 1 Peter 1:1 -2 says:

"Peter, an apostle of Jesus Christ, to the pilgrims of the Dispersion in Pontus, Galatia, Cappadocia, Asia, and Bithynia,

2 elect according to the foreknowledge of God the Father, in sanctification of the Spirit, for obedience and sprinkling of the blood of Jesus Christ: grace to you and peace be multiplied."

In his second epistle, he begins in a similar way, 2Peter 1:1-2 says:

"Simon Peter, a bondservant and apostle of Jesus Christ, to those who have obtained like precious faith with us by the righteousness of our God and Saviour Jesus Christ:

2 grace and peace be multiplied to you in the knowledge of God and of Jesus Christ our Lord."

The key phrase here is 'grace and peace be multiplied to you'. It is the desire of the Almighty God that you live your life and walk in His presence where His favour, mercy and goodness is continually manifested and multiplied daily.

Chapter 17

He Promises To Make You Exceedingly Fruitful

He said when you live and walk in my presence, I will make you exceedingly fruitful.

Summary:

The Lord says I will make you exceedingly fruitful if you walk in my presence.
A fruitful life is a fulfilled and satisfied life.
Fruitfulness makes you satisfied with your life and accomplishments.
Fruitfulness makes others to see you as an imparter and giver of hope and comfort.
Fruitfulness results from walking in obedience to Jesus Christ, in turn it makes the Lord God to be pleased with you.
We need to abide in the Lord Jesus Christ-
(That means continually yielding to His Lordship in the decisions we make).
We need to let His word abide in us (that means daily seeking His word, reading, listening and meditating upon it so that it continually renews our minds.)
We bear fruit for God in our everyday roles and activities for example as we raise children.
We bear fruit for God in our daily activities as we encounter and work with people at school, work, and travels.
We bear fruit for God as we witness and share the good news of salvation through Jesus Christ as the opportunities arise.
In these roles we are salting the earth, giving light to dark places, witnessing the love of the Lord Jesus Christ, doing good works and giving glory to our Father in Heaven.

Covered in Chapter *(all quotations are from the NKJV unless otherwise stated)*
17.1 Understanding the context in which we become exceedingly fruitful.
17.2 Understanding that the source of our fruitfulness
is abiding in obedience to the Lord Jesus Christ.

17.3 Understanding that we bear fruit for the Lord God as we give flavour to society in as much as salt and condiments flavour food.
17.4 Understanding that we bear fruit for the Lord God as we let the light of Christ shine through us to the world.

17.1 Understanding the context in which we become exceedingly fruitful.

When you receive the righteousness of God which we receive by believing on the sacrifice which the Lord Jesus made for us when He suffered, died on the cross of Calvary and rose again from the dead on the third day, repenting and calling on the name of the Lord Jesus Christ, you enter the presence of God.

You then need to understand holiness which is co-operating with the Holy Spirit in thought, word and deed and refuse to co-operate with satan the enemy of God and mankind (see Chapter 9).

You need to continually renew your mind by reading and listening to God's manual which is the word of God.

You also need to understand your sonship, your redemption, and the power of a continuously positive attitude in His presence (see Chapters 10, 11 and 12).

Packaged in these will be an understanding of salvation, being born again and having received forgiveness of sin and eternal life.

You need also to understand the dynamics of faith and the dynamics of talking to God in prayer (see Chapter 3).

You need to belong to a congregation where the Lord Jesus is preached, you have a personal relationship with your Pastor, and you meet with fellow believers regularly to hear the word of God, worship God, receive ministry and have fellowship.

The Pastor will pray for you to be filled with the Holy Spirit and also to have you baptised in water.

In this situation you will begin to grow as a believer and develop a personal relationship with the Lord Jesus through the Holy Spirit.

You are walking and living in His presence.

One of the things The Lord promises you is to make you exceedingly fruitful.

17.2 Understanding that the source of our fruitfulness is abiding in obedience to the Lord Jesus Christ.

In John 15: 1-8 the Lord Jesus said **"I am the vine, and my Father is the vinedresser.**

2 Every branch in Me that does not bear fruit He takes away;
and every branch that bears fruit He prunes, that it may bear more fruit.

3 You are already clean because of the word which I have spoken to you.

4 Abide in Me, and I in you. As a branch cannot bear fruit of itself unless it abides in the vine, neither can you, unless you abide in Me.

5 I am the vine you are the branches. He who abides in Me, and I in him, bears much fruit; for without me you can do nothing.

6 If anyone does not abide in Me, he is cast out as a branch and is withered; and they gather them and throw them into the fire, and they are burned.

7 If you abide in Me and My word abide in you, you will ask what you desire, and it shall be done for you.

8 By this is My Father glorified, that you bear much fruit; so you will be My disciples".

The key to fruitfulness is in abiding in the Lord Jesus who is the vine and being full of His word.

As we read His word, meditate upon it and commit to a life of prayer.

Meditating upon His word with the help of the Holy Spirit makes us to live in obedience to God.

You have a duty as a believer then to share the good news of salvation through the Lord Jesus Christ with your family, friends, and colleagues.

You are now a witness of what the Lord Jesus Christ has done for you.

You are now living as a partner with God to bring salvation to mankind.

You also bear fruit for God in your daily activities and roles.

For example, raising children in a Godly way.

17.3 Understanding that we bear fruit for the Lord God as we give flavour to society in as much as salt and condiments flavour food.

In Matthew 5:13 the Lord Jesus said "You are the salt of the earth;
but if the salt loses it's flavour, how shall it be seasoned?
It is then good for nothing but to be thrown out and trampled underfoot by men."

Here the Lord Jesus Christ uses the examples of salt to demonstrate how we can produce fruit for the Kingdom of God.

Salt gives flavour to food; it is amazing that in every culture most cooked foods need salt to taste and where there is no salt there is no taste.

As believers the Lord wants us to exude flavour in our encounters with people in everyday situations, be it in school, work, travels wherever we are, the Holy Spirit of God wants us by our manner and grace, the smile, the confidence, the goodness, the hope, the attitude- show the goodness of the Lord to the world.

17.4 Understanding that we bear fruit for the Lord God as we let the light of Christ shine through us to the world.

In Mathew 5:14-16 the Lord Jesus said

"You are the light of the world,
a city that is set on a hill cannot be hidden.
Nor do they light a lamp and put it under a basket, but on a lampstand,
and it gives light to all who are in the house.
Let your light so shine before men, that they may see your good works
and glorify your Father who is in heaven".

The Lord Jesus Christ also likens a believer to a lamp that gives light in a dark place.

What is the light He is referring to? Again, our daily conduct should show hope where there is hopelessness and despair, goodness where there is evil, love where there is hate, show forgiveness and tolerance but yet still being firm in what we believe and stand for.

These qualities are exuded in a child of God, most of the time without effort and subconsciously because it is the nature of the Holy Spirit in us. Ephesians 2:10 says

"For we are His workmanship, created in Christ Jesus for good
works, which God prepared beforehand that we should walk in them."

Galatians 5:22 also says

"But the fruit of the Spirit is love, joy, peace, long suffering,
kindness, goodness, faithfulness, gentleness, self-control. Against such
there is no law."

Pray and cry for the multiplication of grace and peace upon your life.

Section 4:

Growing Into Maturity In The Service Of Almighty God

Chapter 18

It Is By Grace – Understanding Dimensions Of Grace

It is important to understand that our salvation and every other ability in us for the service of Almighty God is by grace. Grace can be defined as activity on the side of Almighty God that gives us advantage.

Grace denotes a favour or gift we do not deserve or merit. Grace is a favour of Almighty God to us which we neither deserve nor merit.

It is derived from Greek charis-which means a state of kindness and favour towards someone, with focus on benefit given, gift or credit. Grace therefore means a free gift.

Grace stems from the exceeding riches of Almighty God in kindness, exceeding riches in mercy and exceeding riches in love.

Our salvation is by grace. Ephesians 2:8-9 tells us:

8 "For by grace you have been saved through faith, and that not of yourselves, it is the gift of God,

9 not of works, lest anyone should boast".(NKJV)

In the preceding portion Ephesians 2:4-7 says **"But God who is rich in mercy, because of His great love with which He loved us**

5 even when we were dead in trespasses, made us alive together with Christ (by grace you have been saved)

6 and raised us up together, and made us sit together in heavenly places in Christ Jesus,

7 that in the ages to come He might show the exceeding riches of His grace in His kindness towards us in Christ Jesus". (NKJV).

So, then grace is activity on the side of God, stemming out of His exceeding riches in mercy, kindness, and love.

It is God's undeserved, unmerited favour towards us stemming from His exceeding riches in mercy, kindness, and love.

Our salvation is not by works -lest anyone should boast, but by grace- to receive that grace one needs to believe on the sacrifice made by Jesus Christ on the cross.

Jesus Christ is the embodiment of the grace of God towards us. He is the embodiment of Almighty God's exceeding riches in mercy, kindness, and love. He is full of grace to overwhelming.

That is why His word says in John 1:14 "**And the Word became flesh and dwelt among us, and we beheld His glory, as the glory of the only begotten of the Father, full of grace and truth**".

Key Point: The grace of Jesus Christ to us stems from His overwhelming riches of mercy, kindness, and love for us.

His word goes further to say in John 1:16-17: "**And of His fullness we have all received, and grace for grace**" (**NKJV**).

The Amplified version puts it this way: "**For out of His fullness (abundance) we have all received [all had a share, and we were all supplied with] one grace after another and spiritual blessing upon spiritual blessing and even favour upon favour and gift [heaped] upon gift**".

Please understand that one can only become a vessel of excellence because of the abundance and riches of grace of Almighty God in Jesus Christ, not only grace for salvation but also grace for service of Almighty God- His abilities in us enabled through the abundant riches of His mercy, kindness and love resulting in us being abundantly supplied with one grace after another grace, spiritual gift heaped upon spiritual gift, one ability upon ability, spiritual blessing upon spiritual blessing, one favour upon favour.

I will be explaining this further.

Please note verse 17 of **John 1- "For the law was given through Moses, but grace and truth came through Jesus Christ"**.

The grace of Almighty God works hand in hand with truth- now the truth is the correct understanding of the word of God- truth is the word correctly understood.

Truth is eternal because the word of God is eternal. "**Heaven and earth shall pass away, but my words shall not pass away**" (Matthew 24:35, Mark 13:31).

That is why Jesus Christ said in **John 8:31-32: "If you abide in My word, then are you My disciples indeed. And you shall know the truth and the truth shall make you free"**.

So, it is critical to be a vessel of excellence to continue in the word of God, to be taught and have the correct understanding of the word of God, to be energised by a correct understanding of the Word of God.

The word of God well understood is like food, chewed, swallowed digested and absorbed to give the energy, nutrition, and nourishment. The word of God not understood is like food chewed but not swallowed, it will then not give any benefit.

Key point: Grace works hand in hand with truth- the correct understanding of the word of God- to bring forth fruit in the child of God.

Please also note that because grace comes from exceeding riches in mercy, love and kindness which are in Jesus Christ- it is poured to effect a required purpose in the required measure for the required circumstances.

Let's look at Romans 5:17-21:

"For if by one man's offense death reigned through the one, much more those who receive abundance of grace and of the gift of righteousness will reign in life through the One, Jesus Christ.

18 Therefore, as through one man's offense judgement came to all men, resulting in condemnation, even so through one Man's righteous act the free gift came to all resulting in justification for life.

19 For as by one man's disobedience many were made sinners, so also by one Man's obedience many will be made righteous.

20 Moreover, the law entered that the offense might abound. But where sin abounded, grace abounded much more,

21 so that as sin reigned in death, even so grace might reign through righteousness to eternal life through Jesus Christ our Lord" (NKJV).

So, we notice here that those who receive abundance of grace, and the gift of righteousness will reign in life through the One, Jesus Christ- grace is poured in the measure to allow you to reign in life through Jesus Christ.

Notice further, where sin abounded – grace abounded much more – so that it enables people to reign through righteousness to eternal life through Jesus Christ.

Let's look at some examples to illustrate this point. In Daniel 3:16-30 we read the story of Shadrach, Meshack and Abed-Nego who were Jewish captives in Babylon from the land of Judah who refused to obey king Nebuchadnezzar's instructions to worship an image of gold.

The king was so angry with them, and he instructed that they be through into a burning fiery furnace that had been heated seven times more than normal – so hot was the furnace that the men who threw these men into the furnace were burnt to death.

In the middle of the furnace king Nebuchadnezzar saw, not three but four men and one looked like the Son of God.

The fire had no power over them- it was astonishing. The result was that the king repented and passed a decree saying, **"There is no other God who can deliver like this"**. Yes indeed.

The grace of God, abilities of Almighty God, activity done by Almighty God, was sent in a measure that was equal to the challenge before them.

We can also look at Daniel 6: 10-23 we see the story of Daniel who was Jewish captive in Babylon from the land of Judah. He was thrown into the den of lions because he had been found praying and making supplications before the only true God which was against the law of Medes and Persians.

Almighty God released a standard of grace- grace abounded and angels came to stop the mouth of lions until the morning. God also made the kings sleep to depart before him. Grace, God's ability was sent in a measure equal to the challenge before them.

In both these situations we see Almighty God raising a standard of grace to match the need of the situation.

Key point: The grace of God, abilities of Almighty God, activity done by Almighty God, are sent in a measure that is equal to the challenge before you.

There are other dimensions of grace I need to share with you in the following Chapter.

Chapter 19

Grace Makes You An Extension Of God On The Earth

Almighty God is seeking a people who would be an extension of God on the Earth. This is because there are things which Almighty God cannot do Himself directly. For example, He needs people to preach, He needs people to pray and intercede, He needs people to give substance to support the gospel and the needy.

Those things are however Almighty God's responsibility and being an extension of Almighty God on the Earth becomes a highly privileged position because Almighty God is a rewarder of those who seek Him diligently. (Hebrews 11:6)

Key point: The grace of God in Jesus Christ enables you to accomplish things on behalf of Almighty God on the Earth.

Key point: Almighty God is seeking people who would be an extension of God on the Earth, to do things which He cannot do directly.

The package of grace we receive from the fulness of Jesus Christ was revealed to prophets of old-and they were astonished at the extent of the working of God with human beings- even angels were keen to look further to understand the intricacy of this relationship.

1 Peter 1:10-12 says

"Of this salvation the prophets have inquired and searched carefully, who prophesied of the grace that would come to you,

11 searching what, or what manner of time, the Spirit of Christ who was in them was indicating when He testified beforehand the sufferings of Christ and the glories that would follow.

12 To them it was revealed that, not to themselves, but to us they were ministering the things which now have been reported to you through

those who have preached the gospel to you by the Holy Spirit sent from heaven- things which angels desire to look into".

Prophets of old were shown glimpses of what the grace of God would accomplish in the lives of people, the workings of Almighty God among His people following the sufferings of Jesus Christ. They were shown people being extensions of Almighty God on the Earth. The phenomenon they saw astonished them.

They were shown how Almighty God would dwell in people though the Spirit of Jesus Christ.

They were shown how through Christ people would be adopted into the household of Almighty God.

They were shown transformed lives, transformed character through the working of the Holy Spirit.

They were shown people exhibiting the fruits of the Holy Spirit: love, joy, gladness, peace, patience, an even temper, forbearance, longsuffering, kindness, goodness, benevolence, faithfulness, gentleness, meekness, humility, self-control, self-restraint, continence. (Galatians 5:22-23 AMP).

The Apostle Paul of Tarsus describes in Ephesians 3, how the grace of Almighty God revealed to him the mystery of Christ- the mystery of the grace of God which has not only brought salvation but also a working of Almighty God with and within people to accomplish the purposes of Almighty God on the Earth.

Ephesians 3:1-7

"1 For this reason I, Paul, the prisoner of Jesus Christ for you Gentiles-

2 if indeed you have heard of the dispensation of the grace of God which was given to me for you,

3 how that by revelation He made known to me the mystery (as I have briefly written already,

4 by which, when you read, you may understand my knowledge in the mystery of Christ),

5 which in other ages was not made known to the sons of men, as it has now been revealed by the Spirit to His holy apostles and prophets:

6 that the gentiles being fellow heirs of the same body, and partakers of His promise in Christ through the gospel,

7 of which I became a minister according to the gift of the grace of God given to me by the effective working of His power".

Everything therefore which we do and accomplish for Almighty God is done through His grace working within us.

That is why Paul the Apostle would say in **1 Corinthians 15:10: By the grace of God, I am what I am, and His grace towards me was not in vain, but I laboured more abundantly than they all, yet not I, but the grace of God which was with me.**

Grace is the zeal in you born of the unmerited favour of God,

the ability in you born by the unmerited favour of God-

in short grace is everything enabled in you,

for you and through you by activity on the side of God.

By grace therefore means through the gift of God, through the favour of God, through the blessing of God, given and received by us through His loving kindness.

Glory be to Almighty God- by the grace of God I am what I am- let this be your confession too.

And His grace towards me was not in vain- let this also be your prayer-cry that you accomplish for Him according to the measure of grace that was poured on you.

Chapter 20

When Almighty God Says You Are His Portion

"For the LORD's portion is His people; Jacob is the place of His inheritance."
Deuteronomy 32:9 NKJV

It is the desire of God that you be counted among those He calls His portion, those He calls His inheritance. Wow! In Jesus Christ you were purchased by His blood to be God's own peculiar person, God's own possession. That is why His word says in Ephesians 2:10 NKJV: **"For we are His workmanship, created in Christ Jesus for good works, which God prepared beforehand that we should walk in them."**

In Ephesians 1:11 (AMP): **In Him we also were made [God's] heritage (portion) and we obtained an inheritance; for we had been foreordained (chosen and appointed before-hand) in accordance with His purpose, who works out everything in agreement with the counsel and design of His own will.**

Desire to excel in Jesus Christ. For this you need to set yourself apart, to consecrate yourself for His purpose and will. Seek to accomplish maximums for your God. Seek to be distinguished in your service for God. Seek to be one of those for whom it will be said "The world was not worthy". (Hebrews 11:38).

The word of God distinguishes those who through faith subdued kingdoms, worked righteousness, obtained promises, stopped the mouths of lions, quenched the violence of fire, escaped the edge of the sword, out of weakness were made strong, became valiant in battle, turned to flight the armies of the aliens. (Hebrews 11:33-34 NKJV)

Being part of God's elite is your choice. You become a shaker and a mover and a proof producer in the things of Almighty God. God will not be ashamed to be called your God (Hebrews 11:16). There is a special reward from God. You will leave an indelible mark on Planet Earth. He will call you His portion and His inheritance.

Almighty God is seeking a people He calls His portion and His inheritance. Desire to be counted by almighty God as His portion and His inheritance.

There are multiple benefits of being counted as His portion and His inheritance:

He will find you, encircle you, instruct you, lead you, keep you as the apple of His eye. There will be no strange god with you, you are assured of reaching your destination in Jesus Christ.

His word says in **Deuteronomy 32:10-12:**

"He found him in a desert land and in the wasteland, a howling wilderness; He encircled him, He instructed him, He kept him as the apple of His eye. As an eagle stirs up its nest, hovers over its young, spreading out its wings, taking them up, carrying them on its wings, so the LORD alone led him, and there was no foreign god with him."

He found, He encircled, He instructed, He kept, He carried, He led: there was no foreign, no strange or alien god found with him.

Let the God that found you in a wasteful and howling wilderness, who encircled you to keep you safe and well, who instructed you in His word and in His ways, who carries you on His eagle's wings. Let that God continue to lead and guide you and do not give any opportunity to a foreign, strange god.

There are many potential distractions in your walk with God. There is therefore a need to remain focussed, principled, and spiritually alert.

That is why Jesus Christ said in His word

"My sheep hear my voice; I know them and they follow me." John 10:27 NKJV.

Do you desire to be called my own by the God of heaven?
When you are ready-

Prayer of consecration:

Heavenly Father in the name of Jesus Christ I thank you for finding me today. Thank you that I can declare that you found me in a howling and wasteful wilderness, thank you for encircling me to keep me safe and well. Thank you, Lord, for instructing me in your word and in your ways and for carrying me on eagle's wings. Continue Lord to lead and guide me in all I do every day, guide me into your purposes every day. I set myself apart for you to accomplish your will and your purpose every day. I acknowledge the risen Jesus Christ as Lord of my life today. I reject every working of the enemy satan and his demons upon my life. I ask you Father in the name of Jesus Christ to fill me with your Holy Spirit right now. To you Father I give all the glory. In Jesus Christ's name I pray. Amen.

Chapter 21

Becoming God's Own Special Person

"For the grace of God that brings salvation has appeared to all men,

12 teaching us that, denying ungodliness and worldly lusts, we should live soberly, righteously, and godly in the present age,

13 looking for the blessed hope and glorious appearing of our great God and Saviour Jesus Christ,

14 who gave Himself for us, that He might redeem us from every lawless deed and purify for Himself His own special people, zealous for good works." (Titus 2:11-14 NKJV)

The grace of God, which is His unmerited, undeserved favour powered by activity on the side of God- has appeared to all men.

Point of Reflection:

His grace teaches you, opens the eyes of your understanding so that you can see and have a revelation of God, it also opens your eyes to see and have a revelation of the working of the enemy satan and his demons.

You will be able to say no to ungodliness and worldly lusts.

His grace also works in your life through the word of God to make you know the Father, to make you grow in the knowledge of God so that you live soberly, righteously, and godly, helping you to overcome the challenges of your generation.

By His grace you were redeemed-that means a ransom prize was paid for you- so that satan and demons of every kind, have no legal right over you anymore- you can command them- *"Let me go and serve God, Jesus Christ paid for me by His own blood."*

You can command these demons by name- for example- bad temper, tobacco, drugs, alcohol, sexual uncleanliness, adultery, fornication, anger, impatience, anxiety, depression, inordinate affection, and so forth.

The result will be that you will become God's own special person, equipped and zealous to do good works which please God and waiting for the blessed hope and the glorious appearing of Jesus Christ to take you into eternity.

Do you desire His grace to accomplish its perfect work in you?
When you are ready-

Prayer of commitment:

Heavenly Father, in the name of Jesus Christ, I thank you for your grace in Jesus Christ which has appeared to me. Thank you for your redemption which is in Jesus Christ. I acknowledge the risen Jesus Christ as Lord of my life today. I reject and denounce every working of the enemy satan and his demons. I ask you Father in the name of Jesus Christ to fill me with your Holy Spirit right now. I receive the abundant outpouring of your Holy Spirit upon my life in Jesus Christ's name. I open my heart to your word to accomplish its perfect work in my life and make me God's own special person in the name of Jesus Christ. Amen.

Chapter 22

God's Promise To The Set Apart Ones: No Weapon To Prevail Against You

"No weapon formed against you shall prosper, and every tongue which rises against you in judgement you shall condemn. This is the heritage of the servants of the LORD, and their righteousness is from Me," says the LORD." **Isaiah 54:17 NKJV**

This scripture refers to you servant of God, you who have set himself apart, consecrated yourself for the use of the Master in whatever capacity. You can therefore celebrate this scripture with that knowledge.

Point of Reflection:

Your God needs you. Why? Because there are things that God cannot do -Himself -directly. Those things are however God's responsibilities.

Almighty God needs those things done!

He needs you to couple with Him and take your portion in having those things done.

He needs you to co-operate with Him to have those things done.

When you do, He promises you rewards, blessings, privileges, and a heritage.

Hebrews 11:6 says: But without faith it is impossible to please Him, for he who comes to God must believe that He is, and that He is a rewarder of those who diligently seek Him. (NKJV)

You need faith to please God- to believe that He is- He exists, He is there.

You also need to know and believe that H is a rewarder of them who seek Him diligently.

Diligence in seeking Almighty God means being conscientious, taking care of detail, taking delight in Him, giving business value to the activities you do with Him, for His house, for His cause. (Opposite of diligence is doing it lazily or shoddily).

1 Corinthians 15:58 tells us: Therefore, my beloved brethren, be steadfast, immovable, always abounding in the work of the Lord, knowing that your labour is not in vain in the Lord. (NKJV).

The Amplified Bible puts it this way: Therefore, my beloved brethren, be firm (steadfast), immovable, always abounding in the work of the Lord [always being superior, excelling, doing more than enough in the service of the Lord], knowing and being continually aware that your labour in the Lord is not futile [it is never wasted or of no purpose].

Note here: knowing and being continually aware that your labour in the Lord is never in vain. A lot of times children of God are intermittently aware, sometimes not aware at all- that every single action you do for Almighty God is recorded and rewarded.

Mathew 25:21 and 23 tells us of the servants who went and traded with their master's talents: **His lord said to him, "Well done good and faithful servant; you were faithful over a few things, I will make you ruler over many things. Enter into the joy of your lord".**

When you are faithful with a few Almighty God will make you ruler over more and give you His joy which no-on can take away from you.

Your victory over opposition is one of them.

You need to understand:

1. Your victory is in Jesus Christ- when you believe on the Lord Jesus Christ that He was manifested for you redemption and acknowledge the risen Jesus Christ as Lord of your life, He gives you victory. (Colossians 2:15, 1Corinthians 15:57).

2. You are an ambassador of Jesus Christ- that is why His word says in

   2 Corinthians 5: 20:

   "Now then, we are ambassadors for Christ, as though God were pleading through us: we implore you on Christ's behalf, be reconciled to God."

3. To be effective you need to make a conscious decision to set yourself apart for Jesus Christ.

4. Almighty God is a rewarder of them who diligently seek Him- He gives them victory over the enemy, He gives them rulership, He gives them joy and more.

Do you desire to be an ambassador for Jesus Christ?

When you are ready-

Prayer of consecration:

Heavenly Father in the name of Jesus Christ, I thank you for redemption which is in Jesus Christ.

I acknowledge the risen Jesus Christ as Lord of my life today.

I reject and denounce every working of the enemy satan and his demons upon my life.

I ask you Father in the name of Jesus Christ to fill me with your Holy Spirit right now.

I receive the abundant outpouring of your Holy Spirit upon my life right now in Jesus Christ's name.

I set myself apart and consecrate myself for you alone Lord Jesus, to do your will and to be an ambassador for Jesus Christ.

Thank you that as I serve you, no weapon formed against me shall prosper and every tongue that rises against me in judgement I condemn in the name of Jesus Christ as this is part of my reward, blessing, privilege and heritage. Amen.

Chapter 23

Vessels Of Excellency Receive The Help Of God- God Is Their Ally

In Genesis 49:22-25 we read:

> "Joseph is a fruitful bough, A fruitful bough by a well; His branches run over the wall.

> 23 The archers have bitterly grieved him, shot at him and hated him.

> 24 But his bow remained in strength, and the arms of his hands were made strong by the hands of the Mighty God of Jacob (From there is the Shepherd, the Stone of Israel),

> 25 by the God of your father who will help you, and by the Almighty who will bless you with blessings of heaven above, Blessings of the deep that lies beneath, Blessings of the breasts and of the womb."

Joseph was a man who was fruitful for the kingdom of God, who accomplished the purpose which Almighty God had put before Him. The word here tells us however that in the process he encountered skilled archers who bitterly grieved him, shot at him and hated him. If you read the story of Joseph, the archers were his own brothers, then the wife of Potiphar and all the other people who opposed him, lied against him and hated him. The word of God teaches us that his bow remained strong, and the arms of his hands were made strong by the hands of the mighty God of Jacob.

As you bear fruit for the kingdom of heaven, you need your bow (your offensive weapon launch pad) and your hands which operate it, to remain strong and to be continually strengthened with might in the inner man by His Spirit.

Ephesians 3:16 tells us: **That He would grant you, according to the riches of His glory, to be strengthened with might through His Spirit in the inner man.**

You need strength of conviction (inner man), strength of body (divine health and protection) as well as strength in resources to accomplish the mission before you. Strength of conviction is the most critical need-when you receive that, the rest follows.

The apostle Paul said in **Acts 26:22-23 NKJV: "Having therefore received the help of God to this day I stand, witnessing to both small and great saying no other thing but those which Moses and the prophets said would come to pass that the Christ would suffer, that He would be the first to rise from the dead, and would proclaim light to the Jewish people and to the Gentiles."**

Yes absolutely, you also need to receive, continuously and continually the help of Almighty God. Help of God means God is your ally. From Greek epikouria, epikouros an ally, one fighting with you side by side. Glory be to God forevermore.

Jesus Christ said to a group of fearful, timid and carnal disciples in Luke 24: 46-49 NKJV:

"Thus it is written, and thus it was necessary for the Christ to suffer and to rise from the dead the third day,

47 and that repentance and remission of sins should be preached in His name to all nations, beginning at Jerusalem.

48 And you are witnesses of these things.

49 Behold, I send the Promise of My Father upon you; but tarry in the city of Jerusalem until you are endued with power from on high."

The power from on high was the game changer, nothing else became the same. Even Simon Peter who had denied Jesus Christ three times within earshot could stand up before a large crowd to proclaim salvation through Jesus Christ.

The Holy Spirit charged their strength of conviction, it made the word of God real and alive inside them, and the disciples were totally changed.

Do you desire to be strengthened by the Holy Spirit?

Do you desire to receive the abundance of His grace for service?

When you ready-

Prayer of consecration:

Heavenly Father in the name of Jesus Christ, I thank you for your grace and mercy. Thank you for the gift of eternal life in Jesus Christ my Lord. Today I confess the risen Jesus Christ as my Lord. I denounce every working of the enemy satan and his demons upon my life. I ask you Father in the name of Jesus Christ, to fill and empower me by your Holy Spirit right now. Pour your Spirit upon me Lord abundantly. I receive your grace and wisdom for service in your house. In the name of Jesus Christ, I pray. Amen.

Chapter 24

Vessels Of Excellence Commit Emotionally

Commitment to a Godly vision is emotional.

In John 20:11-13, 17-18 we read:

11 "But Mary stood outside by the tomb weeping, and as she wept she stooped down and looked into the tomb.

12 And she saw two angels in white sitting, one at the head and the other at the feet, where the body of Jesus had lain.

13 Then they said to her, "Woman, why are you weeping?" She said to them, "Because they have taken away my Lord, and I do not know where they have laid Him."

17 Jesus said to her, "Do not cling to Me, for I have not yet ascended to My Father; but go to My brethren and say to them, 'I am ascending to My Father and your Father, and to My God and your God.' "

18 Mary Magdalene came and told the disciples that she had seen the Lord, and that He had spoken these things to her."

The Lord Jesus Christ after the resurrection appeared first to Mary Magdalene, not to the apostles. You could ask why?

I believe it was because of her positioning.

The women followed Jesus to the cross when the men had scattered. They took notice of where He was buried. They departed and started working gathering ointments and spices. Rested the sabbath day, rose early on the first day of the week to go to the tomb to anoint the body of Jesus Christ.

When Mary Magdalene did not find the body; she started weeping in anguish, she wanted to find Him, even His dead body. Jesus Christ seeing her commitment and passion appeared to her- the Lord Jesus had to make an unscheduled detour to come to the tomb while He was on His way to the Father to present His own blood to God the Father. You may ask why? Mary Magdalene was determined and emotionally committed to see Jesus Christ. She wanted to see Him, she was determined to see Him- nothing else was going to do- she wanted results and she was determined to get them. Her request was granted- it had to be granted- her passion and determination moved God. She became the first preacher of the New Testament who went and told the apostles "I have seen the Lord, He is risen". The whole exercise was done with deep conviction and passion.

Praying for planet earth, including every nation in the Middle East to receive the gospel and worship Jesus Christ freely will take praying with conviction and passion.

Communicating the message of living in the presence of Almighty God will take conviction and passion.

To those who will engage with God in sending this message, Jesus Christ will manifest Himself as He did to Mary Magdalene and many others who through faith *"subdued kingdoms, worked righteousness, obtained promises, stopped the mouths of lions, quenched the violence of fire, escaped the edge of the sword, out of weakness were made strong, became valiant in battle, turned to flight the armies of the aliens."* Hebrews 11:33-34 (NKJV)

Do you desire to be part of the team which Almighty God will use to send His message to every corner of Planet Earth?

Do you desire Almighty God to use you to pray for an outpouring of His Spirit that will usher the second coming of Jesus Christ?

Do you desire to leave an indelible mark in the kingdom of Almighty God which cannot be erased for all eternity?

Your God needs you to set yourself apart for Him and allow His Holy Spirit to fill and empower you.

When you are ready-

Prayer:

Heavenly Father in the name of Jesus Christ I thank you for sending Jesus Christ your Son to die for my sin and rise again. Today I confess the risen Jesus Christ as Lord of my life. I set myself apart and consecrate myself to serve you alone Lord. I reject every working of the enemy satan and his demons upon my life in the name of Jesus Christ. I ask you Father in the name of Jesus Christ to fill and empower me by your Holy Spirit right now. I receive the abundant outpouring of your Spirit upon my life in the name of Jesus Christ. Thank you, Father, for it is done. In Jesus Christ's name I pray. Amen.

Chapter 25

Vessels Of Excellency Are Committed To A Godly Vision

There is power in committing to a Godly vision.

Ruth 1:14-17 we read:

Then they lifted up their voices and wept again; and Orpah kissed her mother-in law, but Ruth clung to her.

15 And she said, "Look your sister-in-law has gone back to her people and to her gods; return after your sister-in-law:

16 But Ruth said: "Entreat me not to leave you, Or to turn back from following after you; For wherever you go, I will go; And wherever you lodge, I will lodge; Your people shall be my people, And your God, my God.

17 Where you die, I will die, and there I will be buried. Th Lord do so to me, and more also, if anything but death parts you and me." (NKJV)

The story of Ruth and her mother-in-law Naomi in the book of Ruth teaches us the power of commitment to a Godly vision.

Ruth saw through her mother-in-law and saw the God of Naomi. When the other sister-in-law Orpah decided to return to her own people and to go and worship idols in Moab, she refused and clang to her mother-in-law.

What did Ruth see and what was she after? While Naomi was a very negative woman, Ruth saw through all that negativity and realised the God of Naomi was the true God of Israel, Jehovah, the only true God. She made up her mind, husband, or no husband, she was not going back to worship idols. She committed herself to follow the vision of serving the true God.

Almighty God proved Himself God, He honoured her commitment. Not only did Ruth get married to Boaz, a God fearing and blessed husband she was made by God to be the most blessed woman in her generation by becoming a great, great mother of the Messiah Jesus Christ.

In **Matthew 1:5-6 (NKJV)** we read in the genealogy of Jesus Christ: **"Salmon begot Boaz by Rahab, Boaz begot Obed by Ruth, Obed begot Jesse, and Jesse begot David the king. David the king begot Solomon by her who had been the wife of Uriah."** She also has a book in the Scriptures named after her. Glory be to God forevermore.

Do you desire to commit to a Godly vision?

Do you desire to commit your life to Jesus Christ and to do His desire and will on Planet Earth?

God will honour your commitment in ways that will blow you away. He is a rewarder of those who diligently seek Him (Hebrews 11:6).

When you are ready-

Prayer of commitment:

Heavenly Father in the name of Jesus Christ, I thank you for sending me your one and only Son Jesus Christ to suffer and die for my sin. Today I believe on the name of Jesus Christ and confess the risen Jesus Christ as Lord of my life. I reject every working of the enemy satan and his demons upon my life. I ask you Father in the name of Jesus Christ to fill me with your Holy Spirit right now. I receive the abundant outpouring of your Holy Spirit upon my life. I set myself apart to do your will and to accomplish your purpose on planet earth. In Jesus Christ's name I pray. Amen.

Chapter 26

Vessels Of Excellency Wholly Follow The Lord Their God

The story of Caleb the son of Jephunneh in the books of Numbers and Joshua is revealing for a man who wholly followed the Lord his God, who was a man of faith, who stood at the promise of Almighty God without wavering. He was strong in faith, giving glory to God. The story begins in the book of Numbers 13 when Almighty God asked Moses to send out 12 men to spy out the land of Canaan. He sent 12 men each from each of the twelve tribes of Israel, every one of them was a leader from each of the tribes of Israel.

From the tribe of Judah, he sent Caleb the son of Jephunneh, and from the tribe of Manasseh, Joshua the son of Nun. (Numbers 13:1-15).

When they returned from spying the land, they all agreed the land was good, and flowed with milk and honey, they brought with them some of the fruits- a cluster of grapes, some pomegranates, and figs.

However, ten of the twelve did not believe it was possible for them to possess the land and gave a bad report:

"Nevertheless, the people who dwell in the land are strong; the cities are fortified and very large; moreover we saw the descendants of Anak there." (Numbers 13:28 NKJV).

In Numbers 13:30-33 we read:

Then Caleb quieted the people before Moses, and said, "Let us go up at once and take possession, for we are well able to overcome it.

But the men who had gone up with him said, "We are not able to go up against the people, for they are stronger than we."

32 And they gave the children of Israel a bad report of the land which they had spied out, saying, "The land through which we have gone as spies is a land that devours its inhabitants, and all the people whom we saw in it are men of great stature.

33 There we saw the giants (the descendants of Anak came from the giants); and we were like grasshoppers in our own sight, and so we were in their sight."

The congregation of Israel lifted their voice and cried and wept that night.

But Joshua the son of Nun and Caleb the son of Jephunneh, who were among those who had spied out the land, tore their clothes;

7 and they spoke to all the congregation of the children of Israel, saying: "The land we passed through to spy out is an exceedingly good land.

8 If the LORD delights in us, then He will bring us into this land and give it to us, a land which flows with milk and honey.'

9 Only do not rebel against the LORD, nor fear the people of the land, for they are our bread; their protection has departed from them, and the LORD is with us. Do not fear them."(Numbers 14:6-9 NKJV).

The Lord was angry with the children of Israel because despite the signs which God had performed among them in Egypt and in the wilderness, they could not believe God. Moses had to intercede for the people, asking the Lord to have mercy on the children of Israel:

Then the LORD said: "I have pardoned, according to your word;

21 but truly, as I live, all the earth shall be filled with the glory of the LORD—

22 because all these men who have seen My glory and the signs which I did in Egypt and in the wilderness, and have put Me to the test now these ten times, and have not heeded My voice,

23 they certainly shall not see the land of which I swore to their fathers, nor shall any of those who rejected Me see it.

24 But My servant Caleb, because he has a different spirit in him and has followed the Lord fully, I will bring into the land where he went, and his descendants shall inherit it. Numbers 14:20-24 NKJV.

Notice here the Lord singled out Caleb the son of Jephunneh as a person who had a different spirit- a different attitude of faith and that he had followed the Lord fully. The children of Israel were sentenced to 40 years in the wilderness and all adults except Caleb and Joshua were to die in the wilderness and were not going to enter the promised land due to their unbelief.

Now forty-five years later, Moses had died and Joshua the son of Nun had led the children of Israel into the Promised Land and they came to Gilgal, at this point God remembered Caleb's faithfulness and gave Caleb, the son of Jephunneh, the mountains of Hebron as his inheritance.

We read in Joshua 14:6-14:

Then the children of Judah came to Joshua in Gilgal. And Caleb the son of Jephunneh the Kenizzite said to him: "You know the word which the LORD said to Moses the man of God concerning you and me in Kadesh Barnea.

7 I was forty years old when Moses the servant of the LORD sent me from Kadesh Barnea to spy out the land, and I brought back word to him as it was in my heart.

8 Nevertheless my brethren who went up with me made the heart of the people melt, but I wholly followed the LORD my God.

9 So Moses swore on that day, saying, Surely the land where your foot has trodden shall be your inheritance and your children's forever, because you have wholly followed the LORD my God.'

10 And now, behold, the LORD has kept me alive, as He said, these forty-five years, ever since the LORD spoke this word to Moses while Israel wandered in the wilderness; and now, here I am this day, eighty-five years old.

11 As yet I am as strong this day as on the day that Moses sent me; just as my strength was then, so now is my strength for war, both for going out and for coming in.

12 Now therefore, give me this mountain of which the LORD spoke in that day; for you heard in that day how the Anakim were there, and that the cities were great and fortified. It may be that the LORD will be with me, and I shall be able to drive them out as the LORD said."

13 And Joshua blessed him and gave Hebron to Caleb the son of Jephunneh as an inheritance. Hebron therefore became the inheritance of Caleb the son of Jephunneh the Kenizzite to this day because he wholly followed the LORD God of Israel.

It is the desire of God in Jesus Christ that you wholly follow the Lord your God, that you put on the whole armour of God and that you have a strong conviction of His faithfulness, His power and His might. Caleb the son Jephunneh, wholeheartedly followed the Lord His God and reaped the results. He was of strong conviction concerning what God had spoken- that what Almighty God had spoken He was also able to perform.

The word of God says in Ephesians 6: 10-12 NKJV:

Finally, my brethren, be strong in the Lord and in the power of His might.

11Put on the whole armor of God, that you may be able to stand against the wiles of the devil.

12 For we do not wrestle against flesh and blood, but against principalities, against powers, against the rulers of the darkness of this age, against spiritual hosts of wickedness in the heavenly places.

13 Therefore take up the whole armor of God, that you may be able to withstand in the evil day, and having done all, to stand.

14 Stand therefore, having girded your waist with truth, having put on the breastplate of righteousness,

15 and having shod your feet with the preparation of the gospel of peace;

16 above all, taking the shield of faith with which you will be able to quench all the fiery darts of the wicked one.

17 And take the helmet of salvation, and the sword of the Spirit, which is the word of God;

18 praying always with all prayer and supplication in the Spirit, being watchful to this end with all perseverance and supplication for all the saints—

It is therefore important that you are strong in the Lord- have a strength of conviction that what He has spoken He is faithful to do and that He has the might- or ability to perform His promise.

Here we are also told to put the whole armour of God- like a decorated soldier ready to go for duty on the frontline of battle.

The components of the armour here are described:

First know the nature of the enemy- it is not flesh and blood- it's not things which are visible- our war is with forces of darkness, forces of the enemy satan and their ranks.

Then he says put on the whole armour of God and stand firm:

Your waist girded with truth- truth is the correct understanding of the word of God.

Breastplate- of righteousness- correct understanding of your righteousness in Jesus Christ- you are the righteousness of God in Jesus Christ. (2 Corinthians 5:21 *see Chapter 8*)

Your feet clothed with the readiness to preach the gospel- How beautiful are the feet of them who preach the gospel of peace, who bring glad tidings of good things. (Romans 10:15).

For a shield- take faith- strong conviction on the promises of God with which you will be able to quench the fiery darts of the wicked one- the attacks of the enemy negative talk and any other kind of attack of the enemy- will bounce off to the ground from the shield of faith. Shield is a defensive weapon and so is faith.

For a helmet (over your head) take the full understanding of your salvation- understanding forgiveness of sin, setting yourself apart for Almighty God or consecration, understanding holiness, redemption, your adoption as a child of Almighty God in Jesus Christ and the power of a positive attitude. *(see section 2)*.

For sword- in today's war language he would have said- for a laser guided precision missile- take the word of God. Jesus Christ (the Word of God) has spoken a promise for every single situation you will ever encounter. Hence His word says in Colossians 3:16:

Let the word of Christ dwell in you richly in all wisdom, teaching and admonishing one another in psalms and hymns and spiritual songs, singing with grace in your hearts to the Lord.

Therefore, take time to study the word of God.

And putting all things together – be in prayer- talk to your Father in heaven, commune with Him and bring everything before Him in prayer- remember to pray with your understanding and also to pray in the spirit- praying in tongues- for he who speaks in an unknown tongue speaks not to man but to God- and in the spirit he speaks mysteries. (1 Corinthians 14:2).

Pray then with both your understanding and in the spirit (1 Corinthians 14:15).

The word of God teaches us, that when you hold fast to His word without wavering you will reap the results.

Do you desire to reap the results of wholly following the Lord and having a strong conviction about His word?

When you are ready-

Prayer of consecration:

My Father in the name of Jesus Christ, I thank you for your increased grace and mercy. Thank you for the sacrifice of the cross and the blood that was shed to deliver me from every weapon of the enemy satan. I acknowledge the risen Jesus Christ as Lord of my life from today. I set myself apart to wholly follow the Lord my God and to wait upon His word without wavering. In Jesus Christ's name I pray. Amen.

Chapter 27

Other Attributes Of Vessels Of Excellence

In this chapter we will look at 5 other attributes of Vessels of Excellence:

27.1 Vessels of excellence are builders of the house of God

27.2 Vessels of excellence are granted by Almighty God victory against skilled archers.

27.3 Vessels of excellence are distinguished by God and receive blessing unlimited in scope and in time.

27.4 Vessels of excellence are honoured by Almighty God in this life.

27.5 Vessels of excellence enter maturity, behave with maturity, and show maturity.

27.1 Vessels of excellence are builders of the house of God

In Ruth 4:11 we read:

"And all the people that were in the gate, and the elders, said, We are witnesses. The Lord make the woman that is come into thine house like Rachel and like Leah, which two did build the house of Israel: and do thou worthily in Ephratah, and be famous in Bethlehem:"

It is the desire of God that you be a builder of the house of God just as Rachel and Leah did build the house of Israel.

Point of Reflection:

To build the house of God you need to have wisdom from on high. That is why apostle Paul said in 1Corinthians 3:10-13 KJV:

"According to the grace of God which is given unto me, as a wise masterbuilder, I have laid the foundation, and another buildeth thereon. But let every man take heed how he buildeth thereupon.

11 For other foundation can no man lay than that is laid, which is Jesus Christ.

12 Now if any man build upon this foundation gold, silver, precious stones, wood, hay, stubble;

13 Every man's work shall be made manifest: for the day shall declare it, because it shall be revealed by fire; and the fire shall try every man's work of what sort it is."

Notice:

1. You need wisdom to build the house of God.
2. Build on a foundation which is Jesus Christ.
3. Decide what material to build with- aim for building with gold- high quality, endures, is glorious and of value.

Building with gold means building with love as the only motive-anything built with any other motive is built with wood, hay and stubble (straw).

Remember 1Corinthians 13:13 tells us:

"And now abideth faith, hope, love, these three; but the greatest of these is love."

Do you desire Almighty God to use you to build His house?

Do you desire to receive the wisdom for building the house of God?

Prayer for consecration and wisdom:

Heavenly Father thank you for sending Jesus Christ to suffer and die for the forgiveness of my sin. I receive the risen Jesus Christ as Lord and Saviour of my life today. I set myself apart and consecrate myself Lord to serve you and you alone. I reject every working of the enemy satan and his demons upon my life. I ask you Father in the name of Jesus Christ to fill me and empower me with your Holy Spirit right now. I receive the abundant outpouring of your Spirit upon my life in the name of Jesus Christ. I ask you Father to grant me your wisdom as I build your house in love. In Jesus Christ name I pray. Amen.

27.2 Vessels of excellence are granted by Almighty God victory against skilled archers.

We read in Genesis 49:22-25

"Joseph is a fruitful bough, A fruitful bough by a well; His branches run over the wall.

23 The archers have bitterly grieved him, shot at him and hated him.

24 But his bow remained in strength, And the arms of his hands were made strong by the hands of the Mighty God of Jacob (From there is the Shepherd, the Stone of Israel),

25 By the God of your father who will help you, and by the Almighty who will bless you with blessings of heaven above, Blessings of the deep that lies beneath, Blessings of the breasts and of the womb."

The fruitful for God are always potential targets for the attacks of the enemy satan. You therefore need to be always alert and vigilant.

The scripture above declares **"Skilled archers have bitterly grieved him, shot at him and hated him."(AMP).**

Ephesians 6:16 speaks of the **"fiery darts of the wicked one".**

2 Corinthians 2:11 says **"we are not ignorant of satan's devices".**

So, child of God be always alert and vigilant because you have the victory always through Jesus Christ who was manifested to destroy, loosen, and undo all the works of the devil (1John 3:8 AMP).

Remember also that Jesus Christ on the cross disarmed satan and his demons, undressed them publicly and openly and made them to march down the road naked and in humiliation.

Remember His word also says no weapon formed against you shall prosper but that any tongue that rises against you in judgement you shall condemn (Isaiah 54:17). Remember also you are a blessed person, and no-one can curse one who God has blessed. God has given a command to bless you, and no-one can reverse it. (Numbers 23:8 and 20).

Remember that often satan uses people against you but you need to remember that we do not war after the flesh and that the weapons of our warfare are not physical, but mighty through God to the pulling down of strongholds of the enemy satan.

That is why 1 Corinthians 10: 3-6 tells us:

3 For though we walk in the flesh, we do not war according to the flesh. 4 For the weapons of our warfare are not carnal but mighty in God for pulling down strongholds, 5 casting down arguments and every high thing that exalts itself against the knowledge of God, bringing every thought into captivity to the obedience of Christ, 6 and being ready to punish all disobedience when your obedience is fulfilled.

Do you desire victory against skilled archers?

Know that the enemy was defeated publicly and openly.

Make a declaration to the enemy.

When you are ready-

Prayer:

Heavenly Father in the name of Jesus Christ I thank you for the victory that I have in Jesus Christ. Thank you that Jesus Christ was manifested to destroy all the works of the enemy satan. Thank you that he disarmed satan and his demons. I receive my victory in the name of Jesus Christ always. I reject every working of the enemy upon my life, and I command satan and demons to let me go and serve the only true God. In Jesus Christ' Amen.

27.3 Vessels of excellence are distinguished by God and receive blessing unlimited in scope and in time.

In Genesis 49:26 we read:

"The blessings of your father have excelled the blessings of my ancestors, up to the utmost bound of the everlasting hills. They shall be on the head of Joseph, And on the crown of the head of him who was separate from his brothers."

It is the desire of God that your commitment to faithfulness and fruitfulness distinguishes you from your contemporaries.

The distinguishing feature is desire. Your desire for fruitfulness will make Almighty God put a crown over your head for all eternity- not only that - it also releases for you a blessing pegged to the utmost bounds of the everlasting hills.

This represents a release by Almighty God of an unlimited blessing- unlimited in scope and in time.

Your desire for fruitfulness, your commitment to God's agenda on the earth will:

1. Make you distinguished among your peers.
2. Make Almighty God put a crown of glory over your head for all eternity.
3. Make Almighty God release upon your life a blessing unlimited in scope and in time - pegged to the utmost bounds (ends, limits) of the everlasting hills.

That is why His word says in Malachi 3: 17:

"They shall be Mine, 'says the LORD of hosts, 'On the day that I make them My jewels. And I will spare them as a man spares his own son who serves him.'" NKJV

He desires to make you, His jewel.

His word also says in Revelations 3:12

"He who overcomes, I will make him a pillar in the temple of My God, and he shall go out no more. I will write on him the name of My God and the name of the city of My God, the New Jerusalem, which comes down out of heaven from My God. And I will write on him My new name."NKJV:

Do you desire to be fruitful for Almighty God?

When you are ready-

Prayer of Consecration:

Heavenly Father in the name of Jesus Christ, I thank you for your grace and mercy upon my life. Thank you for sending your Son Jesus Christ to be a sacrifice for our sin, thank you for the redemption from disease and sickness, poverty and lack that I receive through His name. I confess Jesus Christ as Lord of my life today and I set myself apart to do your will and to be fruitful for the kingdom of God. I reject every working of the enemy satan and his demons upon my life. I receive right now in the name of Jesus Christ the in filling of the Holy Spirit upon my life. I receive the abundant outpouring of your Holy Spirit upon my life right now. In Jesus Christ's name I pray. Amen.

27.4 Vessels of excellence are honoured by Almighty God in this life

Almighty God desires to reward the set apart ones in the things of this life. Allowing you and giving you the opportunity to pursue a life associated with standards of quality and excellence.

We read in **Deuteronomy 32:13-14**

13 "He made him ride in the heights of the earth, that he might eat the produce of the fields; He made him draw honey from the rock, and oil from the flinty rock; 14 curds from the cattle, and milk of the flock, with fat of lambs; and rams of the breed of Bashan, and goats, with the choicest wheat; and you drank wine, the blood of the grapes." (NKJV)

Almighty God is **a rewarder of them who diligently seek Him (Hebrews 11:6).**

That is why His word says in **1 Corinthians 15:58 "Therefore, my beloved brethren, be steadfast, immovable, always abounding in the work of the Lord, knowing that your labour is not in vain in the Lord."**

When you set yourself apart and consecrate yourself for God, God will see you as His portion and His inheritance (Deuteronomy 32:9). You will be seen by Almighty God as something special in His hand, an assert in His hands.

He will say about you: **"You shall also be a crown of glory in the hand of the LORD, and a royal diadem in the hand of your God." Isaiah 62:3 NKJV**

He will keep, protect, instruct, and lead you. (Deuteronomy 32:10-12). Not only that but the Lord will also make you experience His goodness, will lift you up and fortify you.

He will shower you with blessing-will make you experience the goodness of God in this life. Glory be to His name forevermore.

Do you desire His fortification and blessing?

These are rewards for obedience, faithfulness, being set apart for Him and being empowered by His Holy Spirit.

When you are ready-

Prayer of setting yourself apart for obedience and service:

Heavenly Father in the name of Jesus Christ, I thank you for salvation in Jesus Christ by whom we have access into your presence. I acknowledge the risen Jesus Christ as Lord of my life. I desire Father to be a crown of glory in your hands. I set myself apart for your will and service. I ask you to empower me by your Holy Spirit in the name of Jesus Christ. Thank you for fortification and unending blessing. In Jesus Christ's name I pray. Amen.

27.5 Vessels of excellency enter maturity, behave with maturity, and show maturity.

The word teaches us in **1 Corinthians 13:11:**

"When I was a child, I spoke as a child, I understood as a child, I thought as a child; but when I became a man, I put away childish things".

Becoming a mature child of Almighty God is a choice you need to make because maturity is entered into. You need to decide to receive, get hold of and begin to make use of the mindset of a mature child of God.

When you make up your mind about putting away childish things and embracing the responsibilities of a mature child of God, that decision opens the door for you to know God the Father.

That is why Jesus Christ says in **John 17:3 "And this is eternal life, that they may know You, the only true God, and Jesus Christ whom You have sent" (NKJV).**

That is why His word also says in **1John 2:13 NKJV "I write to you, fathers, because you have known Him who is from the beginning. I write to you, young men, because you have overcome the wicked one. I write to you, little children, because you have known the Father."**

When you decide to put away childish things, Almighty God decides to fill you with the knowledge of Himself, that knowledge of God exposes the enemy satan to you.

The knowledge of God brings with it strength of conviction to His word which is a critical ingredient for overcoming the wicked one, satan. Glory be to God forevermore.

God wants you to be His extension on the earth and that you be the person who carries and executes His agenda on the earth.

To do this you need to transition to maturity, a mature mind set, the mindset of a responsible child of God.

Do you desire to be an extension of God and to carry out His purposes on the earth?

When you are ready-

Prayer of consecration:

Heavenly Father in the name of Jesus Christ, thank you for sending Jesus Christ to suffer and die for me. I confess the risen Jesus Christ as Lord of my life today. I reject every working of the enemy satan and his demons upon my life. Today I make up my mind to reject childish things and I ask you Father to fill me with your Holy Spirit right now. I receive the abundant outpouring of the Holy Spirit upon my life. Thank you, Father, for hearing me and for revealing the Father to me. In the name of Jesus Christ, I pray. Amen.

Section 5:

Activities of Excellence

Chapter 28

Your Calling To Intercede

Summary:

Your God needs you to stand in the gap on behalf of your family, community, and nation- its people and its leaders. Praying first and foremost for salvation of souls, for people to come to salvation and the knowledge of the truth. Indeed, it is the will of Almighty God that you pray and intercede for whole Planet Earth, countries and regions in conflict or wars, countries, and regions with disasters like famine, disease and hardships caused by natural disasters such as earthquakes, flooding, hurricanes etc.

Covered in this section:

28.1 At the centre of the will of Almighty God is salvation of souls
28.2 He desires that we pray for the opening of eyes.
28.3 Almighty God desires that we plead on behalf of people who do not know Him.
28.4 You are qualified to plead on behalf of Planet Earth because of Jesus Christ.
28.5 You are qualified to join brethren in corporate prayer for God to spare His people and not give them to reproach.
28.6 The power of prayer with fasting.
28.7 Learning from the Lord Jesus Christ.

28.1 At the centre of the will of Almighty God is salvation of soul

His word says in 1 Timothy 2:1-4 (NKJV)

"**Therefore, I exhort first of all that supplications, prayers, intercessions, and giving of thanks be made for all men,
2 for kings and all who are in authority, that we may lead a quiet and peaceable life in all godliness and reverence.
3 For this is good and acceptable in the sight of God our Saviour,
4 who desires all men to be saved and to come to the knowledge of the truth."**

He desires all men to be saved and to come to the knowledge of the truth, He desires that every nation has an environment conducive to the preaching of the gospel to accomplish salvation of souls. We therefore need to intercede for people to be saved, to cry for mercy and the outpouring of His Holy Spirit. To pray for signs, wonders and undeniable miracles to follow the preaching of the gospel as these make people to believe in Almighty God and accept the message of the gospel.

28.2 He desires that we pray for the opening of eyes.

His word says in Acts 26: 16-18 NKJV:

"But rise and stand on your feet; for I have appeared to you for this purpose, to make you a minister and a witness both of the things which you have seen and of the things which I will yet reveal to you.

17 I will deliver you from the Jewish people, as well as from the Gentiles, to whom I now send you,

18 to open their eyes, in order to turn them from darkness to light, and from the power of satan to God, that they may receive forgiveness of sins and an inheritance among those who are sanctified by faith in Me.'

It is the desire of Almighty God that we pray for the opening of eyes- spiritual eyes- people's minds have been darkened, eyes blinded to spiritual and eternal realities- by a working of the enemy satan. As we pray, eyes of people will be opened, the dark cloud will lift and there will be receptive to the preaching of the word of Almighty God and salvation will come to many. As we pray bind and rebuke the spirit of blindness and release the spirit of sight. Rebuke the spirit of darkness and release the light of Almighty God into their lives. Command satan to let the people of Almighty God go and serve their God, command the shackles of the enemy to be broken that people be freed to serve their God. Glory be to God.

28.3 Almighty God desires that we plead on behalf of people who do not know Him.

His word says in **Ezekiel 22: 29-31(NKJV):**

"The people of the land have used oppressions, committed robbery, and mistreated the poor and needy; and they wrongfully oppress the stranger.

30 So, I sought for a man among them who would make a wall, and stand in the gap before Me on behalf of the land, that I should not destroy it; but I found no one.

31 Therefore, I have poured out My indignation on them; I have consumed them with the fire of My wrath; and I have recompensed their deeds on their own heads," says the Lord God.

When He was about to pour His indignation, His wrath upon the people who had done wickedly, Almighty God sought for a man or woman who would plead the cause of the people to Him. A person who would ask for mercy, but He found none- the result was that Almighty God poured His wrath upon the people- today let us answer the call and come and stand in the gap.

Abraham stood and pleaded with Almighty God on behalf of Sodom (Genesis 18:17-32)- until Almighty God promised He would not destroy Sodom if ten righteous people were found there. In the end Almighty God failed to find ten people but found one - Lot and had to rescue Lot out of Sodom before He destroyed it.

Moses interceded for the children of Israel in the wilderness when Almighty God was about to destroy them because of their unbelief. Notice what he said in **Exodus 32:11-14 (NKJV):**

"Then Moses pleaded with the Lord his God, and said: Lord, why does Your wrath burn hot against Your people whom You have brought out of the land of Egypt with great power and with a mighty hand?

12 Why should the Egyptians speak, and say, 'He brought them out to harm them, to kill them in the mountains, and to consume them from the face of the earth'? Turn from Your fierce wrath and relent from this harm to Your people.

13 Remember Abraham, Isaac, and Israel, Your servants, to whom You swore by Your own self, and said to them, 'I will multiply your descendants as the stars of heaven; and all this land that I have spoken of I give to your descendants, and they shall inherit it forever.'

14 So the Lord relented from the harm which He said He would do to His people."

Here the word of Almighty God teaches us that God was so angry with the children of Israel that He wanted to destroy them all and start to raise a new nation through Moses. Moses reasoned with Almighty God, and He relented.

Notice the language Moses used-very forceful persuasive language. Almighty God is looking for men and women who will accept His call to be intercessors.

28.4 You are qualified to plead on behalf of Planet Earth because of Jesus Christ.

Jesus Christ is our High Priest and Chief Intercessor. Through Jesus Christ you are the righteousness of God (2 Corinthians 5:21). You have received adoption to become a child of God (John 1:12-13).

His word also says in **1 Peter 2:9-10 (NKJV)**:

"But you are a chosen generation, a royal priesthood, a holy nation, His own special people, that you may proclaim the praises of Him who called you out of darkness into His marvellous light;

10 who once were not a people but are now the people of God, who had not obtained mercy but now have obtained mercy."

His word says further that you are a member of Almighty God's own household. (Ephesians 2:19).

His word also says **in 2 Chronicles 7:13-14 (NKJV)**:

"When I shut up heaven and there is no rain, or command the locusts to devour the land, or send pestilence among My people,

14 if My people who are called by My name will humble themselves, and pray and seek My face, and turn from their wicked ways, then I will hear from heaven, and will forgive their sin and heal their land.

So, you are qualified by Jesus Christ's salvation to stand before Almighty God on behalf of God's people and plead their case before the Father. As you do Almighty God has promised to hear you. Yes - you are a person called by the name of Jehovah through Jesus Christ. When you seek His face and pray on behalf of God's people - He will hear from heaven and heal our Planet, He will hear from heaven and save souls, He will hear from heaven and heal the politics of Planet Earth, He will hear from heaven and deliver Planet Earth from attacks of the enemy satan and his demons.

28.5 You are qualified to join brethren in corporate prayer for God to spare His people and not give them to reproach.

His word says in Joel 2:15-17 NKJV:

Blow the trumpet in Zion, Consecrate a fast, call a sacred assembly; gather the people, sanctify the congregation, assemble the elders,

16 gather the children and nursing babes; let the bridegroom go out from his chamber, and the bride from her dressing room.

17 Let the priests, who minister to the Lord, weep between the porch and the altar; let them say, 'Spare Your people, O Lord, And do not give Your heritage to reproach, that the nations should rule over them. Why should they say among the peoples, 'Where is their God?'

Here there was reproach, the enemy satan was causing suffering and the heathens were asking: "Where is their God?" God's answer was to call a sacred assembly, to sanctify a fast, to cancel even the honeymoons of newly wedded couples so that everybody would cry to God with one voice "Spare your people O God, do not give your heritage to reproach, that the enemy satan should rule over them- why should they say among the heathens where is their God."

We see a similar situation in the book of Acts when Peter and John were arrested for preaching the gospel:

Acts 4:23-31 (KJV)

"And being let go, they went to their own company, and reported all that the chief priests and elders had said unto them.

24 And when they heard that, they lifted up their voice to God with one accord, and said, Lord, thou art God, which hast made heaven, and earth, and the sea, and all that in them is:

25 Who by the mouth of thy servant David hast said, Why did the heathen rage, and the people imagine vain things?

26 The kings of the earth stood up, and the rulers were gathered together against the Lord, and against his Christ.

27 For of a truth against thy holy child Jesus, whom thou hast anointed, both Herod, and Pontius Pilate, with the Gentiles, and the people of Israel, were gathered together,

28 For to do whatsoever thy hand and thy counsel determined before to be done.

29 And now, Lord, behold their threatenings: and grant unto thy servants, that with all boldness they may speak thy word,

30 By stretching forth thine hand to heal; and that signs and wonders may be done by the name of thy holy child Jesus.

31 And when they had prayed, the place was shaken where they were assembled together; and they were all filled with the Holy Ghost, and they spake the word of God with boldness."

Here Peter and John went to their company where a group of believers were gathered and they raised their voice (one voice) in one accord, in agreement-after prayer there was an earthquake, the Holy Spirit came down and filled the brethren (again) and Almighty God answered their prayers, saved souls, healed the sick and raised the dead.

28.6 The power of prayer with fasting.

Sometimes it is critical to set apart time to pray with fasting. Fasting is going through a period of abstaining from food and drink, for the purpose of seeking the face of Almighty God in the weakness of the body. It is an act of faith and as such it is a supernatural activity. It should be done with full understanding of your body and its limitations. Under certain circumstances it needs to be done under medical counsel and supervision.

Above (Joel 2:15-17), we saw how Almighty God commanded leaders to call upon God's people to gather to pray fasted.

In Isaiah 58:3-9 KJV we read: "Wherefore have we fasted, say they, and thou seest not? wherefore have we afflicted our soul, and thou takest no knowledge?

Behold, in the day of your fast ye find pleasure, and exact all your labours.

4 Behold, ye fast for strife and debate, and to smite with the fist of wickedness: ye shall not fast as ye do this day, to make your voice to be heard on high.

5 Is it such a fast that I have chosen? a day for a man to afflict his soul? is it to bow down his head as a bulrush, and to spread sackcloth and ashes under him?

Wilt thou call this a fast, and an acceptable day to the Lord?

6 Is not this the fast that I have chosen?

To loose the bands of wickedness, to undo the heavy burdens, and to let the oppressed go free, and that ye break every yoke?

7 Is it not to deal thy bread to the hungry, and that thou bring the poor that are cast out to thy house?

When thou seest the naked, that thou cover him; and that thou hide not thyself from thine own flesh?

8 Then shall thy light break forth as the morning, and thine health shall spring forth speedily: and thy righteousness shall go before thee; the glory of the Lord shall be thy rearward.

9 Then shalt thou call, and the Lord shall answer; thou shalt cry, and he shall say, Here I am. If thou take away from the midst of thee the yoke, the putting forth of the finger, and speaking vanity.

Fasting makes your voice be heard on high with a different type of impact. It gives the believer a higher dimension of authority over satan and demons resulting in loosening the bands of wickedness, undoing heavy burdens, breaking yokes of the enemy upon our lives and upon God's people and letting oppressed go free. It takes authority over demons of blindness so that people may see the light of God.

We notice that Moses fasted for 40 days and 40 nights while up the mountain of Almighty God to receive the Ten Commandments.

"And he was there with the Lord forty days and forty nights; he did neither eat bread, nor drink water. And he wrote upon the tables the words of the covenant, the ten commandments." Exodus 34:28 KJV.

Jesus Christ fasted forty days and forty nights before being attempted by the devil:

"Then was Jesus led up of the Spirit into the wilderness to be tempted of the devil. 2 And when he had fasted forty days and forty nights, he was afterward an hungred." Matthew 4:1-2 KJV.

Esther called for three days of prayer and fasting before he appeared before the king with a petition for the Israelites in Babylon:

In Esther 4:15-16 (NKJV) we read:

Then Esther told them to reply to Mordecai:

16"Go, gather all the Jews who are present in Shushan, and fast for me; neither eat nor drink for three days, night or day. My maids and I will fast likewise. And so I will go to the king, which is against the law; and if I perish, I perish!"

Jesus Christ taught that certain demons will not go away except after prayer and fasting:

In Matthew 17:20-21 (NKJV) we read:

So Jesus said to them, "Because of your unbelief; for assuredly, I say to you, if you have faith as a mustard seed, you will say to this mountain, 'Move from here to there,' and it will move; and nothing will be impossible for you.

21 However, this kind does not go out except by prayer and fasting."

The apostle Paul fasted often. (2 Corinthians 11:27).

A word of wisdom regarding fasting if you have certain medical condition such as Type 1 diabetes treated with insulin- you would need to fast with medi cal counsel and supervision. The same applies to anyone under medical supervi sion for heart, kidney or blood disorders such as anaemia.

28.7 Learning from the Lord Jesus Christ.

The Lord Jesus Christ is our intercessor. The scriptures tell us that He is seated a the right hand of the Father making intercessions for us:

> **"Who is he that condemneth? It is Christ that died, yea rather, that is risen again, who is even at the right hand of God, who also maketh intercession for us." Romans 8:34.**

The Holy Spirit in us also intercedes for us when we speak in tongues witl groanings:

> **"Likewise, the Spirit also helpeth our infirmities: for we know not what we should pray for as we ought: but the Spirit itself maketh intercession for us with groanings which cannot be uttered. Romans 8:26 KJV.**

> *Remember the Lord Jesus Christ Himself had a prayer habit:*

> **"And in the morning, rising up a great while before day, he went out, and departed into a solitary place, and there prayed." Mark 1:35 KJV.**

Matthew 14:23 tells us:

> **And when He had sent the multitudes away, He went up on the mountain by Himself to pray. Now when the evening came, He was alone there. (NKJV).**

The scriptures teach us that the day before He appointed His twelve disciple: the Lord Jesus Christ prayed all night:

> **"And it came to pass in those days, that he went out into a mountain to pray, and continued all night in prayer to God. And when it was day, he called unto him his disciples: and of them he chose twelve, whom also he named apostles;" Luke 6:12-13 KJV.**

In the garden of Gethsemane Jesus Christ told His disciples to pray so tha they may not enter into temptation- to intercede for themselves while He inter ceded also for the battles He was going to face:

In **Matthew26:36-42,44:**

Then cometh Jesus with them unto a place called Gethsemane, and saith unto the disciples, Sit ye here, while I go and pray yonder.

And he took with him Peter and the two sons of Zebedee, and began to be sorrowful and very heavy.

Then saith he unto them, My soul is exceeding sorrowful, even unto death: tarry ye here, and watch with me.

he went a little further, and fell on his face, and prayed, saying, O my Father, if it be possible, let this cup pass from me: nevertheless, not as I will, but as thou wilt.

And he cometh unto the disciples, and findeth them asleep, and saith unto Peter, what, could ye not watch with me one hour?

Watch and pray, that ye enter not into temptation: the spirit indeed is willing, but the flesh is weak.

He went away again the second time, and prayed, saying, O my Father, if this cup may not pass away from me, except I drink it, thy will be done.

And he left them, and went away again, and prayed the third time, saying the same words." KJV.

Jesus Christ here asked the disciples to watch and pray with Him - one hour- aim therefore for a cumulative hour of prayer per day.

Jesus Christ prayed and had a victorious night, but His disciples slept, and the result was disastrous for them.

Chapter 29

You Are Witnesses To These Things

Summary:

Every child of God, who has acknowledged Jesus Christ as Lord and has experienced His saving grace in their life, has a calling to be a witness of Jesus Christ. We are ambassadors and representatives of Jesus Christ on the Earth. Apart from praying and interceding we have been sent to be witnesses of Jesus Christ.

We have been sent in the same way as the Lord Jesus Christ was sent, that is, backed by all the power, authority and the hosts and arsenals of heaven.

A witness gives a testimony of what they have seen, heard, handled, and experienced.

As you witness the power of Jesus Christ, He turns up to confirm His word with undeniable miracles. As a witness of Jesus Christ, you cause people who have been captives to the wicked one, to be set free.

As you witness the power of Jesus Christ, you cause their eyes to be opened to see the goodness of God and to also have a revelation on the working of the wicked one, satan.

The word you speak and send forth, will not come back to you void, but will accomplish the purpose for which it is sent.

As you witness the power of Jesus Christ, you cause desolate cities to be inhabited, these are lives of people which have been destroyed by the enemy satan which you will cause to receive healing and hope.

As you witness Jesus Christ you will bring comfort to those who are hurting, joy to those who are anxious and depressed.

Covered in this chapter:

29.1 We are sent and commissioned by Jesus Christ to be witnesses.
29.2 A witness speaks about what they have seen, hard, and handled.
29.3 As you witness the power of Jesus Christ, He turns up to confirm His word with undeniable miracles.
29.4 We have been sent to set the captives free.
29.5 Sent to open eyes.

29.6 When you live and speak His word, it will go and accomplish the purpose for which He sent it.

29.7 As you witness the power of Jesus Christ, you cause desolate cities to be inhabited.

29.8 Sent to comfort those who mourn- healing to those who are hurting.

29.1 We are sent and commissioned by Jesus Christ to be witnesses.

We read in **Luke 24:44-49**:

Then He said to them, "These are the words which I spoke to you while I was still with you, that all things must be fulfilled which were written in the Law of Moses and the Prophets and the Psalms concerning Me."

45 And He opened their understanding, that they might comprehend the Scriptures.

46 Then He said to them, "Thus it is written, and thus it was necessary for the Christ to suffer and to rise from the dead the third day,

47 and that repentance and remission of sins should be preached in His name to all nations, beginning at Jerusalem.

48 And you are witnesses of these things.

49 Behold, I send the Promise of My Father upon you; but tarry in the city of Jerusalem until you are endued with power from on high."

We learn here that Jesus Christ Himself acknowledged that the books of the Law of Moses (Genesis, Exodus, Leviticus, Numbers and Deuteronomy), the prophets and psalms wrote about and foretold the coming and mission of the Messiah Jesus Christ.

We also note that He opened their understanding, so that they may comprehend the scriptures- this is critical for every child of God. The truth that set people free is the correct understanding of the word of God.

He then stated the necessity of the Christ to suffer, die and rise from the dead the third day and that repentance and remission of sins should be preached in His name to all nations beginning at Jerusalem.

Then He stated, "You are witnesses of these things". In other words, go and declare what you have seen, heard, experienced, and touched concerning the salvation in Jesus Christ.

Following this He stated another critical truth- you cannot do this on your own- I will send the Promise of the Father upon you, miracle working power, the

Helper, Comforter, Counsellor, Intercessor, Advocate, Strengthener and Stand-by- the Holy Spirit.

In Matthew 28:18-20 Jesus Christ commissioned His disciples and said:

And Jesus came and spoke to them, saying, "All authority has been given to Me in heaven and on earth.

19 Go therefore and make disciples of all the nations, baptizing them in the name of the Father and of the Son and of the Holy Spirit,

20 teaching them to observe all things that I have commanded you; and lo, I am with you always, even to the end of the age." Amen.

In this He added the dimension of all authority, all power of rule, all political power in heaven and on Earth is given to me and therefore I send you, backed by that authority.

In John 20:21 Jesus Christ said to His disciples:

So Jesus said to them again, "Peace to you! As the Father has sent Me, I also send you.

Jesus Christ was sent by the Father backed by all authority in heaven and on earth- and in exactly the same way He is sending us- backed by the same power and authority- to go and be witnesses of the power of God.

He also said there in Matthew 28:20- teach them to observe all things that I have commanded you and lo I will be with you always- as you witness Me, I will turn up and will be there.

Key points:

- **You need correct understanding of the word- the truth that sets you free.**
- **As the Father sent Jesus Christ, even so He sends us- backed by the same power and authority.**
- **All authority, all power of rule in heaven and on earth has been given to Jesus Christ and He sends us backed by the same power.**
- **You need to be filled with the Holy Spirit- the miracle working power, the Game Changer, the Helper, Comforter, Intercessor, Advocate, Strengthener, Standby, Counsellor and Guide.**
- **As you go, I will be there with you said Jesus Christ.**

29.2 A witness speaks about what they have seen, hard, and handled.

In 1 John 1:1-4 we read:

That which was from the beginning, which we have heard, which we have seen with our eyes, which we have looked upon, and our hands have handled, concerning the Word of life—

2 the life was manifested, and we have seen, and bear witness, and declare to you that eternal life which was with the Father and was manifested to us—

3 that which we have seen and heard we declare to you, that you also may have fellowship with us; and truly our fellowship is with the Father and with His Son Jesus Christ.

4 And these things we write to you that your joy may be full.

You need an experience with God to be a witness of Jesus Christ- to have things you have experienced, things you have seen God do for you, things which you have heard from God and things which you have handled. You need to have experienced something.

In 1 John 1:14 the word declares: And we have seen and do testify that the Father sent the Son to be the Saviour of the world.

So then... see and testify, experience, and testify, hear and testify, handle and testify.

29.3 As you witness the power of Jesus Christ, He turns up to confirm His word with undeniable miracles.

As Jesus Christ preached God the Father attested of Him by miracles, wonders and signs which God did through Him.

Acts 2:22 tells us:

"Men of Israel, hear these words: Jesus of Nazareth, a Man attested by God to you by miracles, wonders, and signs which God did through Him in your midst, as you yourselves also know—."

Jesus Christ has promised to confirm and bear witness to the word we preach by doing miracles, signs and wonders.

The Amplified Bible explains this scripture in a manner that adds another dimension to our sending:

"You men of Israel, listen to what I have to say: Jesus of Nazareth, a Man accredited and pointed out and shown forth and commended and attested to you by God by the mighty works and the power of performing wonders and signs which God worked through Him right in your midst, as you yourselves know." Acts 2:22 AMP

The point here is this- as the Father sent Me even so I send you- said Jesus- He was sent with heavenly accreditation- that means heaven had officially recognised Him and qualified Him to act on behalf of Almighty God and this accreditation was through the miracle power which God did through Him.

In the same way as you witness Jesus Christ, you are an ambassador of heaven, accredited by heaven with power to perform miracles on behalf of heaven.

In 2 Corinthians 5:18-20 we read:

Now all things are of God, who has reconciled us to Himself through Jesus Christ, and has given us the ministry of reconciliation,

19 that is, that God was in Christ reconciling the world to Himself, not imputing their trespasses to them, and has committed to us the word of reconciliation.

20 Now then, we are ambassadors for Christ, as though God were pleading through us: we implore you on Christ's behalf, be reconciled to God.

We have been given a ministry of reconciliation and we are ambassadors of Jesus Christ, His representatives on the Earth, with full powers of accreditation as with earthly ambassadors who represent their home countries in another country.

In Mark 16:20

And they went out and preached everywhere, the Lord working with them and confirming the word through the accompanying signs. Amen.

As you preach Jesus Christ- Almighty God will work with you and confirm the word you preach with accompanying signs.

Hebrews 2:1-4 tells us:

Therefore, we must give the more earnest heed to the things we have heard, lest we drift away.

2 For if the word spoken through angels proved steadfast, and every transgression and disobedience received a just reward,

3 how shall we escape if we neglect so great a salvation, which at the first began to be spoken by the Lord, and was confirmed to us by those who heard Him,

4 God also bearing witness both with signs and wonders, with various miracles, and gifts of the Holy Spirit, according to His own will?

We are carrying the good news of a great salvation and as we do Almighty God will bear witness with various miracles and gifts of the Holy Spirit, transformation of lives, deliverance of lives from the bondage of the enemy satan.

29.4 We have been sent to set the captives free.

"The Spirit of the LORD is upon Me, Because He has anointed Me to preach the gospel to the poor; He has sent Me to heal the broken hearted, to proclaim liberty to the captives and recovery of sight to the blind, to set at liberty those who are oppressed; to proclaim the acceptable year of the LORD." Luke 4:18-19 NKJV.

Every child of God in Jesus Christ has been anointed, commissioned, sent forth, accredited, attested to and commended by God Almighty to preach the gospel and cause healing to the broken hearted, let captives go free, cause the spiritually and physically blind to see, to give liberty and freedom to those who are oppressed by demons of the enemy and to proclaim the year of God's favour. Before you proclaim these things to others, you need to experience them.

Jesus Christ said in John 14:12NKJV:

Most assuredly, I say to you, he who believes in Me, the works that I do he will do also; and greater works than these he will do, because I go to My Father."

The only qualification for you to release the power of Jesus Christ to others is to be a believer who has allowed the power of God to work its perfect work in you. Allow Him to set you completely free from every oppression of the enemy satan, let your eyes be opened to see the exceeding greatness of His resurrection power to you who believe (Ephesians 1:19-20).

Be totally set free from every working of the enemy satan. You need to renounce and denounce every influence and working of satan and his demons upon your life. Allow your mind to be renewed by His word. Receive His unmerited favour, His grace for your total deliverance and salvation. Ask the Father in the name of Jesus Christ to fill you with His Holy Spirit.

Key points:

- **Sent to bring true freedom.**
- **To bring the taste of true freedom.**
- **To set at liberty those who are oppressed.**

The word of God declares in **John 8:36 KJV**

> **"If the Son therefore shall make you free, ye shall be free indeed."**

The enemy satan desires to put people in bondage of various sorts, from bad temper and unforgiveness all the way to substance misuse (alcohol, tobacco, and other illicit drugs).

His word says in **Colossians 2:15:**

> **"Having disarmed principalities and powers, He made a public spectacle of them, triumphing over them in it. (the cross)."**

His word also declares in John 3:8 AMP

> **"[But] he who commits sin [who practices evildoing] is of the devil [takes his character from the evil one], for the devil has sinned (violated the divine law) from the beginning. The reason the Son of God was made manifest (visible) was to undo (destroy, loosen, and dissolve) the works the devil [has done]."**

Jesus Christ on the cross disarmed satan, publicly and openly, He was made manifest to destroy, undo and dissolve all the works the enemy satan had done. In short you have victory over every demon and every bondage of the enemy satan through Jesus Christ. You can command satan and his demons to leave you, to let you go so that you can experience total freedom that comes from Jesus Christ. The freedom to serve God, to release your talent and full potential. The freedom to sing your "song" your way, His way, the way your creator intended it to be sung, under His guidance, direction, wisdom and powered by His Holy Spirit.

Do you desire to be set completely free by the power of Jesus Christ?

Do you desire His unlimited and unmerited favour and grace upon your life?

When you are ready-

Prayer for deliverance:

My Father in the name of Jesus Christ, I thank you for salvation and deliverance through the name of Jesus Christ. Thank you that Jesus Christ was manifested to deliver and set me free from all the power of the enemy. I acknowledge the risen Jesus Christ as Lord of my life and I command the enemy satan and his demons to let me go and serve God. I ask you Father in the name of Jesus Christ to empower and fill me by your Holy Spirit, right now. In the name of Jesus Christ. In Jesus Christ's name I pray. Amen.

29.5 Sent to open eyes.

We have been sent to give spiritual wealth to the poor.
Turn people from darkness to light,
From power of satan to the power of God.
Giving to them an inheritance everything of eternal life.

The gospel, the good news is on a mission to give spiritual wealth to the poor, to heal broken-hearted, to set captives free from the bondage of satan, to give the blind sight and to proclaim the year of God's favour and grace.

The word of God further declares in **Acts 26: 18 NKJV**

"To open their eyes, in order to turn them from darkness to light, and from the power of satan to God, that they may receive forgiveness of sins and an inheritance among those who are sanctified by faith in Me."

Every born-again child of God needs to be aware of their commissioning, their authorization and their sending by Almighty God. Putting it differently, your God needs you, He has authorized you as His vessel to live, speak and spread the good news.

29.6 When you live and speak His word it will go and accomplish the purpose for which He sent it.

His word says in **Isaiah 55: 10-11**

"For as the rain comes down, and the snow from heaven, and do not return there, but water the earth, and make it bring forth and bud, that it may give seed to the sower and bread to the eater,

11 so shall My word be that goes forth from My mouth; It shall not

return to Me void, but it shall accomplish what I please, and it shall prosper in the thing for which I sent it."

Do however seek to grow in grace and in the knowledge of Jesus Christ (2 Peter 3:18).

Study His word to make yourself approved by God (2 Timothy 2:15) and make use of every educational opportunity to become the best you can be in everything you do.

Be equipped for the work of the ministry (Ephesians 4:12).

As you send the word of God, address it to whom it may concern- in other words- sometimes sow the word in love and leave the rest to God- His word accomplishes the mission- sometimes long after it is sent.

29.7 As you witness the power of Jesus Christ, you cause desolate cities to be inhabited

"'Sing, O barren, You who have not borne! Break forth into singing, and cry aloud, you who have not labored with child! For more are the children of the desolate than the children of the married woman,' says the LORD.

2 "Enlarge the place of your tent, and let them stretch out the curtains of your dwellings; do not spare; lengthen your cords, and strengthen your stakes.

3 For you shall expand to the right and to the left, and your descendants will inherit the nations, and make the desolate cities inhabited."

It is amazing when the Lord God Almighty visits your barren areas, areas of your life where you are yearning for productivity and a breakthrough and then asks you to sing, celebrate, jump, shout and break forth into a celebration frenzy.

Why? You are about to experience a visitation from Almighty God in Jesus Christ, your barren areas are being turned productive left, right and centre. The result is desolate cities, which are lives without the light and life of Jesus Christ, will turn to Jesus Christ through your witness and productivity.

Almighty God turns situations around. Remember your God wants to use you in your own way, to make desolate cities to be inhabited. Desolate cities are lives and hearts where there is no life of God, lives in bondage of the enemy. When they discover again the life and joy of Jesus Christ, they move out of darkness to light, their eyes are opened to see and understand spiritual realities (Luke 4:18, Acts 26:18).

This is what you need to do:

1. **Sing, celebrate, the ability of God, His power and goodness in turning your situation around and bringing the growth and improvement you need.**

2. **Visualize increase and enlargement- have a mental picture of what it will look like when God has turned your situation around and increased your productivity.**

3. **Put your faith into action- do the action needed to bring growth and improvement.**

4. **Strengthen areas that needs strengthening to enable and sustain growth- your processes and systems- be the best you can in all you do.**

5. **Give thanks to Almighty God for growth and improvement.**

Remember He declared:

"You shall expand to the right and to the left and your descendants shall inherit the nations and make desolate cities to be inhabited."

Do you desire that?
When you are ready-

Prayer of Faith:

Heavenly Father in the name of Jesus Christ, I thank you for your grace and mercy which is in Jesus Christ. Thank you that you sent Jesus Christ to suffer and die for my sin. Thank you that Jesus Christ died, rose again and is alive today. I acknowledge the risen Jesus Christ as Lord of my life today. I denounce and reject every influence of the enemy satan and his demons upon my life in the name of Jesus Christ.

I ask you Father in the name of Jesus Christ to fill me with your Holy Spirit right now.

I receive the abundant outpouring of your Holy Spirit upon my life right now.

Today Father I celebrate the fruit of the barren, I speak into every barren part of my life and I declare a celebration of growth and improvement.

I declare expansion to the right and to the left, that my spiritual descendants shall inherit the nations and cause the desolate cities to be inhabited.

I release the spread of the word of Almighty God into every nation, every village, and every single person in Planet Earth in the name of Jesus Christ.

I speak the life, the light, the salvation, and deliverance of Jesus Christ into each single life of Planet Earth in the name of Jesus Christ. Amen.

29.8 Sent to comfort those who mourn- to bring healing to those who are hurting.

As you witness the power of Jesus Christ, you bring comfort to those who mourn- healing to those who are hurting.

You give oil of joy for mourning- joy and hope in place of despair and depression through the healing power of the Holy Spirit.

That people may be called trees of righteousness- people established in the faith and planted firmly in the kingdom of God.

His word says in **Isaiah 61:2-4**

To proclaim the acceptable year of the LORD,

And the day of vengeance of our God;

To comfort all who mourn,

3 To console those who mourn in Zion,

To give them beauty for ashes,

The oil of joy for mourning,

The garment of praise for the spirit of heaviness;

That they may be called trees of righteousness,

The planting of the LORD, that He may be glorified."

4 And they shall rebuild the old ruins,

They shall raise up the former desolations,

And they shall repair the ruined cities,

The desolations of many generations.

You shall rebuild the old ruins and raise up former desolations and repair ruined cities and desolations of many generations-these are all referring to restoration of lives through the gospel, rebuilding lives destroyed by the enemy satan lives that are hurting due to broken relationships, financial hardships, disease and sickness, poor character traits and bondages of tobacco, drugs and alcohol gambling addiction etc.

In the process you are taking them through the principles described in Sections 1 to 3 of this book.

Chapter 30

Faithful Stewardship Part 1:

God Wants You To Prosper- Understanding God's Position

Summary:

Almighty God wishes above everything else and desires that you may prosper, be in health even as your soul prospers. Every child of God needs to be fully persuaded about this statement. Your covenant with Almighty God is not established while you are in poverty. He wants that covenant to be established. Prosperity means having enough substance, enough financial resources to feed yourself and your dependants, to clothes yourself and your dependants, to have dignified accommodation for yourself and your dependants and have enough left to accomplish other purposes for which God has raised you up. There are enough resources on Planet Earth for everyone. Jesus Christ redeemed you from the curse of poverty by hanging on a tree so that you can have access to the Holy Spirit who in turn gives us access to the blessing of Abraham. The blessing of Abraham means positive outcomes in every area of your life. He desires you to eat bread without scarcity, He desires to command a blessing into your storehouses. You need to ask for blessing indeed in the way that Jabez prayed and to use Godly wisdom to use every God given potential to make a livelihood and make wealth creation to happen. We need more children of God to be millionaires and multimillionaires.

Covered in this chapter:

30.1 He wishes above all things that you may prosper and be in health as your souls prospers.
30.2 Jesus Christ redeemed you from the curse of the law, so that the blessing of Abraham may come to you.
30.3 God in Jesus Christ is bringing you into a good land in which you shall eat bread without scarcity.
30.4 He wants to command His blessing in your storehouses.

30.5 Jabez asked God for a blessing indeed and God granted his request. 30.6 Use Almighty God given potential and capabilities to make livelihood and wealth creation happen.

30.1 He wishes above all things that you may prosper and be in health as your souls prospers.

It is critical that every child of God knows that God desires you to prosper, He wants you to have substance. He desires you to have food to eat, clothes, a roof over your head as well as enough resources to accomplish the purpose for which He is raising you.

Let's look at the vow Jacob made to God after encountering God at Bethel in Genesis 28:20-22:

> Then Jacob made a vow, saying, "If God will be with me, and keep me in this way that I am going, and give me bread to eat and clothing to put on,
>
> 21 so that I come back to my father's house in peace, then the LORD shall be my God.
>
> 22 And this stone which I have set as a pillar shall be God's house, and of all that You give me I will surely give a tenth to You."

It is the desire of Almighty God that your needs be met.

In 3 John 2 His word also says:

Beloved, I wish above all things that thou mayest prosper and be in health even as thy soul prospereth. (KJV).

Jesus wore a crown of thorns so as to break the curse of poverty and lack from your life. - **In Matthew 27:29 we read:**

When they had twisted a crown of thorns, they put it on His head, and a reed in His right hand. And they bowed the knee before Him and mocked Him, saying, "Hail, King of the Jews!"

Jesus the Son of God- who owns all the gold and silver- He is King of kings and Lord of lords but instead of putting a crown of gold, they put a crown of thorns on His head. The reason was to break the curse of bareness, thorns and briers that came upon mankind at the fall of man. *(See Genesis 3:17-19 below).* He broke the curse of poverty and lack from your life by wearing a crown of thorns on the cross. Please note the opposite of a crown of gold is a crown of thorns.

His word also says in **2 Corinthians 8:9**

For you know the grace of our Lord Jesus Christ, that though He was rich, yet for your sakes He became poor, that you through His poverty might become rich.

Jesus Christ was poor physically not spiritually- the poverty referred to here is physical poverty.

In Matthew 8:20 His word says:

And Jesus said to him, "Foxes have holes and birds of the air have nests, but the Son of Man has nowhere to lay His head."

When Jesus needed to pay temple tax, He asked Simon Peter to go fishing and to get a coin from the mouth of the first fish he caught:

In Matthew 17:27:

Nevertheless, lest we offend them, go to the sea, cast in a hook, and take the fish that comes up first. And when you have opened its mouth, you will find a piece of money; take that and give it to them for Me and you."

Jesus Christ was poor, suffered poverty so that through His suffering poverty and lack, our needs may be met.

30.2 Jesus Christ redeemed you from the curse of the law, so that the blessing of Abraham may come to you.

In Galatians 3:13-14 His word says:

Christ has redeemed us from the curse of the law, having become a curse for us (for it is written, "Cursed is everyone who hangs on a tree"),

14 that the blessing of Abraham might come upon the Gentiles in Christ Jesus, that we might receive the promise of the Spirit through faith.

The word redeem means He bought us back, or He paid the necessary ransom needed to set us free from the curse of the law.

Remember after the fall of man came judgement. Part of judgement was that the land was cursed to bring thorns and thistles- in other words bareness.

Genesis 3:17-19:

Then to Adam He said, "Because you have heeded the voice of your wife, and have eaten from the tree of which I commanded you, saying,

'You shall not eat of it':
"Cursed is the ground for your sake;
In toil you shall eat of it
All the days of your life.
18 Both thorns and thistles it shall bring forth for you,
And you shall eat the herb of the field.
19 In the sweat of your face you shall eat bread
Till you return to the ground,
For out of it you were taken;
For dust you are,
And to dust you shall return."

Jesus Christ the Son of God redeemed us from the curse of the law- by being a curse for us- for cursed is everyone who hangs on a tree- so that the blessing of Abraham may come to the Gentiles through Jesus Christ and that we may receive the promise of the Holy Spirit through faith. The Holy Spirit opens the way for us to receive the blessing of Abraham. The blessing of Abraham means every positive outcome in our lives.

30.3 God in Jesus Christ is bringing you into a good land in which you shall eat bread without scarcity.

In Deuteronomy 8:7-18 we read:

For the LORD your God is bringing you into a good land, a land of brooks of water, of fountains and springs, that flow out of valleys and hills;

8 a land of wheat and barley, of vines and fig trees and pomegranates, a land of olive oil and honey;

9 a land in which you will eat bread without scarcity, in which you will lack nothing; a land whose stones are iron and out of whose hills you can dig copper.

10 When you have eaten and are full, then you shall bless the LORD your God for the good land which He has given you.

11 "Beware that you do not forget the LORD your God by not keeping His commandments, His judgments, and His statutes which I command you today,

12 lest—when you have eaten and are full, and have built beautiful houses and dwell in them;

13 and when your herds and your flocks multiply, and your silver and your gold are multiplied, and all that you have is multiplied;

14 when your heart is lifted up, and you forget the LORD your God who brought you out of the land of Egypt, from the house of bondage;

15 who led you through that great and terrible wilderness, in which were fiery serpents and scorpions and thirsty land where there was no water; who brought water for you out of the flinty rock;

16 who fed you in the wilderness with manna, which your fathers did not know, that He might humble you and that He might test you, to do you good in the end—

17 then you say in your heart, 'My power and the might of my hand have gained me this wealth.'

18 "And you shall remember the LORD your God, for it is He who gives you power to get wealth, that He may establish His covenant which He swore to your fathers, as it is this day.

You will notice here that the land referred to is the experience of the love of God. The land of salvation, of sins forgiven in which you experience the peace, joy and goodness of God.

In that land it is the desire of God that you eat bread without scarcity, that you build goodly houses and dwell in them and that your herds and flocks multiply, that your silver and gold are multiplied- that you have all the resources you need to accomplish the will and purpose of Almighty God upon your life.

Notice also here that God is your senior partner in wealth creation-it is Him who gives you power to get wealth. The word power here means the ability, knowledge, and the wisdom to get wealth.

Notice also that there is a reason given- so that He may establish His covenant which He swore to your fathers, as it is this day- for our day. Our covenant with God is through the blood of Jesus Christ. That covenant must be established in your life and on the earth.

In other words- there is a two-fold reason why God gives you the power to get wealth:

1. That you may have all your needs met-when you are hungry and not clothed and housed- His covenant with you is not established. God is zealous for this to happen.

2. That you can contribute to the preaching of the word of God to establish the covenant in those who have not heard about Jesus Christ in our day. In other words, so that you can give for salvation of souls across Planet earth.

30.4 He wants to command His blessing in your storehouses.

In Deuteronomy 28: 1-14 we read:

"Now it shall come to pass, if you diligently obey the voice of the LORD your God, to observe carefully all His commandments which I command you today, that the LORD your God will set you high above all nations of the earth.

2 And all these blessings shall come upon you and overtake you, because you obey the voice of the LORD your God:

3 "Blessed shall you be in the city and blessed shall you be in the country.

4 "Blessed shall be the fruit of your body, the produce of your ground and the increase of your herds, the increase of your cattle and the offspring of your flocks.

5 "Blessed shall be your basket and your kneading bowl.

6 "Blessed shall you be when you come in, and blessed shall you be when you go out.

7 "The LORD will cause your enemies who rise against you to be defeated before your face; they shall come out against you one way and flee before you seven ways.

8 "The LORD will command the blessing on you in your storehouses and in all to which you set your hand, and He will bless you in the land which the LORD your God is giving you.

9 "The LORD will establish you as a holy people to Himself, just as He has sworn to you, if you keep the commandments of the LORD your God and walk in His ways.

10 Then all peoples of the earth shall see that you are called by the name of the LORD, and they shall be afraid of you.

11 And the LORD will grant you plenty of goods, in the fruit of your body, in the increase of your livestock, and in the produce of your ground, in the land of which the LORD swore to your fathers to give you.

12 The LORD will open to you His good treasure, the heavens, to give the rain to your land in its season, and to bless all the work of your hand. You shall lend to many nations, but you shall not borrow.

13 And the LORD will make you the head and not the tail; you shall be above only, and not be beneath, if you heed the commandments of the LORD your God, which I command you today, and are careful to

observe them.

14 So you shall not turn aside from any of the words which I command you this day, to the right or the left, to go after other gods to serve them.

The word here lists blessings which will come upon you and overtake you. Verse one however gives a condition- if you diligently obey the voice of the Lord your God and observe carefully His instructions. Diligence means taking care of detail and having a business relationship with God. It means taking delight in Him, being conscientious in your dealings with God.

Notice that He would like to impact every area of your life with positive outcomes including the fruit of your body- your offspring, your storehouses-bank accounts and investments, victory over those who fight against you and bless all the work of your hands.

You need to desire, ask for and seek blessing in every area of your life.

30.5 Jabez asked God for a blessing indeed and God granted his request.

We read in 1 Chronicles 4 the story of Jabez:

9 Now Jabez was more honourable than his brothers, and his mother called his name Jabez, saying, "Because I bore him in pain."

10 And Jabez called on the God of Israel saying, "Oh, that You would bless me indeed, and enlarge my territory, that Your hand would be with me, and that You would keep me from evil, that I may not cause pain!" So, God granted him what he requested.

He called on God and asked for blessing indeed, thorough, proper blessing. This includes wisdom, knowledge, understanding, as well as an anointing for might, the Spirit of Counsel and the Spirit of the fear of the Lord- his aim was to get a capacity to accomplish the purpose of God for his life.

Then he asked for enlargement of territory which means more things to command and to control- again to enable him to accomplish the purpose of God for his life.

Further he asked for the hand of God to be upon him- the Spirit of the Lord- the Yahweh anointing to pave the way for him, a strong hand and outstretched arm.

Then he asked for deliverance from the wicked one satan- for judgement to be made by the Most High, who seats on the throne in his favour.

When you ask God who seats on the throne for blessing knowing the purpose of blessing is to establish covenant in your life and on Planet Earth, to accomplish the purpose of God for your life, God will answer your request.

Often however you will need to undergo spiritual training in handling blessing, especially training in handling substance, money and wealth. That includes the discipline needed in handling substance, understanding of the tithes and offerings of your substance as weapons for you to put substance under your feet and use it in the service of Almighty God.

It is important to understand that giving of substance breaks the power of mammon so that it is not an object for worship but an instrument for the service of Almighty God.

There are three main principles you need to understand here which I will explain in some detail in turn. The first is using your Almighty God given potential and capabilities to make wealth creation to happen. The second is understanding the principle of Godly tithing. The third is understanding worshipping God with your substance. The latter two will be explained in the next two chapters. The first of these will be explained below.

30.6 Use Almighty God given potential and capabilities to make livelihood and wealth creation happen.

First – understand that the Lord God Almighty is your Senior partner in wealth creation. He gives you the strength, wisdom and the capacity to get the knowledge you need to create wealth. In other words, every resource you have, you received from Him.

Proverbs 6 admonishes us to take wisdom from the ant who having no guide, overseer or ruler, they gather food in the harvest providing food for the winter. It goes further- a little sleep, a little slumber, a little folding of hands to sleep will cause poverty to come as a robber and want as an armed man. Essentially saying get off your bum and work.

Proverbs 6:6-11:

Go to the ant, you sluggard!
Consider her ways and be wise,
7 Which, having no captain,
Overseer or ruler,
8 Provides her supplies in the summer,
And gathers her food in the harvest.

9 How long will you slumber, O sluggard?
When will you rise from your sleep?
10 A little sleep, a little slumber,
A little folding of the hands to sleep—
11 So shall your poverty come on you like a prowler,
And your need like an armed man. (NKJV).

Use every opportunity before you to get a good education, to acquire knowledge.

Proverbs 22:29 tells us that a person who is skilled in his field will stand before kings – to serve them and will not stand before mean men- in other words his service will be so valuable that important people of substance will want his services and pay for it.

Do you see a man diligent and skilful in his business? He will stand before kings; he will not stand before obscure men. (AMP).

Parents therefore need to do their very best to give children the best education they can, to help them get the best skills they can in line with their calling and desire.

The Apostle Paul in 2 Thessalonians 3:10 even goes further to say:

For even when we were with you, we commanded you this: If anyone will not work, neither shall he eat. (NKJV).

This really means we each have a responsibility to diligently look for ways to have a livelihood. We each need to use the resources that we have received from our Senior Partner- Almighty God to make productivity to happen.

Once we have earned the substance we need to learn to give back to God in tithes, offerings and alms.

The tithe is the first ten percent of our increase.

The offering is giving money to God in an act of worship.

The alms is donating money to those in need as a charitable act.

The spiritual basis of tithing and worshipping Almighty God in offerings will be explained in the next two chapters.

Chapter 31

Faithful Stewardship Part 2:

Understanding The Spiritual Basis Of Tithing

Summary:

One of the most critical thing every child of God in Jesus Christ needs to know, understand and practice is tithing, which is bringing a tenth of one's increase to God. It is an act of honouring God with substance for which God promises to bring efficiency to your finances. The tithes are meant to be used to finance the work of the ministry. Many people argue that tithes are of the Law of Moses and should no longer be brought. However, the first tithing act recorded in the scriptures were done by Abraham the father of faith to Melchizedek, a character in the scriptures who was like the Son of God Jesus Christ and who has an un-ending priesthood. This was an act of faith done well before the Law of Moses was given.

The patriarch Jacob also pledged tithes when he experienced God at Bethel, and this was again an act of faith before the Law of Moses was given. Jesus Christ commended faith. Tithing needs to be done prayerfully, with guidance of the Holy Spirit and not of the letter because the letter kills but the Holy Spirit gives life.

Covered in this chapter:

31.1 Tithing is honouring God with our substance.
31.2 Giving tithes finances the work of the ministry.
31.3 The first tithe was given by our father of faith Abraham to Melchizedek- it was an act of faith, not under the law of Moses.
31.4 Jacob the patriarch pledged tithes to God well before the Law of Moses was given- this was an act of faith.
31.5 Jesus Christ commended tithing.
31.6 Tithe prayerfully, of the Spirit not of the letter because the letter kills but the Spirit gives life.
31.7 Where to put the decimal point.

31.1 Tithing is honouring God with our substance.

In **Proverbs 3:9-10,** we are admonished to honour God with our substance and the first fruits of our increase- the first fruits of increase is the tithe.

Honour the LORD with your possessions,
And with the first fruits of all your increase;
So your barns will be filled with plenty,
And your vats will overflow with new wine. (KJV).

Here we are admonished to honour the Lord with our possessions and with the first fruits of our possessions-the first fruits refers to tithes.

Here the word of God goes further to say- so shall your barns be filled with plenty and your vats overflow with new wine. In other words, these is a promise here that as we give tithes and offering Almighty God will bless us back.

Every child of God needs to understand and practise tithing prayerfully and as an act of faith. Tithing is the principle of giving the first ten percent of your increase, salary, wage or profit to God.

I will take some time to explain this and dispel myths which have often confused children of God.

31.2 The purpose of tithes is to support the work of the ministry.

In Malachi 3:6-12 we read:

"For I am the LORD, I do not change;
Therefore you are not consumed, O sons of Jacob.
7 Yet from the days of your fathers
You have gone away from My ordinances
And have not kept them.
Return to Me, and I will return to you,"
Says the LORD of hosts.
"But you said,
'In what way shall we return?'
8 "Will a man rob God?
Yet you have robbed Me!
But you say,
'In what way have we robbed You?'

In tithes and offerings.
9 You are cursed with a curse,
For you have robbed Me,
Even this whole nation.
10 Bring all the tithes into the storehouse,
That there may be food in My house,
And try Me now in this,"
Says the LORD of hosts,
"If I will not open for you the windows of heaven
And pour out for you such blessing
That there will not be room enough to receive it.
11 "And I will rebuke the devourer for your sakes,
So that he will not destroy the fruit of your ground,
Nor shall the vine fail to bear fruit for you in the field,"
Says the LORD of hosts;
12 "And all nations will call you blessed,
For you will be a delightful land,"
Says the LORD of hosts.

Notice here the word begins by saying I am the Lord; I do not change. Our God does not change with time. Hence Hebrews 13:6 tells us that Jesus Christ is the same, yesterday, today and forever.

Then He says you have gone away from My ordinances- return to Me and I will return to you.

He next poses a question- Will a man rob God? You have robbed Me in tithes and offerings. Then He says you are cursed with a curse- but bring all the tithes to the storehouse so that there may be food in My house and try Me and see if I will not open the windows of heaven and pour you out a blessing and there will not be room enough for you to receive it and I will rebuke the devourer for your sake so that he will not destroy the fruit of your ground nor cause your vine to fail to produce fruit for you in the field. Then Hs word goes on to say -And all nations will call you a delightful land. Wow.

Notice here that bringing tithes and offering has a purpose of financing the work of the ministry. Providing resources for the work of God which includes financial support for servants of God and ministers in the house of God. It also comes with a promise – God says He will open the windows of heaven and pour a blessing and there will not be room enough to receive it- this speaks of not just financial blessing but also the joy, peace, protection and deliverance from attacks of the enemy and emotional fortification we receive as we become faithful stewards.

Notice that His word here also says I will rebuke the devourer for your sake-the devourer is a demon of inefficiency, waste and destruction. It is a demon spirit which only God can rebuke after you have given your tithes.

As a growing child of God, I got a revelation of the importance of tithing. I had a repeated amazing experience. I walked from Medical School Residence to our church office in Harare City centre to bring my tithes. As I walked, I would be shown in the spirit, the devourer. I needed to give my tithes before I would start my shopping. As soon as I handed over the envelope with my tithe's money, that demon would just vanish and go away. At one point I tried to command the demon away- it never worked- the demon would look at me.

One day I passed through a departmental shop to buy some clothes before I handed over my tithes- but I realise I was scatterbrain-my head was scattered everywhere-I could not think straight at all- then I went and handed over the envelop of tithes- immediately I could think straight and concisely again. Once or twice, I made the mistake of buying staff before I gave my tithes – often it was clothes I would never wear or that food I would eventually throw away. The devourer is a spirit of in-efficiency in one's finances.

I believe in these episodes God was training me in the importance of tithing.

Also remember this- as a child of God filled with the Holy Spirit who is our guide and teacher- you need to tithe prayerfully.

31.3 The first tithe was given by our father of faith Abraham to Melchizedek- it was an act of faith, not under the law of Moses.

Many children of God argue that since we are under the grace of God in Jesus Christ and not under the Law of Moses, we should no longer give tithes. It is important that we understand the origin of tithes, that it is of faith and not a product of the Law of Moses.

The word teaches us in John 1:17:

For the law was given through Moses, but grace and truth came through Jesus Christ. (KJV).

Now we see from the scriptures that the tithe anteceded the Law of Moses, the first act of tithing recorded in the scriptures occurred well before the Law of Moses was given.

The first act of giving tithes in the scriptures was done by our father of faith Abraham to Melchizedek (King of Righteousness, King of Peace, without father and without mother and made like the Son of God) as described in **Genesis 14:14-20:**

> **Now when Abram heard that his brother was taken captive, he armed his three hundred and eighteen trained servants who were born in his own house, and went in pursuit as far as Dan.**
>
> **15 He divided his forces against them by night, and he and his servants attacked them and pursued them as far as Hobah, which is north of Damascus.**
>
> **16 So he brought back all the goods, and also brought back his brother Lot and his goods, as well as the women and the people.**
>
> **17 And the king of Sodom went out to meet him at the Valley of Shaveh (that is, the King's Valley), after his return from the defeat of Chedorlaomer and the kings who were with him.**
>
> **18 Then Melchizedek king of Salem brought out bread and wine; he was the priest of God Most High.**
>
> **19 And he blessed him and said:**
>
> **"Blessed be Abram of God Most High,**
>
> **Possessor of heaven and earth;**
>
> **20 And blessed be God Most High,**
>
> **Who has delivered your enemies into your hand."**
>
> **And he gave him a tithe of all.(NKJV).**

Here we read the story of Lot, Abram's brother's son who dwelt in Sodom being taken captive and all his goods were also taken. When Abram heard that his brother was taken captive, he armed three hundred and eighteen men and pursued the enemy, brought back all the goods as well as his brother Lot as well as the women and the people.

As Abram came back, he met Melchizedek king of Salem who did three things:

1. Brought out bread and wine – like the last supper which Jesus Christ did before He was crucified.
2. He blessed Abram- "Blessed be Abram of God Most High Possessor of heaven and earth and blessed be God Most High, who has delivered your enemies into your hand."
3. Melchizedek received tithes from Abram- Abram gave him a tithe of all the spoil.

The question here is who was Melchizedek and what qualified him to receive tithes from Abram?

To understand this, we need to look at Psalms 110:4 and Hebrews 7:1-9

Psalms 110:4 The LORD has sworn

And will not relent,

"You are a priest forever

According to the order of Melchizedek."(NKJV).

This was a prophecy referring to our Lord Jesus Christ. So, Jesus Christ is a Priest of the order of Melchizedek.

Hebrews 7:1-9 explains further:

For this Melchizedek, king of Salem, priest of the Most High God, who met Abraham returning from the slaughter of the kings and blessed him,

2 to whom also Abraham gave a tenth part of all, first being translated "king of righteousness," and then also king of Salem, meaning "king of peace,"

3 without father, without mother, without genealogy, having neither beginning of days nor end of life, but made like the Son of God, remains a priest continually.

4 Now consider how great this man was, to whom even the patriarch Abraham gave a tenth of the spoils.

5 And indeed those who are of the sons of Levi, who receive the priesthood, have a commandment to receive tithes from the people according to the law, that is, from their brethren, though they have come from the loins of Abraham;

6 but he whose genealogy is not derived from them received tithes from Abraham and blessed him who had the promises.

7 Now beyond all contradiction the lesser is blessed by the better.

8 Here mortal men receive tithes, but there he receives them, of whom it is witnessed that he lives.

9 Even Levi, who receives tithes, paid tithes through Abraham, so to speak, for he was still in the loins of his father when Melchizedek met him. (NKJV).

Melchizedek is therefore a mysterious figure who appeared to Abram – this is what we know about him:

He had no father, and he had no father, he had no genealogy, no beginning of days or end of life- that basically means he was God, or a manifestation of Jesus Christ.

He was made like the Son of God and remains a priest continually.

His name Melchizedek means My King is Righteousness, his name was also king of Salem meaning king of peace- these are both attributes of Jesus Christ.

Jesus Christ is a priest forever of the order or rank of Melchizedek- that must mean this Melchizedek was a form of God.

He blessed Abram- that means he was greater than Abram- for without contradiction, the greater blesses the lesser.

Levi- who received tithes according to the law of Moses- paid tithes to Melchizedek as he was still in the loins of Abram.

Here men receive tithes but there He receives them of whom it is witnessed that He lives: in other words, tithes are ultimately received by him who lives forever and ever- that is Almighty God.

The conclusion therefore is that the father of faith- Abram gave tithes to Melchizedek as an act of faith as he was not under the law. This was such a critical event in the calendar of Lord God Almighty, that He saw it fit for Melchizedek to appear from heaven to receive tithes and bless Abraham.

31.4 Jacob the patriarch pledged tithes to God well before the Law of Moses was given- this was an act of faith.

The second witness to giving tithes well before the of Moses was given, comes from Jacob in **Genesis 28:11-22:**

We read:

So he came to a certain place and stayed there all night, because the sun had set. And he took one of the stones of that place and put it at his head, and he lay down in that place to sleep.

12 Then he dreamed, and behold, a ladder was set up on the earth, and its top reached to heaven; and there the angels of God were ascending and descending on it.

13 And behold, the LORD stood above it and said: "I am the LORD God of Abraham your father and the God of Isaac; the land on which you lie I will give to you and your descendants.

14 Also your descendants shall be as the dust of the earth; you shall spread abroad to the west and the east, to the north and the south; and in you and in your seed all the families of the earth shall be blessed.

15 Behold, I am with you and will keep you wherever you go and will bring you back to this land; for I will not leave you until I have done what I have spoken to you."

16 Then Jacob awoke from his sleep and said, "Surely the LORD is in this place, and I did not know it."

17 And he was afraid and said, "How awesome is this place! This is none other than the house of God, and this is the gate of heaven!"

18 Then Jacob rose early in the morning, and took the stone that he had put at his head, set it up as a pillar, and poured oil on top of it.

19 And he called the name of that place Bethel; but the name of that city had been Luz previously.

20 Then Jacob made a vow, saying, "If God will be with me, and keep me in this way that I am going, and give me bread to eat and clothing to put on,

21 so that I come back to my father's house in peace, then the LORD shall be my God.

22 And this stone which I have set as a pillar shall be God's house, and of all that You give me I will surely give a tenth to You." (NKJV).

Here we see again Jacob the patriarch, pledging to God- if you will be with me God, and keep and protect me in this way I am going, and give me food to eat and clothes to wear, so that I come again to my father's house in peace- in other words- if you will be God to me I will accomplish your purpose for my life on the earth and of everything you give to me I will give a tenth back to you. This was a statement of faith not of the law. A statement borne out of revelation that if Lord God Almighty is my everything, my all in all, my defining attribute and senior partner in wealth creation then surely, I should give Him a tenth of all I get for the purpose of establishing Your hand on the earth.

31.5 Jesus Christ commended tithing.

What did Jesus Christ say about tithing?
In Matthew 23:23 we read:

"Woe to you, scribes and Pharisees, hypocrites! For you pay tithe of mint and anise and cummin, and have neglected the weightier matters of the law: justice and mercy and faith. These you ought to have done, without leaving the others undone."

Here the Lord Jesus Christ castigated and reprimanded the Pharisees for they were gave tithes even of herbs they grew in their back garden but neglected other weightier matters of the law such as justice, showing mercy and living by faith. Notice here the Lord Jesus said these you ought to have done without leaving the other undone. Jesus Christ therefore commended tithing.

31.6 Tithe prayerfully, of the Spirit not of the letter because the letter kills but the Spirit gives life.

2 Corinthians 3:4-6 tells us

And we have such trust through Christ toward God.

5 Not that we are sufficient of ourselves to think of anything as being from ourselves, but our sufficiency is from God,

6 who also made us sufficient as ministers of the new covenant, not of the letter but of the Spirit; for the letter kills, but the Spirit gives life (NKJV).

Tithe of the spirit not of the letter- for the letter kills but the spirit gives life.

You have a business, tithe your increase or profit. You earn a wage or salary – tithes your wage or salary but allow the Holy Spirit to guide you.

Your tithes and offering needs to be the first fruit- tithe first and decide on your offering target prayerfully and then lay out the rest of your budget for the week or for the month.

The wrong way to do it is to say I will lay out my whole budget, and whatever is left is what I will give to God. This way tithing and giving will not happen because you will have opened a way for the devourer into your finances.

Tithing and giving an offering is a spiritual fight which needs to done with spiritual alertness and prayerfully.

Sometimes the Holy Spirit Himself will instruct you that the money you are holding is not for tithing.

This happened to me once- I was not on regular employment at the time and got some temporary work over a weekend, I had some very important bills that needed paying. As I got the job the Holy Spirit spoke to me clearly, that the money you will be earning on this job on this occasion is not tithable- get your bills paid. That is what I did.

My point here is that let the Spirit lead you. The Holy Spirit is the Spirit of Jesus Christ. He will be present with you on the day of judgement. Obey Him and follow His guidance.

When God gave me instruction to start Planet Ministries, before we opened a bank account for the ministry, one of the first instructions I received was "Take my money which is in your account and go buy Me a keyboard". That was how I bought the very first Keyboard we used for our worship service. God was talking about the tithe of my salary which was in my account. So, the Holy Spirit is your partner- obey HIM.

31.7 Where to put the decimal point.

The tithe is ten percent of your increase. If you run a business, ten percent of your profit is your tithe. If you earn a wage or salary however, the exact calculation is not always straight forward. Do you tithe your gross salary or after income-tax deductions? Whichever way you do it, be at peace within yourself and do it prayerfully. Jesus Christ said in **John 10:27: "My sheep hear My voice, and I know them, and they follow Me."(NKJV)**.

I come back again to the point raised in the previous section- the letter kills but the Spirit gives life. Tithe prayerfully, let the Holy Spirit help you and use the ten percent decimal point as a guide. Since Almighty God asked me to oversee Planet Ministries, I have largely used my own tithes (and offerings) to run the work of the Ministry for ten years. During this time, I have learnt to obey the Holy Spirit with my tithe and offerings. I have also learnt that God expects my tithe. We have bought equipment, hired premises paid for transport costs, paid for on-line streaming services among many other things using largely my tithes and offerings. Whenever I slipped and forgot to separate the tithe for God, He reminded me of the omission. I am therefore speaking here as a person who has brought tithe more than who has received tithes.

Chapter 32

Faithful Stewardship Part 3:

Understanding Worshipping God With The Offering Of Substance.

Summary:

It is critical for every child of God to understand the power of the offering of substance. The Lord Jesus Christ is our example in offering in that He offered Himself as a sacrifice for our sins. In the same way when we give an offering of substance, we are giving of ourselves, of our worth and value to God. Your offering appears before the throne of God as a sweet-smelling aroma and your offering has a witness voice at the judgement seat of God. Always aim to give an excellent offering, an offering from your heart. Also understand that giving to God is like sowing a seed from which you should expect a harvest. Almighty God has promised a hundred-fold return to your investment into the gospel, and it is a godly thing to give expecting to receive back from Almighty God multiplied. The earth is founded on a principle of seedtime being followed by harvest time. You need therefore to be spiritually sensitive to times of sowing and times of reaping as it applies to giving. One therefore needs to apply diligence in giving so that you purpose your giving prayerfully knowing that your giving is a strong determining factor to your future financial capacity in the service of Almighty God. He who sows sparingly will also reap sparingly but he who sows bountifully, will reap bountifully.

You need to give diligently and in proportion to what you have. Always begin by giving yourself to God and to His servants by the will of God. As you give you are laying your treasures in heaven and where your treasure is, there your heart will be also, giving therefore locks your heart to the Kingdom of Heaven.

Covered in this chapter:

32.1 Jesus Christ offered Himself as an offering for sin.

32.2 When you give an offering of substance, you are giving of yourself, your worth and value to God.

32.3 Your offering appears before God as a sweet-smelling aroma.

32.4: Always aim to give an excellent offering, from the heart, learn from Abel, King Solomon and Cornelius.

32:5 Giving is sowing a seed and Almighty God has made a hundred-fold return promise to your giving to the gospel.

32.6 As the earth remains, seed time and harvest time shall not cease.

32:7 Apply diligence to your giving.

32.8 Purpose and give prayerfully knowing that he who sows bountifully will reap bountifully, he who sows sparingly will reap sparingly.

32.9 Your giving needs to be in proportion to what you have- the widow who gave two mites, gave more than all.

32.10 Give yourself first to God then to His servants.

32.11 Lay your treasures in heaven, where your treasure is, that is where your heart will be also.

32.1 Jesus Christ offered Himself as an offering for sin.

It is very critical that every child of God understands the importance of giving an offering of substance to God.

Remember that Jesus Christ offered Himself as a sacrifice for sin, as an offering for sin.

Hebrews 10:12-14 tells us:

But this Man, after He had offered one sacrifice for sins forever, sat down at the right hand of God,

13 from that time waiting till His enemies are made His footstool.

14 For by one offering He has perfected forever those who are being sanctified. (NKJV).

Jesus Christ offered Himself for the remission of our sins, to perfect us forever.

32.2 When you give an offering of substance, you are giving of yourself, your worth and value to God.

I want you to understand that when you give an offering, you are giving of yourself to God in worship, you are giving of your substance, of your sweat, and of your worth and value to God.

32.3 Your offering appears before God as a sweet-smelling aroma.

This offering appears before God as a sweet-smelling aroma.
    In Philippians 4:18-19 we read:

Indeed I have all and abound. I am full, having received from Epaphroditus the things sent from you, a sweet-smelling aroma, an acceptable sacrifice, well pleasing to God.

19 And my God shall supply all your need according to His riches in glory by Christ Jesus.(NKJV).

When you give from a sincere heart your offering ascends to the throne of God as a sweet-smelling aroma, well pleasing to God. Your offering also has a voice by the throne of God which is the judgement seat in the courtroom of heaven from where the Lord God Almighty releases judgements against the enemy satan, the accuser of the brethren, in favour of the saints for the different situations they face.

32.4: Always aim to give an excellent offering, from the heart, learn from Abel, King Solomon and Cornelius.

Let us explore offerings from the word of God.
    The first recorded offering was given to God by Abel recorded in Genesis 4:3-7

And in the process of time it came to pass that Cain brought an offering of the fruit of the ground to the LORD.

4 Abel also brought of the firstborn of his flock and of their fat. And the LORD respected Abel and his offering,

5 but He did not respect Cain and his offering. And Cain was very angry, and his countenance fell.

6 So the LORD said to Cain, "Why are you angry? And why has your

countenance fallen? If you do well, will you not be accepted?
7 And if you do not do well, sin lies at the door. And its desire is for
you, but you should rule over it."(NKJV).

We learn here that God respected, looked with favour the sacrifice which
Abel had offered but not one which Cain had offered. God even explained to
Cain- this is not because somehow, I favour Abel but if you do well, your own
offering will be accepted also.

How did Abel do it- He took the first born and the fat portions- that was his
attitude of faith. I will give to God the first born and take the fat portions, the
good portions. The attitude was of respect and honouring God by giving a more
excellent sacrifice.

In Hebrews 11:4, the scriptures explain further:

By faith Abel offered to God a more excellent sacrifice than Cain,
through which he obtained witness that he was righteous, God
testifying of his gifts; and through it he being dead still speaks.
(NKJV).

Here we learn- it was a more excellent sacrifice that that which Cain gave, it
was given by faith and through which Abel was declared righteous by God and
his offering continues to speak to this day. That is the power of an offering given
from the heart, with the correct attitude of respecting and honouring God.

If we move further to 2 Chronicles 1:6-7

And Solomon went up there to the bronze altar before the LORD,
which was at the tabernacle of meeting, and offered a thousand burnt
offerings on it.

7 On that night God appeared to Solomon, and said to him, "Ask!
What shall I give you?"(NKJV).

King Solomon went to the alter and offered a thousand burnt offerings on
it- that night God appeared and asked him a question that was to change his life
forever- Ask what shall I give you?

We know that following this Solomon asked for wisdom and knowledge
which God granted but also gave him wealth and honour, glory, a long life and
victory over his enemies.

In Acts 10:1-6 we read:

There was a certain man in Caesarea called Cornelius, a centurion
of what was called the Italian Regiment, a devout man and one who
feared God with all his household, who gave alms generously to the

people, and prayed to God always. About the ninth hour of the day he saw clearly in a vision an angel of God coming in and saying to him, "Cornelius!"

And when he observed him, he was afraid, and said, "What is it, lord?"

So he said to him, "Your prayers and your alms have come up for a memorial before God. Now send men to Joppa, and send for Simon whose surname is Peter. He is lodging with Simon, a tanner, whose house is by the sea. He will tell you what you must do."(NKJV).

Cornelius was a devout man, who feared God and gave generously to the poor and prayed to God always. Here an angel of the Lord was sent to him and declared: your alms and prayers have come for a memorial before God, or have been remembered by God, now send to Joppa.

What happened next was that Cornelius was the first gentile to whom God sent an apostle to preach the gospel and he and his household were the first gentile to receive the Holy Spirit. This was all possible because his prayers and alms came for a memorial before God.

32:5 Giving is sowing a seed and Almighty God has made a hundred-fold return promise to your giving to the gospel.

As we move further in the Gospels in Mark 10:28-30 we read

Then Peter began to say to Him, "See, we have left all and followed You."

29 So Jesus answered and said, "Assuredly, I say to you, there is no one who has left house or brothers or sisters or father or mother or wife or children or lands, for My sake and the gospel's,

30 who shall not receive a hundredfold now in this time—houses and brothers and sisters and mothers and children and lands, with persecutions—and in the age to come, eternal life. (NKJV).

Here Peter the apostle went to Jesus and said look, we have left all and followed you- Jesus answered- no-one has left or given for My sake and the sake of the gospel, who will not receive a hundred-fold now in this time and in the age to come eternal life.

Giving to the gospel is backed by a hundred-fold return promise from God.

Let's look at another aspect of giving offering – the aspect of sowing and reaping.

32.6 As the earth remains, seed time and harvest time shall not cease.

In Genesis 8:20-22 we read:

Then Noah built an altar to the LORD, and took of every clean animal and of every clean bird, and offered burnt offerings on the altar.

21 And the LORD smelled a soothing aroma. Then the LORD said in His heart, "I will never again curse the ground for man's sake, although the imagination of man's heart is evil from his youth; nor will I again destroy every living thing as I have done.

22 "While the earth remains,

Seedtime and harvest,

Cold and heat,

Winter and summer,

And day and night

Shall not cease."(NKJV).

Noah built an alter and offered a massive offering- every clean animal and every clean bird- this offering ascended before God as a soothing aroma, a sweet-smelling odour, a scent of satisfaction to His heart (AMP)- God made a vow- never again to destroy every living thing as He had done. The next verse then says; while the earth remains, seedtime shall be followed with harvest time.

Please understand that a seed is anything you have with which you can add value to someone else.

Invention is a seed from which you can reap rewards.

Labour is seed- you work for someone and after an agreed period to receive a wage or salary.

Education is a seed- after an agreed period and satisfying the conditions of the school, college or university, you receive a certificate after gaining skills with which you will be of value to someone or some employer.

You can sow seeds of love, encouragement, a smile, goodness etc.

The beginning point of all success therefore is asking: What do I have? Or how can I get a seed?

The sowing of money seed for the gospel however remains a critical way of serving God from which God promises a harvest in monetary terms and more- in things which money cannot buy- like joy, peace, self-satisfaction, self -fulfilment and a feeling of personal worth and fulfilment.

Quite a few years ago – God spoke to me a statement I will never forget-

"For you to accomplish the purpose for which I have called you, you will need to operate at a certain level of finance and for you to reach that level you need to start sowing money seed now". I was a medical student on a Ministry of Health cadetship scholarship which means I was paid a monthly salary as opposed to my colleagues who were paid every semester. So I understood this statement to some degree and started giving in the offering in cash and sometimes cheques. I gave very prayerfully allowing the Holy Spirit to lead me. I felt it was time to sow seed.

32:7 Apply diligence to your giving.

Ecclesiastes 11:1-6 tells us:

1 Cast your bread upon the waters,

For you will find it after many days.

2 Give a serving to seven, and also to eight,

For you do not know what evil will be on the earth.

3 If the clouds are full of rain,

They empty themselves upon the earth;

And if a tree falls to the south or the north,

In the place where the tree falls, there it shall lie.

4 He who observes the wind will not sow,

And he who regards the clouds will not reap.

5 As you do not know what is the way of the wind,

Or how the bones grow in the womb of her who is with child,

So you do not know the works of God who makes everything.

6 In the morning sow your seed,

And in the evening do not withhold your hand;

For you do not know which will prosper,

Either this or that,

Or whether both alike will be good. (NKJV).

Here we are admonished to cast your bread upon the waters of the word of God- give believing God, and you will find it after many days- allow time for your seed to germinate, grow and give a harvest.

Verse 4 then says -He who observes the wind will not sow and he who regards the clouds shall not reap. This talks about waiting for an ideal time to sow- there is none.

Verse 5 there says in the morning sow your seed and in the evening do not withhold your hand.

When I started giving and sowing a financial seed – there are many things I could have used the money for- I had no bicycle, I had no bed of my own as I was living in a furnished university accommodation. I felt it was time to sow seed.

Psalms 126:1-6 tells us:

1 When the LORD brought back the captivity of Zion,

We were like those who dream.

2 Then our mouth was filled with laughter,

And our tongue with singing.

Then they said among the nations,

3 "The LORD has done great things for them."

The LORD has done great things for us,

And we are glad.

4 Bring back our captivity, O LORD,

As the streams in the South.

5 Those who sow in tears

Shall reap in joy.

6 He who continually goes forth weeping,

Bearing seed for sowing,

Shall doubtless come again with rejoicing,

Bringing his sheaves with him. (NKJV).

This psalm starts by saying- when the Lord brought back the captivity of Zion- or when the people were released from captivity – we were like those who dream- our mouth were filled with laughter and our tongues with singing and celebrating.

Then it goes on to say that those who sow in tears will reap in joy, and he who continually goes forth weeping carrying precious seed to sow, with doubtlessly return rejoicing carrying their harvest.

One way in which the Lord will turn away your captivity to poverty and lack is by learning to sow in tears- this speaks of giving a purposeful offering which often is sacrificial. The opposite of this is discretionary giving- when one gives change and left-over money-that you will not feel and will not hurt. God loves givers who give meaningfully and often this giving is associated with a degree of weeping or pain- His word then says they will doubtlessly come back rejoicing carrying their harvest. Giving therefore needs to be done prayerfully and purposefully.

Please understand again that sowing is not limited to giving an offering as stated before, because doing anything that adds value to yourself or others is sowing a seed. Examples are preaching the gospel, teaching others add value to others, receiving an education- that adds value to yourself, working for a wage or salary- that adds value to the organisation you work for, acts of kindness, acts of goodness etc.

It is important to always ask the question- what do I have to give, what seed can I sow?

32.8 Purpose and give prayerfully knowing that he who sows bountifully will reap bountifully, he who sows sparingly will reap sparingly.

Then remember to sow bountifully, to give with a good measure.

Let's examine the scriptures:

2 Corinthians 9:5-8
5 Therefore I thought it necessary to exhort the brethren to go to you ahead of time, and prepare your generous gift beforehand, which you had previously promised, that it may be ready as a matter of generosity and not as a grudging obligation.
6 But this I say: He who sows sparingly will also reap sparingly, and he who sows bountifully will also reap bountifully.
7 So let each one give as he purposes in his heart, not grudgingly or of necessity; for God loves a cheerful giver.
8 And God is able to make all grace abound toward you, that you, always having all sufficiency in all things, may have an abundance for every good work. (NKJV).

This portion of scripture is referring specifically to giving an offering.

The apostle was addressing believers in Macedonia who had pledged an offering, or a financial gift.

He urged the brethren to prepare their generous gift beforehand and make it ready before the apostle arrived.

Purpose in your heart- and this purposing needs to be done prayerfully- so that you receive wisdom from the Holy Spirit.

It says here do not give grudgingly- do not feel pushed or compelled to give.

Do not give of necessity- that is under pressure to meet a need.

Rather give purposefully, prayerfully and cheerfully, for God loves a cheerful giver.

Note again: He who sows sparingly will reap sparingly, he who gives bountifully will also reap bountifully.

32.9 Your giving needs to be in proportion to what you have- the widow who gave two mites, gave more than all.

Please note the amount here has to be proportionate to what you have, to make it an honourable offering.

Remember the widow who gave two mites as described in Luke 21:1-4:

1 And He (Jesus) looked up and saw the rich putting their gifts into the treasury,

2 and He saw also a certain poor widow putting in two mites.

3 So He said, "Truly I say to you that this poor widow has put in more than all;

4 for all these out of their abundance have put in offerings for God, but she out of her poverty put in all the livelihood that she had." (NKJV).

Jesus Christ here remarked that this widow had given more than all in proportion with what she had. She had given sacrificially, from her heart. It is therefore important to give prayerfully and meaningfully.

32.10 Give yourself first to God then to His servants by the will of God.

The apostle Paul commended the churches in Macedonia for the grace they showed in their giving. They gave more than would have been expected.

In **2 Corinthians 8:1-9 we read:**

Moreover, brethren, we make known to you the grace of God bestowed on the churches of Macedonia:

2 that in a great trial of affliction the abundance of their joy and their deep poverty abounded in the riches of their liberality.

3 For I bear witness that according to their ability, yes, and beyond their ability, they were freely willing,

4 imploring us with much urgency that we would receive the gift and the fellowship of the ministering to the saints.

5 And not only as we had hoped, but they first gave themselves to the Lord, and then to us by the will of God.

6 So we urged Titus, that as he had begun, so he would also complete this grace in you as well.

7 But as you abound in everything—in faith, in speech, in knowledge, in all diligence, and in your love for us—see that you abound in this grace also.

8 I speak not by commandment, but I am testing the sincerity of your love by the diligence of others.

9 For you know the grace of our Lord Jesus Christ, that though He was rich, yet for your sakes He became poor, that you through His poverty might become rich.

So here the people in the churches at Macedonia managed to give more than expected. We learn a few lessons from them.

First there was a grace of God upon them to give- an ability granted to them by the working of the Spirit of God in their lives, this grace enabled them to give themselves first to God and then to the servants of God by the will of God. To give, you need to give yourself to God and then to the servants of God who minister to you. This grace is needed to give you a revelation of an opportunity to sow a seed into the work of the gospel. Personal needs will always be there, but you need to prayerfully decide how much to give.

Secondly there was a deep yearning to serve, a deep desire to give, which the apostle here refers to as deep poverty.

Thirdly the apostle here reminds us of the grace of our Lord Jesus Christ whom though He was rich, owned the universe as the Son of God yet for our sake He became poor so that through His poverty we may be made rich.

32.11 Lay your treasures in heaven, where your treasure is that is where your heart will be also.

In Matthew 6:19-21 Jesus Christ said:

19 Do not lay up for yourselves treasures on earth, where moth and rust destroy and where thieves break in and steal;

20 but lay up for yourselves treasures in heaven, where neither moth nor rust destroys and where thieves do not break in and steal.

21 For where your treasure is, there your heart will be also.

When you give for the gospel, you are investing into the Kingdom of God. Not only are you promised a hundred-fold return, but also your investment is safe. Not only that, but it is an insurance policy to keep your heart on God, for where your treasure is, there your heart will be also. Giving therefore locks you into God.

In 1 Timothy 6:17-19 we read:

Command those who are rich in this present age not to be haughty, nor to trust in uncertain riches but in the living God, who gives us richly all things to enjoy.

18 Let them do good, that they be rich in good works, ready to give, willing to share,

19 storing up for themselves a good foundation for the time to come, that they may lay hold on eternal life.

Here again we are instructed to command the rich not to trust in uncertain riches, but to trust in the living God, to be ready to give and willing to share thereby storing up for themselves a good foundation for the time to come and that they may lay hold of eternal life.

Chapter 33

Faithful Stewardship Part 4:

Making Prosperity To Happen-

Summary:

33.1 Almighty God desires you to prosper and be in health as your soul prospers.

33.2 God can prosper you anywhere.

33:3 Understanding the principle of seed time and harvest time.

33.4 Use sound financial principles.

33.5 The wealth of the wicked shall be laid up for the just.

33.6 Give it a fight- You need a strong conviction about the following:

33.1 Almighty God desires you to prosper and be in health as your soul prospers.

His word in **3 John 2** says:

Beloved, I wish above all things that you may prosper and be in health even as your soul prospers. (KJV)

Dear friend, I hope all is well with you and that you are as healthy in body as you are strong in spirit. (NLT).

Beloved I pray that you may prosper in every way and [that your body] may keep well, even as [I know] your soul keeps well and prospers. (AMP).

Please note here- as your soul prospers. The soul is basically our mind (intellect, will, emotions and conscience). Prosperity of the soul means your mind is being renewed with the word of God and you are growing in the knowledge of Jesus Christ and you are being transformed to think like God. That means you are taking Godly principles to keep money, substance, mammon under your feet. It means you are using Godly principles of tithing and giving to serve God with your substance. Understand that tithing and giving offering breaks the power of money so that it is no longer an object of worship but something we use to serve God.

In Matthew 6: 24 and Luke 16:13 we read: **No one can serve two masters; for either he will hate the one and love the other, or else he will be loyal to the one and despise the other. You cannot serve God and mammon. (NKJV).**

Here Jesus said you cannot serve God and mammon.

We need however to use mammon to serve God.

Another scripture often misquoted is in 1 Timothy 6:10 which says:

For the love of money is a root of all kinds of evil, for which some have strayed from the faith in their greediness and pierced themselves through with many sorrows.

Notice it says **the love** of money is the root of all evil, not money itself.

Ecclesiastes 10:19 tells us: A feast is made for laughter, And wine makes merry; But money answers everything.

We need money to live, and we need also to learn to serve God with money.

Jesus Christ said in **Mark 8:36: For what shall it profit a man if he gains the whole world and loses his own soul. (NKJV). See also Matthew 16:26.**

Your spiritual prosperity should always stay ahead of your material or financial prosperity so that you use your financial prosperity to serve Almighty God through giving tithes, offerings and alms to the less fortunate.

The critical point here is that tithing a million pounds and giving a good offering breaks the power of a million pounds. Hence 1 Timothy 6:17-19 tells us

Command those who are rich in this present age not to be haughty, nor to trust in uncertain riches but in the living God, who gives us richly all things to enjoy.

18 Let them do good, that they be rich in good works, ready to give, willing to share,

19 storing up for themselves a good foundation for the time to come, that they may lay hold on eternal life.

God gives us all things richly to enjoy, therefore serve God with your wealth by giving a tithe, offerings and sharing generously.

33.2 God can prosper you anywhere.

Please understand that Godly prosperity is not situational. There are resources for God to prosper you in every nation on Earth. The point here is that, as a child of God, you seek the will of God rather than moving from nation to nation seeking opportunities to prosper.

In Genesis 26:1-6, 12-14 we read about Isaac who wanted to flee a famine and go to Egypt and God stopped him and gave him a word of promise. That same year he sowed in that land and in spite of the famine, he reaped a hundred-fold.

1 There was a famine in the land, besides the first famine that was in the days of Abraham. And Isaac went to Abimelech king of the Philistines, in Gerar.

2 Then the LORD appeared to him and said: "Do not go down to Egypt; live in the land of which I shall tell you.

3 Dwell in this land, and I will be with you and bless you; for to you and your descendants I give all these lands, and I will perform the oath which I swore to Abraham your father.

4 And I will make your descendants multiply as the stars of heaven; I will give to your descendants all these lands; and in your seed all the nations of the earth shall be blessed;

5 because Abraham obeyed My voice and kept My charge, My commandments, My statutes, and My laws."

6 So Isaac dwelt in Gerar. ....

12 Then Isaac sowed in that land and reaped in the same year a hundredfold; and the LORD blessed him.

13 The man began to prosper, and continued prospering until he became very prosperous;

14 for he had possessions of flocks and possessions of herds and a great number of servants. So the Philistines envied him. (NKJV).

Isaac here obeyed a promise of God and reaped a hundred-fold, he became very prosperous. We read here that the Lord blessed him. God can bless and prosper you anywhere He has placed you. The temptation with Isaac was to run to Egypt and God said no. Why did Isaac want to go to Egypt? The reason is that there was no reported famine in Egypt at the time. So, in the natural going to Egypt made sense but it was not in the purpose of God for Isaac at that time. Isaac then obeyed God and sowed in Gerar and he reaped that year a hundred fold. The point here is that we need to seek the will and purpose of God. His will and purpose for you has a geographical location and definition.

Many years ago now, on a Sunday afternoon, while in the nation of Zimbabwe in Southern Africa, God spoke to my spirit very clearly. "I have opened a door for you to go to England". In my naivety I thought God was speaking about going on holiday. I was sitting outside on a patio bench at the house I lived in on the hospital in Mutare. I called my sister and told her – we will be going to

England. When I eventually came to England five years later- I thought it was for a short time. Eventually God revealed that I was to launch the work of Planet Ministries in England.

33:3 Understanding the principle of seed time and harvest time.

Understanding the principle of seed time and harvest time is critical.

God will prosper you through the principle of sowing and reaping. You therefore need a seed to begin with, something you can give.

If you are a student studying at whatever level, you are sowing skills, education into yourself, following that you may reap a certificate as evidence of the skills you obtained. You use the certificate to look for a job. When you get a job, you are sowing your skill and your time and at the end of an agreed period, be it weekly or monthly you reap a reward in the form of wages or salary.

Because Almighty God is your partner in wealth creation you need to honour Him with the first fruits in the form of tithes and then prayerfully sow seeds into the offering. You then need to be conscious of the time to sow financial seed into the work of the ministry as you believe God for reaping further rewards as God blesses you and prospers you.

Sometimes you may be in a situation where there is no formal employment. You need to ask yourself- what do I have? What is my seed?

For example, you feel a calling of God as a Pastor, your seed is time and the word of God. You want opportunities to share that word and raise a church. Share the gospel with as diverse people as possible, including colleges and schools, teachers and students. This is best done under mentorship of an established servant of God. As the church grows you will have the opportunity to reap support from the church.

The word of God teaches us in **Galatians 6:6**

"Let him who is taught the word share in all good things with him who teaches". (NKJV).

If say you have a plot and you have time to farm- grow crops and sell your produce. If doing horticulture, find ways to diversify for example by growing short season crops and poultry farming. You will need diligence in making a start as you may need capital.

In many places- where formal employment opportunities are low; you can begin as a market trader and build yourself up from there.

2 Corinthians 9:10-11 tells us:

10 Now may He who supplies seed to the sower, and bread for food, supply and multiply the seed you have sown and increase the fruits of your righteousness,

11 while you are enriched in everything for all liberality, which causes thanksgiving through us to God.

God supplies seed to the sower. That means He is the One who gives you a beginning point, use it with diligence and wisdom.

In **Deuteronomy 8:18** we read: **And you shall remember the LORD your God, for it is He who gives you power to get wealth, that He may establish His covenant which He swore to your fathers, as it is this day.**

You can look at this chapter 8 from verse 1 – it is describing the desire of God for you- that He wants all to be well with you. In verse 18 there the word teaches us to remember the Lord our God for it is Him who gives us power to get wealth. So that He may establish His covenant with you- when you have no food, His covenant is not established. When you have no clothing or accommodation, His covenant with you is not established.

You need therefore to ask the question- what seed do I have? Take that seed as a starting point- Almighty God gives everybody seed to sow, and bread to eat. He gives you power to get wealth, so that He may establish His covenant with you. The covenant says He wants to be your God, your everything, your giver of righteousness, your provider, your healer, your giver of victory, your peace, your ever present One, your shepherd to guide, shield and feed you.

33.4 Use sound financial principles.

It is important that you learn sound financial principles, and this sometime means dealing with wisdom and shrewdness.

We read in **Luke 16:8**

So the master commended the unjust steward because he had dealt shrewdly. For the sons of this world are more shrewd in their generation than the sons of light.

The King James Version uses the word 'wiser' in place of 'more shrewd'. The meaning reflected here is more cunning.

The Oxford English dictionary defines shrewd as "having or showing sharp powers of judgement; astute." Other synonyms of shrewd include sharp-witted, alert, intelligent and clever.

It is therefore important that while heavenly wisdom takes precedence as you make financial decisions prayerfully, you need to be armed with knowledge of all financial options available to you. You need financial intelligence. For example, one need to understand the difference in the mindset of those who make it big in finance and the mindset of the ordinary person. For example, the rich have a mindset that understand delayed gratification as well as taking intelligent risks. (1, 2). One also need to understand the power of vision, the power of dreaming big (3).

It is also important to understand the cash flow quadrants. That while one may begin as employed or self employed you can also move or concurrently plan to be a business owner or an investor. (4).

The use of and power in investing in Real Estate to grow one's portfolio is another key opportunity which one needs to look at and consider. There are several books and guides to do this on the internet and elsewhere.

33.5 The wealth of the wicked shall be laid up for the just.

Proverbs 13:22 tells us:

A good man leaves an inheritance to his children's children, but the wealth of the sinner is stored up for the righteous.

Statistics show that one percent of the world's wealthiest possess more than the rest of the population of Planet Earth combined and that more than 1 billion people live on less than US$ 1.25 per day across Planet Earth. In these last days we are living in, there is a spiritual shaking of wealth from the unrighteous to the righteous. The reason is that God has given the Earth to mankind and the only way He can cause a more just distribution of wealth is by moving the hearts of His children with wealth to share with those without and also for the financing of the gospel for the end time harvest of souls.

Matthew 24:14 tells us:

And this gospel of the kingdom will be preached in all the world as a witness to all the nations, and then the end will come.

The second coming of Jesus Christ cannot happen until the gospel is preached to all nations and every single individual is given an opportunity to say "yes" or "no" to Jesus Christ. The reason is that on that day ignorance of the gospel will no longer be an excuse as Jesus Christ will take up to heaven those who believe and those who do not will enter the period of the great tribulation.

1 Corinthians 4:2 tells us:

Moreover, it is required in stewards that one be found faithful.
His word also tells us in Luke 16:10-12
He who is faithful in what is least is faithful also in much; and he who
is unjust in what is least is unjust also in much.
11 Therefore if you have not been faithful in the unrighteous mammon,
who will commit to your trust the true riches?
12 And if you have not been faithful in what is another man's, who will
give you what is your own?

We saw earlier in **Deuteronomy 8:18:**

And you shall remember the LORD your God, for it is He who gives
you power to get wealth, that He may establish His covenant which He
swore to your fathers, as it is this day.

We saw also in **Matthew 25:21 and 23:**

His lord said to him, 'Well done, good and faithful servant; you were
faithful over a few things, I will make you ruler over many things.
Enter into the joy of your lord.'

When you are faithful over a few, God will make you ruler over more. If you are faithful in what is least, you will also be faithful over much. If you are faithful with another Man's goods- in this case God, He will give you what will be your own.

The power to get wealth is from God, He is our Senior Partner in wealth creation, and we need to be faithful in bringing our tithes and offerings to Him so that we establish the covenant as in our day.

Tithes and offerings break the power of mammon so that it is no longer an object of worship but something we can use to serve God. We need more children of God to learn to put mammon under their feet, use it to serve God and to fight for more wealth because there is right now a shaking of wealth from the unrighteous to the righteous.

His word says in **Haggai 2:1-9**

In the seventh month, on the twenty-first of the month, the word of
the LORD came by Haggai the prophet, saying:
2 "Speak now to Zerubbabel the son of Shealtiel, governor of Judah,
and to Joshua the son of Jehozadak, the high priest, and to the remnant
of the people, saying:

3 Who is left among you who saw this temple in its former glory? And how do you see it now? In comparison with it, is this not in your eyes as nothing?

4 Yet now be strong, Zerubbabel,' says the LORD; 'and be strong, Joshua, son of Jehozadak, the high priest; and be strong, all you people of the land,' says the LORD, 'and work; for I am with you,' says the LORD of hosts.

5 'According to the word that I covenanted with you when you came out of Egypt, so My Spirit remains among you; do not fear!'

6 "For thus says the LORD of hosts: Once more (it is a little while) I will shake heaven and earth, the sea and dry land;

7 and I will shake all nations, and they shall come to the Desire of All Nations, and I will fill this temple with glory,' says the LORD of hosts.

8 'The silver is Mine, and the gold is Mine,' says the LORD of hosts.

9 The glory of this latter temple shall be greater than the former,' says the LORD of hosts. 'And in this place I will give peace,' says the LORD of hosts."

We notice here God is making a comparison between the glory of the former house and the glory of the latter house of God, the glory of the church as we prepare for the return of Jesus Christ will be greater than the glory of the former house of God.

He says here that He will shake the heavens, the earth, the sea and the dry land and also shake all nations. The result of the shaking will be twofold: 1. People will come to the Desire of All Nations- which is Jesus Christ the Messiah and 2. He will fill His house with glory and part of that glory will be a flow of gold and silver to the house of God and for the alleviation of poverty across the nations of Planet Earth.

Then He says -the gold is mine and the silver is mine and the glory of the latter house will greater than the glory of the former house. There is an exhortation to the people of God to be of strong conviction and to work. God says because I am with you and My Spirit remains among you. Do not fear.

Please understand that the glory and splendour of the house of God is referring to here requires gold and silver and among other things, requires the church to build beautiful, well-designed places of worship across the nations of Planet Earth.

For this to happen we need a people of God to rise with conviction to work with God as He causes a shaking of wealth from the wicked into the hands of children of God. Wealth in the hands of the wicked is of no value to the kingdom of God. God needs gold and silver in the hands of people who can hear God and share with the poor and also share with Him to build His house across the nations of Planet Earth.

He says in **Hebrews 12:26-28**

Whose voice then shook the earth; but now He has promised, saying, "Yet once more I shake not only the earth, but also heaven."

27 Now this, "Yet once more," indicates the removal of those things that are being shaken, as of things that are made, that the things which cannot be shaken may remain.

28 Therefore, since we are receiving a kingdom which cannot be shaken, let us have grace, by which we may serve God acceptably with reverence and godly fear.

For the child of God reading this to benefit, you need to understand faithful stewardship of substance:

1. That means understanding bringing tithes and offering.

2. Understanding that when you are faithful over little, he will make you ruler over much.

33.6 Give it a fight- You need a strong conviction about the following:

33.6.1 **God wants you to prosper, He desires you to prosper above everything else.**

33.6.2 **He wants you to experience the promised land- both spiritually (His love, peace and joy) and physically (His provision, health and victory).**

33.6.3 **Almighty God desires every positive outcome for you in Jesus Christ**

33.6.4 **Remember- Jesus Christ redeemed us from the curse of the law and opened access for us to receive the Holy Spirit through faith, the Holy Spirit in turn opens the way for gentiles to receive the blessing of Abraham.**

33.6.5 **It was necessary for the Christ to suffer- so that you can have not only forgiveness of sin but also blessing.**

33.6.1 God wants you to prosper, He desires you to prosper above everything else.

Remember 3 John 2: Beloved I wish above all things that you may proper and be in health even as your soul prospers.

Almighty God desires above everything else that you prosper, that your needs be met every day and that you be in health as your soul prospers. In other words, as you keep nourishing your soul with the correct understanding of the word of God, which is the truth, as you grow in the knowledge of God, that knowledge should also translate into God meeting your every financial need as well as your health needs.

33.6.2 He wants you to experience the promised land- both spiritually (His love, peace and joy) and physically (His provision, health and victory).

Remember Deuteronomy 8: 1-18:

Every commandment which I command you today you must be careful to observe, that you may live and multiply, and go in and possess the land of which the LORD swore to your fathers.

2 And you shall remember that the LORD your God led you all the way these forty years in the wilderness, to humble you and test you, to know what was in your heart, whether you would keep His commandments or not.

3 So He humbled you, allowed you to hunger, and fed you with manna which you did not know nor did your fathers know, that He might make you know that man shall not live by bread alone; but man, lives by every word that proceeds from the mouth of the LORD.

4 Your garments did not wear out on you, nor did your foot swell these forty years.

5 You should know in your heart that as a man chastens his son, so the LORD your God chastens you.

6 "Therefore you shall keep the commandments of the LORD your God, to walk in His ways and to fear Him.

7 For the LORD your God is bringing you into a good land, a land of brooks of water, of fountains and springs, that flow out of valleys and hills;

8 a land of wheat and barley, of vines and fig trees and pomegranates, a land of olive oil and honey;

9 a land in which you will eat bread without scarcity, in which you will lack nothing; a land whose stones are iron and out of whose hills you can dig copper.

10 When you have eaten and are full, then you shall bless the LORD your God for the good land which He has given you.

11 "Beware that you do not forget the LORD your God by not keeping His commandments, His judgments, and His statutes which I command you today,

12 lest—when you have eaten and are full, and have built beautiful houses and dwell in them;

13 and when your herds and your flocks multiply, and your silver and your gold are multiplied, and all that you have is multiplied;

14 when your heart is lifted up, and you forget the LORD your God who brought you out of the land of Egypt, from the house of bondage;

15 who led you through that great and terrible wilderness, in which were fiery serpents and scorpions and thirsty land where there was no water, who brought water for you out of the flinty rock;

16 who fed you in the wilderness with manna, which your fathers did not know, that He might humble you and that He might test you, to do you good in the end—

17 then you say in your heart, 'My power and the might of my hand have gained me this wealth.'

18 "And you shall remember the LORD your God, for it is He who gives you power to get wealth, that He may establish His covenant which He swore to your fathers, as it is this day.

He desires good things for you. He is bringing you into a good land- with brook of water and food provisions. That you eat bread without scarcity, where you have clothing to put on, where your herds and flocks multiply- that speaks of your farming, where your gold and silver can multiply- that speaks of investment and where you will have a place of your own to live in dignity and where you will lack nothing.

Then in verse 18 He says you shall remember the Lord your God for it is Him who gives you power to get wealth so that He may establish His covenant as it is today. You need a strong conviction that your God is your senior partner in wealth creation, you also need to understand the reason- His covenant with you includes Him being your God- your everything including Him being your Provider- Jehovah Jireh. When you are in poverty, His covenant with you is not established. When your needs are met you need to give so that He establishes His covenant with others by getting the good news of salvation in Jesus Christ to them and by abolishing poverty across the nations of Planet Earth.

33.6.3 Almighty God desires every positive outcome for you in Jesus Christ

In **Deuteronomy 28:1-14** we read.

Now it shall come to pass, if you diligently obey the voice of the LORD your God, to observe carefully all His commandments which I command you today, that the LORD your God will set you high above all nations of the earth.

2 And all these blessings shall come upon you and overtake you, because you obey the voice of the LORD your God:

3 "Blessed shall you be in the city and blessed shall you be in the country.

4 "Blessed shall be the fruit of your body, the produce of your ground and the increase of your herds, the increase of your cattle and the offspring of your flocks.

5 "Blessed shall be your basket and your kneading bowl.

6 "Blessed shall you be when you come in and blessed shall you be when you go out.

7 "The LORD will cause your enemies who rise against you to be defeated before your face; they shall come out against you one way and flee before you seven ways.

8 "The LORD will command the blessing on you in your storehouses and in all to which you set your hand, and He will bless you in the land which the LORD your God is giving you.

9 "The LORD will establish you as a holy people to Himself, just as He has sworn to you, if you keep the commandments of the LORD your God and walk in His ways.

10 Then all peoples of the earth shall see that you are called by the name of the LORD, and they shall be afraid of you.

11 And the LORD will grant you plenty of goods, in the fruit of your body, in the increase of your livestock, and in the produce of your

ground, in the land of which the LORD swore to your fathers to give you.

12 The LORD will open to you His good treasure, the heavens, to give the rain to your land in its season, and to bless all the work of your hand. You shall lend to many nations, but you shall not borrow.

13 And the LORD will make you the head and not the tail; you shall be above only, and not be beneath, if you heed the commandments of the LORD your God, which I command you today, and are careful to observe them.

14 So you shall not turn aside from any of the words which I command you this day, to the right or the left, to go after other gods to serve them.

Notice here that verse one begins by giving a condition- if you diligently obey the voice of the Lord and observe His instructions- these blessings shall come upon you. Blessings are positive outcomes in every area of your life. These blessings include blessing in the fruit of your body- that is your offspring's, your wealth, victory over your enemies, blessing in your storehouses- that is your bank accounts and investments. Notice verse 11- the Lord will grant you plenty of goods and verse 12 – He will open for you His good treasure and bless all the work of your hands. You will lend to many nations, and you will not borrow. Being in debt is not the will of God for you.

Then from verse 15 comes the curses of disobedience. I recommend that you read through these as well.

33.6.4 Remember- Jesus Christ redeemed us from the curse of the law and opened access for us to receive the Holy Spirit through faith, the Holy Spirit in turn opens the way for gentiles to receive the blessing of Abraham.

In Galatians 3:13-14 we read:

Christ has redeemed us from the curse of the law, having become a curse for us (for it is written, "Cursed is everyone who hangs on a tree"),

that the blessing of Abraham might come upon the Gentiles in Christ Jesus, that we might receive the promise of the Spirit through faith.

Deuteronomy 8: 1-18 and 28: 1-14 above describe the blessing of Abraham which essentially mean positive outcomes in every area of your life- you notice here that Jesus Christ redeemed us from the curse of the law which is described in Deuteronomy 28:15-68 so that the blessing of Abraham may come your way.

That blessing includes the blessing unto the utmost bounds of the everlasting hills- His promise to the fruitful child of God (Genesis 49:26). A blessing unlimited in scope and in time.

33.6.5 It was necessary for the Christ to suffer- so that you can have not only forgiveness of sin but also blessing.

In Luke 24: 44-49 we read:

Then He said to them, "These are the words which I spoke to you while I was still with you, that all things must be fulfilled which were written in the Law of Moses and the Prophets and the Psalms concerning Me."

45 And He opened their understanding, that they might comprehend the Scriptures.

46 Then He said to them, "Thus it is written, and thus it was necessary for the Christ to suffer and to rise from the dead the third day,

47 and that repentance and remission of sins should be preached in His name to all nations, beginning at Jerusalem.

48 And you are witnesses of these things.

49 Behold, I send the Promise of My Father upon you; but tarry in the city of Jerusalem until you are endued with power from on high."

Notice here that Jesus states Himself that there are many prophesies written in the Law of Moses, the Prophets and the Psalms concerning Himself and that these were now fulfilled. The next verse then says that He opened their understanding, that they might comprehend the scriptures.

You need to pray for your mind to be opened so that you understand the scriptures.

Understanding the scriptures also means you have a revelation of the scriptures.

The word of God correctly understood is the truth and it is the truth that sanctifies, sets people apart for God and it is the truth that sets people free.

In **John 17:17** Jesus said:

Sanctify them by Your truth, Your word is truth.

In John 8:31-32 He said this:

Then Jesus said to those Jews who believed Him, "If you abide in My word, you are My disciples indeed. And you shall know the truth, and the truth shall make you free."

Understanding the word of God gives you nourishment, energy and zeal to act. Without understanding of the word of God, you are like a person who puts food in the mouth and chews it and spits it to the ground without swallowing and absorbing it- the food would not benefit you and you would starve.

Once swallowed food is absorbed, goes into bloodstream and goes into every part of the body to nourish, energise and cause growth.

Now the point you need to understand here is this- **it was necessary for the Christ to suffer.** Why was it necessary? - for us to receive redemption from sin, poverty, disease and sickness and mental oppression by the enemy satan.

The word necessary means it needed to be done, it was required, it was mandatory. It was essential for Jesus Christ to accomplish His mission on the Earth. It was obligatory. It was vital, it was critical. It was all-important.

The opposite of necessary is optional or discretionary.

I am emphasising this point so that you can understand the following:

Jesus Christ suffered poverty so that you may have-

2 Corinthians 8:9 says: For you know the grace of our Lord Jesus Christ, that though He was rich, yet for your sakes He became poor, that you through His poverty might become rich.

They put a crown of thorns on His head, He suffered pain and humiliation from it (John 19:2, Mark 15:17) to break the curse of poverty, thorns and briers that came upon mankind at the fall of man (Genesis 3:17-18). The result is that you may have a crown of gold, may have honour and your needs may be met.

He was cursed by hanging on a tree so that the blessing of Abraham may come to you, and you may have access to the Holy Spirit. As you meditate on these truths, let them give you the understanding, the energy, the zeal to rise up in faith and rebel against poverty and lack. Let the Holy Spirit give you wisdom and the direction to act and turn your situation around. It was necessary for the Christ to suffer so that you and me can be redeemed from poverty and lack and may receive the blessing and resources we need for life as well as to accomplish the purpose of God for our lives on the Earth.

References

Kiyosaki Robert T- *Rich Dad, Poor Dad*. TechPress Inc. ISBN 096438561-9
Moore Rob- *Money*. John Murray Learning. ISBN 978-1-473-64133-4
Hill Napoleon. *Think and Grow Rich*. Capstone. ISBN 978-1-906-46559-9
Kiyosaki Robert T. *Cash Flow Quadrant*. Plata Publishing. ISBN 978-1-61268-006-4.

Chapter 34

Conclusion

I have set out in this book how you can translate the historical knowledge of the greatest person who ever lived on Planet earth- Jesus Christ-to an experience o: Jesus Christ as your Lord and Saviour.

It needs to start with a quest to know God, to discover His presence and live your life in His presence. He is giving this invitation to every single person who is on Planet Earth.

The beginning point is repentance and acknowledging the risen Jesus Chris as Lord of your life.

What will follow is forgiveness of sin and the experience of eternal life. You become born-again into the household of God.

As you get filled with the Holy Spirit- the Promise of the Father- the Game Changer, the abilities of heaven will descend upon you. You will experience the grace of God- His favour upon favour, blessing upon blessing, His gift heaped upon gift.

In the process He will enable you to be the best you can be.

You will have ignited power and strength from within you.

You will be connected to the source of unending power and strength

He will enable you to make change happen from within you, making you a person of character, stature, achievement, and self- assurance.

You will experience life fulfilment and satisfaction.

You will discover joy unspeakable, joy inexpressible, glorious, triumphant heavenly joy.

You will discover the peace of God that passes all understanding, which wil garrison and keep guard of your heart and minds in Jesus Christ.

You will experience the love of Christ which passes knowledge so that you experience all the fullness of God.

You will discover your purpose, which comes with self-fulfilment.

Your life will be anchored to faith, hope and love.

You will be given true freedom, authenticity, and excellence.

You will exude hope and confidence and become a condiment in the life o other people, become a light that shines into the dark places of other people lives. People who interact with you, will say to themselves "There is something different about that person, it seems he knows something I need to know; He has experienced something I need to experience."

This has happened to me on a few occasions but on one of these occasions, it was dramatic. I was working as a Senior House Officer at a Hospital in Dudley in the West Midlands of the United Kingdom when a group of six nurses came to me and asked, 'There is something different about you, tell us what is it?" I told them I had encountered Jesus Christ and took it as an opportunity to share the love of God in Jesus Christ with them.

You will then become a type, a kind called the God-kind and God will want you to go on and multiply after your kind as you pray for the Planet Earth harvest, as you witness the power and love of Jesus Christ and as you become a faithful steward of the time you have been given, the substance given to you and the mysteries of God.

What is stopping you? Go on tell others and let's make the earth to be filled with the knowledge of the glory of God as the waters cover the sea.

Some of the sections in this book will need re-visiting repeatedly. As you do, you gain a different understanding, a deeper understanding. This is the amazing thing about scripture, with each teaching there is a virtual 360-degree journey you can travel in terms of depth of understanding. In the process you grow in your knowledge of the Lord Jesus Christ, knowledge of the Father and knowledge of the Holy Spirit.

To the Lord God Almighty, we give all the glory. *Amen.*

About the Author

Max Matonhodze is an Apostle, medical practitioner, and author who, in his own words, "has a message to Planet Earth from Almighty God." As the Founder and General Overseer of *Planet Ministries*, Dr Max serves the people of *Planet Ministries* church and the world at large, and he has a message of hope and glad tidings for the hurting, the guilty, the lonely, and the discouraged.

His book *Vessels of Excellence* is a result of 40 years of an experience with Almighty God of Jesus Christ and teaching which has been delivered over the same period. It is written for anyone, irrespective of nationality, language, or tribe and irrespective of whether you were brought up as a Sikh, Hindu, Muslim, Protestant, Catholic, Buddhist, Jain or Communist. Or whether you consider yourself Atheist, Agnostic or anything else.

If you are sincerely asking the question- is there God?

And you are saying God if you are there, reveal yourself to me. This book will usher you into an experience of the God of Jesus Christ.

This book is also for any child of God, who wants to develop in their knowledge of God. It is also intended to be used as a resource manual for training church leaders and pastors.

Dr Max Matonhodze is a qualified Respiratory and General Internal Medicine Specialist. His medical qualifications include Bachelor of Medicine and Bachelor of Surgery (Mb ChB) from University of Zimbabwe, Master's Degree in Medicine from University of Zimbabwe, Member of the Royal College of Physicians of Ireland (MRCPI), Certificate of Completion of Specialist Training (CCST-UK) from the Joint Royal Colleges of Physicians Training Board of the United Kingdom (JRCPTB). He is Fellow of the Royal College of Physicians of London (FRCP) and holds a Master of Arts in Medical Education (M A Med Ed) form Keele University.

After medical qualification worked in the health service in Zimbabwe for 9 years before coming to England in December 1993. After working in various training grades, was appointed Consultant Physician in General and Respiratory Medicine for Walsall Healthcare NHS Trust on the 10th of June 2002, a post he has held for 20 years.

Having been brought up Catholic including spending six years in a Catholic boarding school (Gokomere High School in Masvingo, Zimbabwe) he had a personal experience of the love of Jesus Christ while an undergraduate medical student in August 1980 when he became a born-again Christian. Following this he felt God was calling him to become a preacher of the gospel.

Almighty God subsequently revealed to him that his calling was in the capacity of an Apostle. What followed were dramatic experiences with Almighty God as described in the preface of this book. Notable among these experiences is that on the 30th of November 1987, the Lord Jesus Christ appeared in his bedroom in visual form and commissioned him to send the message in this book to Planet Earth.

Planet Ministries was launched on the 18th of May 2012 following another encounter with Almighty God that night. On the 11th of August 2015, He was instructed by God to send out the Planet Daily, a daily devotional message. This has been sent as a daily blog from the *Planet Ministries* website (https://planet-ministries.org.uk) as well as on social media and WhatsApp groups. At the time of writing of this book, he has sent out more than two thousand daily blogs over the last six years.